An Outline of the Science of Political Economy

AN
OUTLINE
OF THE
SCIENCE
OF
POLITICAL ECONOMY

By

Nassau W. Senior

[1836]

REPRINTS OF ECONOMIC CLASSICS

Augustus M. Kelley, Bookseller
New York 1965

First edition, in quarto, 1836

Subsequent editions in 8vo:

Second	1850
Third	1854
Fourth	1858
Fifth	1863
Sixth	1872

Original edition 1939.
Reprinted 1965 by arrangement with Allen & Unwin.

The present edition contains an Appendix:

"On certain terms which are peculiarly liable to be used ambiguously in Political Economy," published originally in *Elements of Logic* by Richard Whately (1836)

Library of Congress Catalogue Card Number
65 - 16991

PRINTED IN THE UNITED STATES OF AMERICA
by SENTRY PRESS, NEW YORK, N. Y. 10019

CONTENTS

PAGE

POLITICAL ECONOMY DEFINED AS, THE SCIENCE WHICH TREATS OF THE
NATURE, THE PRODUCTION, AND THE DISTRIBUTION OF WEALTH,   1

NATURE OF WEALTH.

WEALTH defined, as comprehending all those things, and those things
only, which are *Transferable, Limited in Supply*, and directly or
indirectly *productive of pleasure or preventive of pain*, or, to use an
equivalent expression, *which are susceptible of Exchange*, or, to use a
third equivalent expression, *which have Value*,   .   .   .   6

Constitutents of WEALTH :

   1. *Utility*, ... 6
   2. *Limitation in Supply*, ... 7
   3. *Transferableness*, ... 8
   Limitation in Supply the most important,   . . . 11

VALUE defined as, *The quality in any thing which fits it to be given and
received in Exchange*, ... 13

The *intrinsic* causes of the Value of a commodity defined as, Those which
give to it Utility and Limit it in Supply,   . . . 16

The *extrinsic* as, Those which Limit the Supply and occasion the Utility
of the commodities for which it is to be exchanged,   . . 16

Steadiness in Value depends on the permanence of the *intrinsic* causes
of value, ... 20

Objections to the Definition of Wealth considered,   . . 22

STATEMENT OF THE FOUR ELEMENTARY PROPOSITIONS OF THE SCIENCE:—

   1. *That every man desires to obtain additional Wealth with as little
sacrifice as possible.*
   2. *That the Population of the world, or, in other words, the number of
persons inhabiting it, is limited only by moral and physical evil, or
by fear of a deficiency of those articles of wealth which the habits
of the individuals of each class of its inhabitants lead them to
require.*
   3. *That the Powers of Labour, and of the other Instruments which
Produce Wealth, may be indefinitely increased by using their
products as the means of further production.*
   4. *That, agricultural skill remaining the same, additional Labour
employed on the land within a given district produces in general a
less proportionate return, or, in other words, that though, with every
increase of the labour bestowed, the aggregate return is increased,
the increase of the return is not in proportion to the increase of the
labour*, ... 26

PAGE

Development of the First Elementary Proposition, namely, the *General Desire of Wealth,* 27

Development of the Second Elementary Proposition, namely, *the Causes which Limit Population,* 30

Development of the Third Elementary Proposition, namely,

Production defined as *the occasioning an alteration in the condition of the existing particles of matter, for the occasioning of which alteration, or for the things thence resulting, something may be obtained in Exchange. This alteration is a Product,* 50

Products divided into *Services* and *Commodities.* A *Service* is *the act of* occasioning the above mentioned alteration. A *Commodity* is *the thing as altered,* 51

Consumption defined as *the making use of a thing,* . . 53

Productive Consumption defined as *that use of a product which occasions an ulterior product.* Unproductive Consumption as *that use which occasions no ulterior product,* 54

INSTRUMENTS OF PRODUCTION :—

Primary : 1. Labour ; 2. Natural Agents :— . . . 57

    1. *Labour* defined as *the voluntary exertion of bodily or mental faculties for the purpose of Production,* 57

    2. Natural Agents defined as *those Productive Agents which do not derive their powers from man,* 58

Secondary : Abstinence.

    3. Third and secondary Instrument of Production. Abstinence defined as *the conduct of a person who either abstains from the unproductive use of what he can command, or designedly prefers the production of remote, to that of immediate, results,* . . 58

Abstinence, combined with one or both of the other two Instruments of Production, occasions the existence of CAPITAL. *Capital* defined as *an article of Wealth, the result of human exertion, employed in the Production or Distribution of Wealth,* 59

Different modes in which *Capital* may be employed, . . 60

Statement of the advantages derived from the use of Capital.

    1. The Use of *Implements,* 67

    2. The *Division of Labour,* 73

Development of the Fourth Elementary Proposition of the Science, namely, Additional Labour when employed in Manufactures is *more,* when employed in Agriculture is *less,* efficient in proportion, . 81

DISTRIBUTION OF WEALTH.

Society divided into *three classes, Labourers, Capitalists, and Proprietors of Natural Agents,* each class having a different *Instrument,* a different *Conduct,* and a different *Remuneration,* . . . 88

Nomenclature applicable to the first class, the *Labourers,* . . 89

Nomenclature applicable to the second class, the *Capitalists,* . . 89

Nomenclature applicable to the third class, the *Proprietors of Natural Agents,* 89

EXCHANGE, ... 95

Cost of Production defined as *the sum of the Labour and Abstinence necessary to Production,* 97

Divided into Cost of Production on the part of the *Producer,* and Cost of Production on the part of the *Consumer,* . . . 101

These are the same, unless the Production be subject to a *Monopoly,* . 103

Monopolies divided into four kinds :—

PAGE

    1. A Monopoly under which the Monopolist has not the exclusive power of Producing, but exclusive facilities as a Producer, which may be employed indefinitely with equal or increasing advantage, ... 103

    2. A Monopoly under which the Monopolist is the only Producer, and cannot increase the amount of his Produce, 104

    3. A Monopoly under which the Monopolist is the only Producer, and can increase indefinitely with equal or increasing advantage the amount of his Produce, . . . 105

    4. A Monopoly under which the Monopolist is not the only Producer, but has peculiar facilities which diminish and ultimately disappear as he increases the amount of his produce, . . 105

The last is the great Monopoly of Land, . . . 105

Effects of the Cost of Production on Price, . . . 111

Effects of Monopolies on Price, ... 114

Consequences of the proposition that additional Labour when employed in Manufactures is *more*, and when employed in Agriculture is *less*, efficient in proportion.

I. Different effects of increased Demand on the Prices of Manufactured, and of Raw, Produce, ... 119

II. Different effects of Taxation on the Prices of Manufactured, and of Raw, Produce, ... 120

Discussion whether certain Revenues ought to be called Rent, Profit, or Wages, ... 128

Causes on which the *proportionate amount of Rent* depends, . . 135

Proportionate Amounts of Profit and Wages, . . 139

Discussion of the circumstances which decide what, at a given time and in a given place, shall be the average rate of Wages and the average rate of Profit, ... 141

Meaning of the words *high* and *low* as applied to *Wages*, . . 141

Difference between the *Amount of Wages* and the *Price of Labour*, . 149

Proximate cause deciding the Rate of Wages stated to be *the extent of the Fund for the Maintenance of Labourers compared with the Number of Labourers to be maintained*, ... 153

Discussion of seven opinions inconsistent with this proposition :—

    1. The doctrine that the Rate of Wages depends solely on the proportion which the number of Labourers bears to the amount of *Capital* in the Country, ... 154

    2. The doctrine that Wages depend on the proportion borne by the number of Labourers to the whole *Revenue* of the society of which they are members, ... 154

    3. The doctrine that the Non-residence of unproductive Consumers can be detrimental to the Labouring inhabitants of a Country which does *not* export raw produce, . . . 155

    4. The doctrine that the general rate of Wages can, except in two cases, be diminished by the introduction of Machinery, 162

    5. The doctrine that the general rate of Wages can be reduced by the Importation of Foreign Commodities, . . 168

    6. The doctrine that the Unproductive Consumption of Landlords and Capitalists is beneficial to the Labouring classes because it furnishes them with employment, . . 169

    7. The doctrine that it is more beneficial to the Labouring Classes to be employed in the production of Services than in the production of Commodities, ... 170

PAGE

Statement of the causes on which the extent of the Fund for the Maintenance of Labourers really depends. 1. The productiveness of labour in the direct or indirect production of the commodities used by the labourers. 2. The number of persons directly or indirectly employed in the production of things for the use of labourers compared with the whole number of labouring families, ... 173

I. Causes on which the Productiveness of Labour depends :—
    1. The corporeal, intellectual, and moral Qualities of the Labourer, 175
    2. The assistance of Natural Agents, ... 175
    3. The assistance of Capital, ... 176
    4. The existence or the absence of Government interference, . 176

II. Causes which divert Labour from the production of Commodities for the use of Labouring families :—
    1. Rent, ... 180
    2. Taxation, ... 182
    3. Profit, ... 185

Profit consists of the difference between the value of the Advance made by the Capitalist and the value of the Return, . . . 185

How that value should be estimated, ... 185

The facts which decide in what proportion the Capitalists and Labourers share the Common Fund after the deduction of Rent and Taxation stated to be two: first, *the general rate of profit in the Country on the advance of capital for a given period:* and, secondly, *the period which in each particular case has elapsed between the advance of the capital and the receipt of the profit,* 185

Cause regulating the Rate of Profit ascertained to be *the proportion which the supply of Capital employed in providing Wages bears to the supply of Labourers,* 193

Causes regulating the period of Advance of Capital incapable of a general statement, ... 194

Capitalists and Labourers interested in the period of Advance of Capital only so far as they are Consumers, ... 196

Causes of variation in the Amount of Wages and the Rate of Profits in different employments of Labour and Capital assigned by Adam Smith :—
    1. Agreeableness, ... 200
    2. Facility of learning the business, ... 204
    3. Constancy of employment, ... 207
    4. Trustworthiness, ... 208
    5. Probability of success, ... 208

Variations occasioned by the difficulty of Transferring Labour and Capital from one employment to another, . . . 217

From one country to another, ... 220

APPENDIX

On certain Terms which are peculiarly liable to be used ambiguously in Political Economy, from *Elements of Logic* by Richard Whately, D.D. 227

Note on the variations between the first and subsequent editions . 240

AN

OUTLINE OF THE SCIENCE

OF

POLITICAL ECONOMY.

BY

NASSAU W. SENIOR, A.M.,

FORMERLY FELLOW OF MAGDALEN COLLEGE, AND PROFESSOR OF POLITICAL ECONOMY, IN THE
UNIVERSITY OF OXFORD.

LONDON:

PRINTED BY W. CLOWES AND SONS, STAMFORD STREET.

1836.

Facsimile of first edition
title page

POLITICAL ECONOMY

INTRODUCTION

Definition of the Science.—We propose in the following Treatise to give an outline of the Science which treats of the Nature, the Production, and the Distribution of Wealth. To that Science we give the name of Political Economy. Our readers must be aware that that term has often been used in a much wider sense. The earlier writers who assumed the name of Political Economists avowedly treated not of Wealth but of Government. Mercier de la Riviere entitled his Work *The Natural and Essential Organization of Society*, and professed to propose an organization " which shall necessarily produce all the happiness that can be enjoyed on earth."[1] Sir James Steuart states, that " the principal object of the Science is to secure a certain fund of subsistence for all the inhabitants, to obviate every circumstance which may render it precarious, and to provide every thing necessary for supplying the wants of the society."[2] The modern continental writers have in general entered into an equally extensive inquiry. " Political Economy," says M. Storch, " is the Science of the natural laws which determine the prosperity of nations, that is to say, their wealth and their civilization."[3] M. Sismondi considers " the physical welfare of man, so far as it can be the work of government, as the object of Political Economy."[4] " Political Economy," says M. Say, " is the economy of society; a Science combining the results of our observations on the nature and functions of the different parts of the social body."[5] The modern writers of the English school have in general professed to limit their attention to the theory of Wealth; but some of the most eminent among them, after having expressed their intention to confine themselves within what appears to us to be their proper province, have invaded that of the general legislator or the statesman. Thus Mr. M'Culloch, after having defined Political Economy to be " the Science of the laws which regulate the production, accumulation, distribution, and consumption of those articles or products that are necessarily useful or agreeable to man, and possess exchangeable

[1] *Discourse Préliminaire*, liv. vi.
[2] Vol. I. p. 2.
[3] Tom. I. p. 21.
[4] *Nouveaux Principes d'Economie Politique*, liv. i. ch. ii.
[5] *Cours Complet*, Tom. I. pp. 1, 2.

value ;"[6] or, "the Science of Values ;" adds, that "its object is to point out the means by which the industry of man may be rendered most productive of wealth, to ascertain the circumstances most favourable to its accumulation, the proportions in which it is divided, and the mode in which it may be most advantageously consumed."[7]

Limits of the Science.—It is impossible to overstate the importance of these inquiries, and it is not easy to state their extent. They involve, as their general premises, the consideration of the whole theory of morals of government, and of civil and criminal legislation; and, for their particular premises, a knowledge of all the facts which affect the social condition of every community whose conduct the Economist proposes to influence. We believe that such inquiries far exceed the bounds of any single Treatise, and indeed the powers of any single mind. We believe that by confining our own and the reader's attention to the Nature, Production, and Distribution of Wealth, we shall produce a more clear, and complete, and instructive work than if we allowed ourselves to wander into the more interesting and more important, but far less definite, fields by which the comparatively narrow path of Political Economy is surrounded. The questions, To what extent and under what circumstances the possession of Wealth is, on the whole, beneficial or injurious to its possessor, or to the society of which he is a member ? What distribution of Wealth is most desirable in each different state of society? and What are the means by which any given Country can facilitate such a distribution ? —all these are questions of great interest and difficulty, but no more form part of the Science of Political Economy, in the sense in which we use that term, than Navigation forms part of the Science of Astronomy. The principles supplied by Political Economy are indeed necessary elements in their solution, but they are not the only, or even the most important elements. The writer who pursues such investigations is in fact engaged on the great Science of legislation ; a Science which requires a knowledge of the general principles supplied by Political Economy, but differs from it essentially in its subject, its premises, and its conclusions. The subject of legislation is not Wealth, but human Welfare. Its premises are drawn from an infinite variety of phenomena, supported by evidence of every degree of strength, and authorizing conclusions deserving every degree of assent, from perfect confidence to bare suspicion. And its expounder is enabled, and even required, not merely to state general facts, but to urge the adoption or rejection of actual measures or trains of action.

On the other hand, the subject treated by the Political Economist, using that term in the limited sense in which we apply it, is not Happiness, but Wealth ; his premises consist of a very few general propositions, the result of observation, or consciousness, and scarcely requiring

Principles, &c. p. 1.   [7] Ibid. p. 8.

proof, or even formal statement, which almost every man, as soon as he hears them, admits as familiar to his thoughts, or at least as included in his previous knowledge; and his inferences are nearly as general, and, if he has reasoned correctly, as certain, as his premises. Those which relate to the Nature and the Production of Wealth are universally true; and though those which relate to the Distribution of Wealth are liable to be affected by the peculiar institutions of particular Countries, in the cases for instance of slavery, legal monopolies, or poor laws, the natural state of things can be laid down as the general rule, and the anomalies produced by particular disturbing causes can be afterwards accounted for. But his conclusions, whatever be their generality and their truth, do not authorize him in adding a single syllable of advice. That privilege belongs to the writer or the statesman who has considered all the causes which may promote or impede the general welfare of those whom he addresses, not to the theorist who has considered only one, though among the most important, of those causes. The business of a Political Economist is neither to recommend nor to dissuade, but to state general principles, which it is fatal to neglect, but neither advisable, nor perhaps practicable, to use as the sole, or even the principal, guides in the actual conduct of affairs. In the meantime the duty of each individual writer is clear. Employed as he is upon a Science in which error or even ignorance, may be productive of such intense and such extensive mischief, he is bound, like a juryman, to give deliverance true according to the evidence, and allow neither sympathy with indigence, nor disgust at profusion or at avarice—neither reverence for existing institutions, nor detestation of existing abuses—neither love of popularity, nor of paradox, nor of system, to deter him from stating what he believes to be the facts, or from drawing from those facts what appear to him to be the legitimate conclusions. To decide in each case how far those conclusions are to be acted upon, belongs to the art of government, an art to which Political Economy is only one of many subservient Sciences; which involves the consideration of motives, of which the desire for Wealth is only one among many, and aims at objects to which the possession of Wealth is only a subordinate means.

The confounding Political Economy with the Sciences and Arts to which it is subservient, has been one of the principal obstacles to its improvement. It has acted thus in two different modes:—

First, by exciting, in the public unfavourable prejudices.

And, secondly, by misleading Economists, both with respect to the object of their Science and the means of attaining it.

With respect to the first of these obstacles, it has often been made a matter of grave complaint against Political Economists, that they confine their attention to Wealth, and disregard all consideration of Happiness or Virtue. It is to be wished that this complaint were better founded; but its general existence implies an opinion that it is

the business of Political Economists not merely to state propositions, but to recommend actual measures; for on no other supposition
could they be blamed for confining their attention to a single subject.
No one blames a writer upon tactics for confining his attention to
military affairs, or, from his doing so, infers that he recommends
perpetual war. It must be admitted that an author who, having
stated that a given conduct is productive of Wealth, should, on that
account alone, recommend it, or assume that, on that account alone, it
ought to be pursued, would be guilty of the absurdity of implying that
Happiness and the possession of Wealth are identical. But his error
would consist not in confining his attention to Wealth, but in confounding Wealth with Happiness. Supposing that error, and it is a
very obvious one, to be avoided, the more strictly a writer confines
his attention to his own Science, the more likely he is to extend its
bounds.

Secondly, The confounding the Science of Political Economy with
the Sciences and Arts to which it is subservient, has seduced Economists sometimes to undertake inquiries too vague to lead to any
practical results, and sometimes to pursue the legitimate objects of
the Science by means unfit for their attainment. To their extended
view of the objects of Political Economy is to be attributed the undue
importance which many Economists have ascribed to the collection of
facts, and their neglect of the far more important process of reasoning
accurately from the facts before them. We are constantly told that
it is a Science of facts and experiment, a Science *avide de faits*. The
practical applications of it, like the practical applications of every other
Science, without doubt, require the collection and examination of
facts to an almost indefinite extent. The facts collected as materials
for the amendment of the poor-laws, and the opening of the trade to
China, fill more than twice as many volumes as could be occupied by
all the Treatises that have ever been written on Political Economy;
but the facts on which the general principles of the Science rest may
be stated in a very few sentences, and indeed in a very few words. But
that the reasoning from these facts, the drawing from them correct
conclusions, is a matter of great difficulty, may be inferred from the
imperfect state in which the Science is now found after it has been so
long and so intensely studied.

This difficulty arises partly from the extremely complicated nature
of the subjects which it investigates, and the consequent abstractness
and generality of its terms. A description, if it were possible, of all
the different things which are designated by the word "Wealth," or
even by the less comprehensive word "Capital," would fill an Encyclopædia. It arises partly, also, from the circumstance, that the
terms which we are forced to use as signs for these abstractions are
taken from ordinary language, commonly used in senses too wide or
too narrow for scientific purposes. In the case therefore, both of the

writer and of the reader, they are often associated with ideas which are intended to be excluded, or separated from ideas which are meant to be comprehended. Thus, in ordinary language, the word Capital is sometimes used as comprehending every species of Wealth, and sometimes as confined to Money.

If Economists had been aware that the Science depends more on reasoning than on observation, and that its principal difficulty consists not in the ascertainment of its facts, but in the use of its terms, we cannot doubt that their principal efforts would have been directed to the selection and consistent use of an accurate nomenclature. So far is this from having been the case, that it is only within a very short period that serious attention has been given to its nomenclature. *The Wealth of Nations* contains scarcely a definition: most of the modern French writers, and some indeed of our own, have not only neglected definitions, but have expressly reprobated their use; and the English Work which has attracted the most attention during the present century, Mr. Ricardo's *Principles of Political Economy*, is deformed by a use of words so unexplained, and yet so remote from ordinary usage, and from that of other writers on the same subject, and frequently so inconsistent, as to perplex every reader, and not unfrequently to have misled the eminent writer himself. We do not complain of all his innovations in language: such innovations are, for scientific purposes, frequently indispensable, and we shall be forced to make many ourselves. What we do complain of is, that his innovations, such, for instance, as the substitution of the word *Value* for *Cost*, are frequently unnecessary, and are almost always made without any warning to his readers; and that the same words, such, for example, as the adjectives *high* and *low*, when applied to wages, are used by him sometimes in their popular sense, as expressing an amount, and sometimes in a technical sense of his own, as expressing a proportion.

Our object in these remarks has been not only to account for the slow progress which has as yet been made by Political Economy, and to suggest means by which its advancement may be accelerated, but also to warn the reader of the nature of the following Treatise. He will find it consist, in a great degree, of discussions as to the most convenient use of a few familiar words. Such discussions it is impossible to render amusing, but we trust that they will be useful, by directing his attention to the great difficulties of the Science, though he may often disapprove our classification or nomenclature.

NATURE OF WEALTH

Wealth defined.—Having stated that the Science which we propose to consider, and to which we apply the term Political Economy, is the Science which treats of the Nature, the Production, and the Distribution of Wealth, our first business is to explain the meaning in which we use the word Wealth.

Under that term we comprehend all those things, and those things only, which are transferable, are limited in supply, and are directly or indirectly productive of pleasure or preventive of pain; or, to use an equivalent expression, which are susceptible of *exchange;* (using the word exchange to denote hiring as well as absolute purchase;) or, to use a third equivalent expression, which have *Value;* a word which, in a subsequent portion of this Treatise, we shall explain at some length, merely premising at present that we use it in its popular sense, as denoting the capacity of being given and received in exchange.

CONSTITUENTS OF WEALTH.

1. **Utility.**—Of the three qualities which render any thing an article of Wealth, or, in other words, give it Value, the most striking is the power, direct or indirect, of producing pleasure, including under that term gratification of every kind, or of preventing pain, including under that term every species of discomfort. Unfortunately, we have no word which precisely expresses this power; *utility*, which comes nearest to it, being generally used to express the quality of preventing pain or of indirectly producing pleasure, as a means. We shall venture to extend the signification of that word, and consider it as also including all those things which produce pleasure directly. We must admit that this is a considerable innovation in English language. It is, however, sanctioned by Mr. Malthus, (*Definitions*, p. 234,) and has been ventured by M. Say in French, a language less patient of innovation than our own. Feeling the same difficulty, he has solved it in the same way by using the term *utilité* as comprehending every quality that renders any thing an object of desire. Attractiveness and desirableness have both been suggested to us as substitutes, but on the whole they appear to us more objectionable than *utility*, objectionable as we must admit that word to be.

Utility, thus explained, is a necessary constituent of value; no man would give any thing possessing the slightest utility for a thing possessing none; and even an exchange of two useless things would be, on the part of each party to the exchange, an act without a motive. Utility, however, denotes no intrinsic quality in the things which we call useful; it merely expresses their relations to the pains and pleasures of mankind. And, as the susceptibility of pain and pleasure from particular objects is created and modified by causes innumerable, and constantly varying, we find an endless diversity in the relative utility of different objects to different persons, a diversity which is the motive of all exchanges.

2. **Limitation in Supply.**—The next constituent of value is *limitation in supply*. It may appear inaccurate to apply this expression to any class of things, as it, in fact, belongs to all; there being nothing which, strictly speaking, is unlimited in supply. But, for the purposes of Political Economy, every thing may be considered as unlimited in supply *in its existing state*, of which a man may have as much as he pleases for the mere trouble of taking it into his possession. Thus the water of the open sea is, in our use of the term, unlimited in supply; any man who chooses to go for it may have as much of it as he pleases: that portion of it which has been brought to London is limited in supply, and is to be obtained not merely by going to the reservoir and taking possession of it, but by giving for it an equivalent. The copper ores which Sir John Franklin discovered on the shores of the Arctic Sea may be considered, *in their existing state*, as unlimited in supply; any man may have as much of them as he has strength and patience to extract. The extracted portion would be limited in supply, and therefore susceptible of value. Many things are unlimited in supply for some purposes, and limited for others. The water in a river is in general more than sufficient for all the domestic purposes for which it can be required; nobody pays therefore for permission to take a bucketfull: but it is seldom sufficient for all those who may wish to turn their mills with it; they pay, therefore for that privilege.

It must be further observed that, for economical purposes, the term *limitation in supply* always involves the consideration of the causes by which the existing supply is limited. The supply of some articles of Wealth is limited by insurmountable obstacles. The number of Raphael's pictures, or of Canova's statues, may be diminished, but cannot possibly be increased. There are others of which the supply may be increased to an indefinite extent. Such things may be considered as comparatively limited in supply, in proportion, not to the existing supply of each, but to the force of the obstacles opposed to their respective increase. It is supposed that there is now about forty-five times as much of silver extracted from the mines, and current in Europe, as there is of gold. Human exertion is the only means by which the supply of either can be increased, and they may both be increased by human exertion to an amount of which we do not know the limit. The obstacle, therefore, by which they are each limited in supply is, the amount of human exertion necessary to their respective increase. About sixteen times more exertion is necessary to produce an ounce of gold than an ounce of silver. The obstacle, therefore, which limits the supply of gold is sixteen times more powerful than that which limits the supply of silver. In our sense of the term, therefore, gold is only sixteen times more limited in supply than silver, though the actual weight of silver in Europe is forty-five times as great as that of gold. To take a more familiar example, the number of coats and waistcoats in England is perhaps about equal. The supply of each may be increased by human exertion to an indefinite extent ; but it requires about three times as much exertion to produce a coat as to produce a waistcoat. As the obstacle, therefore, which limits the supply of coats is three times as forcible as that which limits the supply of waistcoats, we consider coats three times more limited in supply than waistcoats, though the existing supply of each may perhaps be equal. Whenever, therefore, we apply the words *limited in supply*, as a comparative expression, to those commodities of which the quantity can be increased, we refer to the comparative force of the obstacles which limit the respective supplies of the objects compared.

3. **Transferableness.**—The third and last quality which a thing must possess to constitute it an article of Wealth, or, in other words, to give it value, is *Transferableness*, by which term (we are sorry to say, an unusual one) we mean to express that all or some portion of its powers of giving pleasure, or preventing pain, are capable of being transferred, either absolutely, or for a period. For this purpose it is obvious that it must be capable of appropriation; since no man can give what he cannot refuse. The sources of pleasure and preventives of pain which are absolutely incapable of appropriation are very few. We almost doubt whether there are any, and we are sure that the instances which are usually given are incorrect. " The earth," observes M. Say, *Econ. Pol.* Liv. ii. Ch. ix. " is not the only material agent with productive power, but it is the only one, or nearly so, that can be appropriated. The water of rivers and of the sea, which supplies us with fish, gives motion to our mills, and supports our vessels, has productive powers. The wind gives us force, and the sun heat, but happily no man can say, ' The wind and the sun belong to me, and I will be paid for their services.' " Now, in fact, air and sunshine are local. This is so obvious that it would be absurd to prove, by serious induction, that some situations have too much wind, and others too little, or that the sun's rays are more powerful productive agents in England than in Melville Island, or in the Tropics than in England. And as the land is every where capable of appropriation, the qualities of climate, which are attributes of that land, must be so too. What gives their principal value to the vineyards of the Côte Rotie, but the warmth of their sun ? or to the houses which overlook Hyde Park,

but the purity of their air ? Rivers and the sea are equally unfortunate illustrations. Many of the rivers of England are not less strictly appropriated, and are far greater sources of wealth, than any equal superficies of land. When M. Say visited Lancashire, he must have found every inch of fall in every stream the subject of lease and purchase. And so far are the services of the sea from being incapabe of appropriation, that, during the late war, £60,000 was sometimes paid for a license to make use of it for a single voyage; and the privilege of fishing in particular parts of it has been the subject of wars and treaties.

The things of which the utility is imperfectly transferable may be divided into two great classes. The first comprises all those material objects which are affected by the peculiar mental associations, or adapted to the peculiar wants, of individuals. A mansion may flatter the pride of its owner as having been the residence of his ancestors, or be endeared to him as the scene of his childhood; or he may have built it in a form which pleases no eye, or laid it out in apartments that suit no habits but his own. Still its substantial powers of affording warmth and shelter will obtain him purchasers or tenants, though they may demand a reduction from the price in consequence of those very qualities which, with him, formed its principal merits. The palace of St. James's is full of comfort and convenience, and would supply a man of large fortune with an excellent residence; but the long suite of apartments within apartments, which is admirably adapted to holding a Court, would be a mere incumbrance to any but a royal personage. Any individual might hire Alnwick or Blenheim, and enjoy their mere beauty and magnificence, perhaps, more than their owners who have been long familiarized to them; but he could never feel the peculiar pleasure which they seem fitted to give to a Percy and a Churchhill. There are many things, such as clothes and furniture, which sink in utility in the estimation of every one but their purchaser, from the mere fact of having changed hands. A hat or a table which has just been sent home does not appear to the purchaser less useful than when he saw it in the shop; but if he attempt to resell either, he will find that with the rest of the world it has sunk into the degraded rank of second-hand.

The second class of things imperfectly transferable includes the greater part, perhaps all, of our personal qualities. This classification, which places talents and accomplishments among the articles of wealth, may appear at first sight strange and inconvenient; it certainly is different from that of most Economists. We will therefore venture to illustrate it more fully.

Health, strength, and knowledge, and the other natural and acquired powers of body and mind, appear to us to be articles of wealth, precisely analogous to a residence having some qualities that are universally useful, and others peculiarly adapted to the tastes of its owner. They are limited in supply, and are auses of pleasure and preventives of pain far more effectual than the possession of Alnwick or of Blenheim. A portion of the advantages which arise from them are inseparably annexed to their possessor, like the associations of an hereditary property: another portion, and often a very large one, is as transferable as the palpable convenience of the mansion, or beauty of the gardens. What cannot be transferred are the temporary pleasure which generally accompanies the exercise of any accomplishment, and the habitual satisfaction arising from the consciousness of possessing it. What can be transferred are the beneficial results which follow from its having been employed during the period for which its services have been hired. If an Erskine or a Sugden undertakes my cause, he transfers to me, for that occasion, the use of all his natural and acquired ability. My defence is as well conducted as if I had myself the knowledge and the eloquence of an accomplished advocate. What he cannot transfer is the pleasure which he feels in the exercise of his dexterity; but how small is his pleasure compared to mine, if he succeeds for me! A passenger may envy the activity and intrepidity of the crew; they cannot actually implant in him their strength, or their insensibility to danger; but so far as these qualities are means towards an end, so far as they enable him to perform his voyage with quickness and safety, he enjoys the use of them as fully as if they belonged to himself. A hunter probably feels somewhat the same sort of pleasure in the chase which Erskine felt in court; and this pleasure cannot be transferred any more than his muscles or his lungs; but, so far as his strength, speed, and bottom are means towards the end of enabling his rider to keep up with the hounds, they can be purchased or hired as effectually as his bridle or saddle. In the greater part of the world a man is as purchasable as a horse. In such Countries the only difference in value between a slave and a brute consists in the degree in which they respectively possess the saleable qualities that we have been considering. If the question whether personal qualities are articles of wealth had been proposed in classical times, it would have appeared too clear for discussion. In Athens, every one would have replied that they, in fact, constituted the whole value of an εμψυχον οργανον. The only differences in this respect between a freeman and a slave are, first, that the freeman sells *himself*, and only for a period, and to a certain extent, the slave may be sold by others, and absolutely; and, secondly, that the personal qualities of the slave are a portion of the wealth of his master; those of the freeman, so far as they can be made the subjects of exchange, are a part of his own wealth. They perish indeed by his death, and may be impaired or destroyed by disease, or rendered valueless by any changes in the customs of the Country which shall destroy the demand for his services; but, subject to these contingencies, they are wealth, and wealth of the most valuable kind. The amount of revenue derived from their exercise in England far exceeds the rental of all the lands in Great Britain.

Limitation in Supply the most important.—Of the three conditions of value, utility, transferableness, and limitation in supply, the last is by far the most important. The chief sources of its influence on value are two of the most powerful principles of human nature, the love of variety, and the love of distinction. The mere necessaries of life are few and simple. Potatoes, water, and salt, simple raiment, a blanket, a hut, an iron pot, and the materials of firing, are sufficient to support mere animal existence in this climate: they do, in fact, support the existence of the greater part of the inhabitants of Ireland; and in warmer countries much less will suffice. But no man is satisfied with so limited a range of enjoyment. His first object is to vary his food; but this desire, though urgent at first, is more easily satisfied than any other, except perhaps that of dress. Our ancestors, long after they had indulged in considerable luxury in other respects, seem to have been contented with a very uniform though grossly abundant diet. And even now, notwithstanding the common declamation on the luxury of the table, we shall find that most persons, including even those whose appetites are not controlled by frugality, confine their principal solid food to but a few articles, and their liquids to still fewer.

The next desire is variety of dress; a taste which has this peculiarity, that, though it is one of the first symptoms that a people is emerging from the brutishness of the lowest savage life, it quickly reaches its highest point, and, in the subsequent progress of refinement, in one sex at least, diminishes until even the highest ranks assume an almost quaker-like simplicity.

Last comes the desire to build, to ornament, and to furnish: tastes which are absolutely insatiable where they exist, and seem to increase with every improvement in civilization. The comforts and conveniences which we now expect in an ordinary lodging, are more than were enjoyed by people of opulence a century ago: and even a century ago a respectable tradesman would have been dissatisfied if his bed-room had been no better furnished than that of Henry VIII., which contained, we are told, only a bed, a cupboard of plate, a joint-stool, a pair of andirons, and a small mirror.[8] And yet Henry was among the richest and the most magnificent sovereigns of his times. Our great grand-children perhaps will despise the accommodations of the present Age, and their poverty may, in turn, be pitied by their successors.

It is obvious, however, that our desires do not aim so much at quantity as at diversity. Not only are there limits to the pleasure which commodities of any given class can afford, but the pleasure diminishes in a rapidly increasing ratio long before those limits are

---

[8] Henry, *History of Great Britain*, Book vi. Ch. vii.

reached. Two articles of the same kind will seldom afford twice the pleasure of one, and still less will ten give five times the pleasure of two. In proportion, therefore, as any article is abundant, the number of those who are provided with it, and do not wish, or wish but little, to increase their provision, is likely to be great; and, so far as they are concerned, the additional supply loses all, or nearly all, its utility. And in proportion to its scarcity the number of those who are in want of it, and the degree in which they want it, are likely to be increased; and its utility, or, in other words, the pleasure which the possession of a given quantity of it will afford, increases proportionally.

But strong as is the desire for variety, it is weak compared with the desire for distinction: a feeling which, if we consider its universality and its constancy, that it affects all men and at all times, that it comes with us from the cradle, and never leaves us till we go into the grave, may be pronounced to be the most powerful of human passions.

The most obvious source of distinction is the possession of superior wealth. It is the one which excites most the admiration of the bulk of mankind, and the only one which they feel capable of attaining. To seem more rich, or, to use a common expression, to keep up a better appearance, than those within their own sphere of comparison, is, with almost all men who are placed beyond the fear of actual want, the ruling principle of conduct. For this object they undergo toil which no pain or pleasure addressed to the senses would lead them to encounter; into which no slave could be lashed or bribed. But this object is attained by appearances, and, indeed, cannot be attained by any thing else. All the gold in the Pactolus, even if the Pactolus were as rich as when Midas had just washed in it, would obviously confer no distinction on the man who was unable to exhibit it. The only mode by which wealth can be exhibited is, by the apparent possession of some object of desire which is limited in supply. Mere limitation of supply, indeed, unless there be some other circumstance constituting the article in question an object of desire, or, in other words, giving it utility, is insufficient. This circumstance must be its having some quality to which some person beside the owner annexes the notion of utility. The original manuscript of every schoolboy's exercise is as limited in supply as any thing can be, but there is nothing to make it an object of desire after it has served its purpose in school. It is merely a blotted manuscript, unique certainly, but valueless. But if the original manuscript of the *Wealth of Nations* could be discovered, it would excite an interest throughout Europe. Curiosity would be eager to trace the first workings of a mind whose influence will be felt as long as civilized society endures. It might, perhaps, be purchased by some ignorant collector only for the purposes of ostentation, but it could not serve even those purposes unless recommended by some circumstance beyond mere singularity.

It is impossible, however, to conceive any thing more trifling or more capricious than the circumstances which may make a thing an object of desire, and therefore, in our extended use of that word, give to it utility when its supply is narrowly limited.

The substance which at present is the greatest object of desire, and of which, therefore, a given quantity will exchange for the greatest quantity of all other things, is the diamond. A bracelet belonging to the king of Persia, the stones in which do not weigh two ounces, is said to be worth a million sterling. Now, a million sterling would command the whole labour of about thirty thousand English families for a year. If that labour were employed in producing and reproducing commodities for the purposes of sale, it would probably give for ever a clear annual income equal to the labour of three thousand families, or twelve thousand individuals. It would place at the disposal of its owner all the commodities that could be produced by all the labour of all the inhabitants of a considerable town. And a few pieces of mineral, not weighing two ounces, capable of gratifying no sense but the sight, and which any eye would be tired of looking at for a minute, is invested by our caprice with a value equal to that of the commodities which would give comfortable support to thousands of human beings in an advanced state of civilization. Hardness and brightness must have been the qualities which first attracted notice to the diamond. They enabled it to please the eye and adorn the person, and thus associated with it the notion of utility. But a diamond weighing an ounce is not found once in a century; there are not five such known to exist. The possession of an object of desire so limited in supply soon became one of the most unequivocal proofs of wealth. And, as to appear rich is the ruling passion of the bulk of mankind, diamonds will probably continue the objects of eager competition while the obstacles that limit their supply are undiminished. If a Sinbad should discover a valley of diamonds, or we should succeed in manufacturing them from charcoal, they will probably be used only as ornaments for savages, playthings for children, and as affording tools and raw materials for some of the Arts; and we may send cargoes of diamonds to the coast of Guinea to be bartered for equal quantities of ivory or gum.

VALUE.

Value defined.—Our definition of Wealth, as comprehending all those things, and those things only which have *Value*, requires us to explain at some length the signification which we attribute to the word Value; especially as the meaning of that word has been the subject of long and eager controversy. We have already stated that we use the word VALUE in its popular acceptation, as signifying *that quality in any thing which fits it to be given and received in Exchange*; or, in other words, to be lent or sold, hired or purchased.

So defined, Value denotes a relation reciprocally existing between two objects, and the precise relation which it denotes is the quantity of the one which can be obtained in exchange for a given quantity of the other. It is impossible, therefore, to predicate value of any object, without referring, expressly or tacitly, to some other object or objects in which its value is to be estimated; or, in other words, of which a certain quantity can be obtained in exchange for a certain quantity of the object in question.

We have already observed that the substance which at present is most desired, or, in other words, possesses the highest degree of value, is the diamond. By this we meant to express that there is no substance of which a given quantity will exchange for so large a quantity of every other commodity. When we wished to state the value of the king of Persia's bracelet, we stated first the amount of gold, and afterwards of English labour, which it would command in exchange. If we had attempted to give a perfect account of its value, we could have done so only by enumerating separately the quantity of every other article of wealth which could be obtained in exchange for it. Such an enumeration, if it could have been given, would have been a most instructive commercial lesson, for it would have shown not only the value of the diamond in all other commodities, but the reciprocal value of all other commodities in one another. If we had ascertained that a diamond weighing an ounce would exchange for one million five hundred thousand tons of Hepburn coal, or one hundred thousand tons of Essex wheat, or two thousand five hundred tons of English foolscap paper, we might have inferred that the coal, wheat, and paper would mutually exchange in the same proportions in which they were exchangeable for the diamond, and that a given weight of paper would purchase six hundred times as much coal, and forty times as much wheat.

Demand and Supply.—The causes which determine the reciprocal values of commodities, or, in other words, which determine that a given quantity of one shall exchange for a given quantity of another, must be divided into two sets; those which occasion the one to be limited in supply and useful, (using that word to express the power of occasioning pleasure and preventing pain,) and those which occasion those attributes to belong to the other. In ordinary language, the *force* of the causes which give utility to a commodity is generally indicated by the word *Demand*; and the *weakness* of the obstacles which limit the quantity of a commodity by the word *Supply*.

Thus the common statement that commodities exchange in proportion to the Demand and Supply of each, means that they exchange in proportion to the force or weakness of the causes which give utility to them respectively, and to the weakness or force of the obstacles by which they are respectively limited in supply.

Unfortunately, however, the words Demand and Supply have not been always so used. Demand is sometimes used as synonymous with consumption, as when an increased production is said to generate an increased demand; sometimes it is used to express not only the desire to obtain a commodity, but the power to give the holder of it something which will induce him to part with it. " A Demand," says Mr. Mill, *Political Economy*, p. 23, 3d edition, "means the will to purchase and the power of purchasing." Mr. Malthus, *Definitions in Political Economy*, p. 244, states that "Demand for commodities has two distinct meanings: one in regard to its extent, or the quantity of commodities purchased; the other in regard to its intensity, or the sacrifice which the demanders are able and willing to make in order to satisfy their wants."

Demand.—Neither of these expressions appears to be consistent with common usage. It must be admitted that the word Demand is used in its ordinary sense when we say that a deficient wheat harvest increases the Demand for oats and barley. But this proposition is not true if we use the word Demand in any other sense than as expressing the increased utility of oats and barley; or, in other words, the increased desire of the community to obtain them. The deficiency of wheat would not give to the consumers of oats and barley any increased power of purchasing them, nor would the quantity purchased or consumed be increased. The mode of consumption would be altered; instead of being applied to the feeding of horses, or to the supply of stimulant liquids, a certain portion of them would be used as human food. And, as the desire to eat is more urgent than the desire to feed horses, or drink beer or spirits, the desire to obtain oats and barley, or, in other words, the pleasure given, or the pain averted, by the possession of a given quantity of them, or, in other words, the *utility* of a given quantity of them, would increase. A fact which, in ordinary language, would be expressed by saying, that the demand for them was increased.

But though the vagueness with which the word Demand has been used renders it an objectionable term, it is too useful and concise to be given up; but we shall endeavour never to use it in any other signification than as expressing the utility of a commodity; or, what is the same, for we have seen that all utility is relative, the degree in which its possession is desired.

Supply.—We cannot complain of equal vagueness in the use of the word Supply. In ordinary language, as well as in the writings of Political Economists, it is used to signify the quantity of a commodity actually brought to market. The complaint is, not that the word Supply has been used in this sense, but that, when used in this sense, it has been considered as a cause of value, except in a few cases, or for very short periods. We have shown, in the examples of coats and waistcoats, and gold and silver, that the reciprocal value of any two commodities depends, not on the quantity of each brought to market, but on the comparative force of the obstacles which in each case oppose any increase in that quantity. When, therefore, we represent increase or diminution of supply as affecting value, we must be understood to mean not a mere positive increase or diminution, but an increase or diminution occasioned by a diminution or increase of the obstacles by which the supply is limited.

Intrinsic and Extrinsic Causes of the Value of a Commodity.—To revert to our original proposition, the reciprocal Values of any two commodities must be determined by two sets of causes; those which determine the Demand and Supply of the one, and those which determine the Demand and Supply of the other. The causes which give utility to a commodity and limit it in supply may be called the *intrinsic* causes of its value; those which limit the supply and occasion the utility of the commodities for which it is to be exchanged, may be called the *extrinsic* causes of its value. Gold and silver are now exchanged for one another in Europe in the proportion of one ounce of gold for about sixteen ounces of silver. This proportion must arise partly from the causes which give utility to gold and limit its supply, and partly from those which create the utility and limit the supply of silver. When talking of the value of gold we may consider the first set of causes as influencing its general value, since they affect its powers of commanding every commodity in exchange. The second set of causes affect gold only so far as it is to be exchanged for silver, which may be called one of its specific values; the aggregate of its specific values forming its general value. If while the causes which give utility to silver and limit it in supply were unaltered, those which affect gold should vary; if, for instance, fashion should require every well-dressed man to have all his buttons of pure gold, or the disturbances in South America should permanently stop all the gold works of Brazil and Colombia, and thus (as would be the case) intercept five-sixths of our supplies of gold, the reciprocal values of gold and silver would in time be materially varied. Though silver would be unaltered both as to its utility and as to its limitation in supply, a given quantity of it would exchange for a less quantity of gold, in the proportion perhaps of twenty to one, instead of sixteen to one. As between one another the rise and fall of gold and silver would precisely correspond, silver would fall and gold would rise one-fourth. But the fall of silver would not be general but specific; though fallen as estimated in gold, it would command precisely the same quantities as before of all other commodities. The rise of gold would be general; a given quantity of it would command one-fourth more not only of silver, but of all other commodities. The holder of a given quantity of silver would be just as rich as before for all purposes except the purchase of gold; the holder of a given quantity of gold would be richer than before for all purposes.

The circumstances by which each different class of commodities is invested with utility and limited in supply are subject to perpetual

variation. Sometimes one of the causes alone varies. Sometimes
they both vary in the same direction; sometimes in opposite directions.
In the last case the opposite variations, wholly or partially, neutralize
one another.

The effects of an increased Demand concurrent with increased
obstacles to Supply, and of diminished Demand concurrent with
increased facility of Supply, are well exemplified by hemp. Its
average price before the revolutionary war, exclusive of duty, did not
exceed £30 per ton. The increased Demand, occasioned by a maritime war, and the natural obstacles to a proportionate increase of
Supply, raised it, in the year 1796, to above £50 a ton; at about
which price it continued during the next twelve years. But in 1808,
the rupture between England and the Baltic powers, the principal
source of our supplies, suddenly raised it to £118 a ton, being nearly
four times the average price in peace. At the close of the war, both
the extraordinary demand and the extraordinary obstacles to the
supply ceased together, and the price fell to about its former average.

We have already stated that the utility of a commodity, in our
extended sense of the term utility, or, in other words, the demand for
it as an object of purchase or hire, is principally dependent on the
obstacles which limit its supply. But there are many cases in which,
while the existing obstacles remain unaltered, the demand is affected
by the slightest suspicion that their force may at a future period be
increased or diminished. This occurs with respect to those commodities
of which the supply is not susceptible of accurate regulation, but is
afforded either in uncertain quantities and at stated periods, between
which it cannot be increased or diminished,—in the case for instance
of the annual products of the earth,—or is dependent on our relations
with foreign Countries. If a harvest deficient by one-third should
occur, that deficiency must last for a whole year, or be supplied from
abroad at an extravagant cost. If we should go to war with Russia,
the obstacles to the supply of hemp would be increased while the war
lasted. In either case the holders of corn or hemp would obtain great
profits. In all rich Countries, and particularly in our own, there is a
great number of persons who have large masses of wealth capable of
being suddenly applied to the purchase of any given objects. The
instant such persons suspect that the obstacles to the supply of any
article are likely to be increased, they are anxious to become holders
of it. They enter the market as new demanders; the price rises,
and the mere fact that it has risen is a cause of its rising further.
The details of commerce are so numerous, the difficulty of obtaining
early and accurate information is so great, and the facts themselves
are so constantly changing, that the most cautious merchants are
often forced to act upon very doubtful premises; and the imprudent,
dazzled by the chance of an enormous gain, which will be their own,
and little restrained by the fear of a loss which may principally fall

upon their creditors, are often ready to act upon scarcely any premises at all.   They see that the price of some article has risen, and they suppose that there must be some good cause for it.   They see that if they had purchased a month ago, they would have been gainers now, and conclude that if they purchase now they will be gainers a month hence.   So far is this reasoning, if it can be called reasoning, carried, that a rise in the price of any one important commodity is generally found to occasion a rise in the price of many others.   "A" (thinks a speculator) "bought hemp before the price had risen, and has resold it at a profit.   Cotton has not yet risen, nor do I see clearly why it should rise, any more than I see why hemp should have risen, but it probably will rise like hemp, therefore I will purchase."

Those who are not practically conversant with commercial transactions, and who are probably accustomed to consider our merchants and capitalists as men of sober minds, and cautious conduct, may perhaps think that we exaggerate the influence of imagination over judgment when we suppose that large fortunes are often risked on such reasoning as this.   We cannot support our view better than by the authority of Mr. Tooke, a merchant of great talent and knowledge, and, at the period when he wrote, forced, for his own safety, to watch narrowly the phenomena which he described.   The passages which we subjoin are taken from his account of the circumstances which occasioned the extraordinary rise of prices in the beginning of 1825. "The close of each year [9] is the period at which, by annual custom, the stocks of goods on hand, and the prospects of supply and consumption for the coming season, are stated and reasoned upon by merchants and brokers in circular letters addressed to their correspondents and employers.   By these circulars it appeared (at the close of 1824) that, of some important articles, the stock on hand fell short of that at the close of the preceding year.   From this the conclusion was more or less plausibly deduced, that the rate of the annual consumption of those articles was outrunning the rate of the annual supply, and that an advance in price ought to take place; and at the same time, there were, as in the case of cotton and silk, confident reports of the failure of crops or other causes which would inevitably diminish the forthcoming supply.   Expectation of scarcity was thus combined with actual deficiency in exciting the spirit of speculation.   This was directed in the first instance to the articles which, upon fair mercantile grounds, justified and called for some advance in price, inasmuch as the rate of the consumption of them had outrun the average rate of supply.   The rise, however, which would have been requisite to increase the supply, or to diminish the consumption, would, in most of the cases in question, have been trifling.

"But when speculation is once on foot, the rise of any one article

---

[9] *Considerations on the State of the Currency*, p. 43.

may not only be in a ratio far greater than the occasion really calls for, but may cause indirectly a rise in other commodities.

" The impulse, therefore, to a rise being given, and every succeeding purchaser having realized, or appearing to have the power of realizing, a profit, a fresh inducement appeared in every step of the advance to bring forward new buyers. These were no longer such only as were conversant with the market: many persons were induced to go out of their own line, and to embark their funds, or stretch their credit, with a view to engage in what was represented to them by the brokers a certain means of realizing a great and immediate gain.

" Cotton exhibited the most extraordinary instance of speculation carried beyond all reasonable bounds. Silk, wool, and some other articles, in which some advance was justified by the relative state of the supply and demand, became the subjects of a speculative anticipation, and advanced much beyond the occasion, as the event proved, though not in so great a degree as cotton.

" Never did the public, that part of it at least which entered into the vortex of the operations in question, exhibit so great a degree of infatuation, so complete an abandonment of all the most ordinary rules of mercantile reasoning since the celebrated bubble year 1720, as it did in the latter part of 1824, and in the first three or four months of 1825.

" The speculative anticipation of an advance was no longer confined to articles which presented a plausible ground for some rise however small. It extended itself to articles which were not only not deficient in quantity but which were actually in excess. Thus coffee, of which the stock was increased compared with the average of former years, advanced from 70 to 80 per cent. Spices rose in some instances from 100 to 200 per cent. without any reason whatever, and with a total ignorance on the part of the operators of every thing connected with the relation of the supply to the consumption.

" In short, there was hardly an article of merchandise which did not participate in the rise. For it became the business of the speculators or the brokers, who were interested in raising and keeping up prices, to look minutely through the general Price Currents with a view to discover any article which had not advanced, in order to make it the subject of anticipated demand.

" If a person not under the influence of the prevailing delusion ventured to inquire for what reason any particular article had risen, the common answer was, ' Every thing else has risen, and therefore this ought to rise.' "

When we consider that the supply of large classes of commodities is dependent on our amicable or hostile relations with foreign States, and on the commercial and financial legislation both of those States and of our own Country, and that the supply of still larger classes is dependent not only on those contingencies, but on the accidents of the

seasons,—and when we consider how the demand is affected not merely
by the existing, or the anticipated obstacles to the supply, but often
by a spirit of speculation as blind as that of a gambler ignorant of the
odds and even of the principles of his game,—it is obvious that the
general value of all commodities, the quantity of each which will
exchange for a given quantity of every other, can never remain the
same for a single day. Every day there will be a variation in the
demand or the supply of one or more of the innumerable classes of
commodities which are the objects of exchange in a commercial
Country. A given quantity of the commodity which has varied will
consequently exchange for a greater or a less quantity of all other
commodities. All other commodities, therefore, will have varied in
value as estimated in the first-mentioned commodity. It is as impossible for one commodity to remain perfectly unaltered in value while
any other is altered, as it would be for a lighthouse to keep at the
same distance from all the ships in a harbour while any one of them
should approach it or recede.

Steadiness in Value, on what it depends.—But it may be asked, what
do we mean when we say that a commodity has, for a given period,
remained *steady* in value?

The question must be answered by referring to the different effects
produced on the value of a commodity by an alteration in the intrinsic,
or an alteration in the extrinsic, causes on which value depends. If
the causes which give utility to a commodity and limit its supply, and
which we have called the intrinsic causes of its value, are altered, the
rise or fall in its value will be general. A given quantity of it will
exchange for a greater or a less quantity than before of every other
commodity which has not also varied at the same time, in the same
direction, and in the same degree; a coincidence which rarely occurs.
Every other commodity must also rise or fall in value as estimated in
the first-mentioned commodity, but not generally.

The fluctuations in value to which a commodity is subject by alterations, in what we have called the extrinsic causes of its value, or, in
other words, by alterations in the demand or supply of other commodities, have a tendency, like all other extensive combinations of
chances, to neutralize one another. While it retains the same utility,
and is limited in supply by the same causes, a given quantity of it,
though it may exchange for a greater or a less quantity of different
specific commodities, will in general command the same average
quantity as before of the general mass of commodities; what it gains
or loses in one direction being made up in another. It may be said,
without impropriety, therefore, to remain steady in value. But the
rise or fall in value which a commodity experiences in consequence of
an alteration in its utility, or in the obstacles to its supply, is, in fact,
entirely uncompensated. It is compensated only with regard to those
commodities of which the utility or the supply has also varied at the

same time and in the same direction. And as quite as many are likely to experience a similar variation, but in an opposite direction, there is really *no* compensation. A commodity, therefore, which is strikingly subject to such variations, is properly said to be unsteady in value.

But we may be asked to account for another and not unfrequent statement, that at particular periods *all* commodities have been observed to rise or fall in value. Literally taken, this statement involves a contradiction in terms, since it is impossible that a given quantity of every commodity should exchange for a greater or a less quantity of every other. When those who make this statement have any meaning, they always tacitly exclude some one commodity, and estimate in that the rise or fall of all others. The excluded commodity is, in general, money or labour.

Estimated in labour, all commodities, money included, have fallen in value in England since the XVIth Century. It is scarcely possible to mention one of which a given quantity will not purchase less labour than it did at the close of Elizabeth's reign; estimated in money, almost all commodities, labour included, have fallen in England since the termination of the late war.

The last remark which we shall now make on value is, that, with a very few exceptions, it is strictly local. A ton of coal at the bottom of the pit near Newcastle is perhaps worth 2s. 6d., at the pit's mouth it is perhaps worth 5s., at ten miles off 7s., at Hull 10s. By the time the collier has reached the Pool, its cargo is seldom worth less than 16s. a ton; and the inhabitant of Grosvenor Square may perhaps think himself fortunate if he can fill his coal cellars at 25s. a ton,[10] A ton of coal, though physically identical, must be considered, for economical purposes, as a different commodity at the bottom of the pit and at its mouth, in Hull and in Grosvenor Square. At every different stage of its progress it is limited in supply by different obstacles, and consequently exchangeable for different things and in different proportions. Supposing that at Newcastle a ton of the best wheat is now worth about twenty tons of the best coal: the same wheat and coal at the west end of London may probably exchange in the proportions of about four tons of coal for one of wheat. At Odessa, they may perhaps exchange about weight for weight.

Whenever, therefore, we speak of the value of a commodity, it is necessary to state the locality both of the commodity in question, and of the commodity in which its value is estimated. And in most cases we shall find their respective proximity to the places where they are respectively to be made use of one of the principal constituents of their respective values. The purchaser of the distant commodity has to consider the labour of transporting it to the place of consumption, the

[10] These prices are merely assumed for the purpose of illustration.

time for which that labour must be paid in advance, and the taxation, and the risk of injury or loss to which it may be subject in its transit. Nor is this all. He must also consider the danger that its quality may not correspond with the description or sample which guided him in making the purchase. The whole expense and risk attending the transport of a diamond from Edinburgh to London are but trifling; but its value is so dependent on its form and lustre, and those are qualities as to which it is so difficult to satisfy any purchaser who cannot ascertain them by inspection, that it would be difficult to obtain in London a fair price for a diamond in Edinburgh. Again, though a given quantity of coal from a given mine is generally of an ascertained quality, yet the expense, loss of time, risk, and taxation, which must be incurred in its transport from Newcastle to Grosvenor Square, are such, that a ton of coal, when it has reached Grosvenor Square, may be of nearly five times the value which it bore at Newcastle.

OBJECTIONS TO THE DEFINITION OF WEALTH CONSIDERED.

The definition of Wealth, as comprehending all those things, and those things only, which have Value, or, in other words, which may be purchased or hired, does not, we believe, precisely agree with that adopted by any Economist except Archbishop Whately.

The principal differences are these: some writers confine the term Wealth to what have been termed material products; some to those things which have been produced or acquired by human labour; and some object to the ideas of value or exchange being introduced into the definition of Wealth.

The question whether the things which have been called immaterial ought to be considered articles of wealth, we shall consider when we treat of production.

Some of the writers who, expressly or impliedly, restrict the term Wealth to the things, the production or appropriation of which has cost human labour, as for instance Mr. Mill, Mr. M'Culloch, Colonel Torrens, Mr. Malthus, and M. Flores-Estrada, appear to suppose that a definition so restricted will comprise every thing that can properly be termed wealth; others, among whom is Mr. Ricardo, admit that there are some things falling within that term which have not been acquired by human exertion, but think them so few or unimportant that it is better to omit them than to disorder the symmetry of the Science by extending it to any thing that is not the result of labour.

The former doctrine is clearly stated in the following passages from Mr. Malthus, Colonel Torrens, and Mr. M'Culloch.

"Wealth. The material things necessary, useful, or agreeable to man, which have required some portion of human exertion to appropriate or produce."[11]

---

[11] Malthus, *Definitions*, p. 234.

" Wealth, considered as the object of economical Science, consists of those material articles which are useful or desirable to man, and which it requires some portion of voluntary exertion to procure or to preserve. Thus two things are essential to wealth : the possession of utility, and the requiring some portion of voluntary exertion or labour. That which has no utility, which serves neither to supply our wants, nor to gratify our desires, is as the dust beneath our feet, or as the sand upon the shore, and obviously forms no portion of our wealth ; while, on the other hand, things which possess the highest utility, and which are even necessary to our existence, come not under the denomination of wealth, unless to the possession of utility be superadded the circumstance of having been procured by some voluntary exertion. Though the air which we breathe and the sunbeams by which we are warmed are in the highest degree useful and necessary, it would be a departure from the precision of language to denominate them articles of wealth. But the bread which appeases the cravings of hunger, and the clothing which protects us from the rigour of the season, though not more indispensably requisite than the former, are with propriety classed under the term wealth ; because to the possession of utility they add the circumstance of having been produced by labour." [12]

" Labour is the only source of wealth. Nature spontaneously furnishes the matter of which all commodities are made ; but until labour has been expended in appropriating matter, or in adapting it to our use, it is wholly destitute of value, and is not, nor ever has been, considered as forming wealth. Place us on the banks of a river, or in an orchard, and we shall inevitably perish of thirst or hunger, if we do not, *by an effort of industry*, raise the water to our lips, or pluck the fruit from its parent tree.

" An object which it does not require any portion of labour to appropriate or to adapt to our own use, may be of the very highest utility, but, as it is the free gift of nature, it is utterly impossible it can possess the smallest value." [13]

Mr. M'Culloch appears to use the word labour as including all voluntary action. And without doubt, if we use the word labour in so extended a sense, it is true that labour is almost necessarily incidental to the *enjoyment* of wealth. If it be an act of industry to gather an apple, it is equally an act of industry to raise it from one's plate ; and every guest at a festival earns his food by the labour which he exerts in appropriating his own portion. Such attempts as these to bend facts and language into accordance with hasty generalization, have thrown on Political Economy a degree of ridicule which is one of the principal obstacles to its progress.

Mr. Malthus, Colonel Torrens, and the other Economists who consider labour, using that word in its popular sense, as a necessary

---

[12] Torrens, *Production of Wealth*, Ch. i.   [13] *Principles of Political Economy*, 66—72.

constituent of wealth, appear to have been led to that opinion by observing, first, that some quality besides mere utility is necessary to value; secondly, that all those things which are useful, and are acquired by labour, are valuable; and thirdly, that almost every thing which is valuable *has* required some labour for its acquisition. But the fact that that circumstance is not essential to value will be demonstrated if we can suppose a case in which value could exist without it. If, while carelessly lounging along the sea-shore, I were to pick up a pearl, would it have no value? Mr. M'Culloch would answer that the value of the pearl was the result of my appropriative industry in stooping to pick it up. Suppose then that I met with it while eating an oyster? Supposing that aerolithes consisted of gold, would they have no value? Or, suppose that meteoric iron were the only form in which that metal were produced, would not the iron supplied from heaven be far more valuable than any existing metal? It is true that, wherever there is utility, the addition of labour as necessary to production constitutes value, because, the supply of labour being limited, it follows that the object, to the supply of which it is necessary, is by that very necessity limited in supply. But any other cause limiting supply is just as efficient a cause of value in an article as the necessity of labour to its production. And, in fact, if all the commodities used by man were supplied by nature without any intervention whatever of human labour, but were supplied in precisely the same quantities as they now are, there is no reason to suppose either that they would cease to be valuable, or would exchange in any other than their present proportions.

The reply to Mr. Ricardo is, first, that the articles of wealth which do not owe the principal part of their value to the labour which has been bestowed on their respective actual production, form, in fact, the bulk of wealth, instead of a small and unimportant portion of it; and secondly, that, as limitation of supply is essential to the value of labour itself, to assume labour, and exclude limitation of supply, as the condition on which value depends, is not only to substitute a partial for a general cause, but pointedly to exclude the very cause which gives force to the cause assigned.

We have lastly to consider the objections which have been raised to the definition of wealth as a general name for the things which have value. Those who use the word value as synonymous with *cost*, or as comprehending whatever is useful, of course object to its introduction into the definition of wealth; and so should we do if we used the word value in either of those senses. But other writers, using the word value in its popular sense, have objected that, according to the definition which we have adopted, the same thing will be wealth to one person and not to another. This consequence is evident; and it is evident that even to the same person the same quality may be wealth under some circumstances, and not so under others. The knowledge

of English law is profitable in England, that of French law in France ;
if an English lawyer, with no other property but his knowledge, were
to settle in France, or a French lawyer in England, he would find
himself instantly reduced from affluence to poverty.   The power of
telling long stories is a source of profit in Asia, but valueless in
Europe.   According to our nomenclature, therefore, it would be
wealth in Persia, and cease to be so in England.   If an actress should
embrace a religious sect of which the tenets should be incompatible
with the stage, her vocal and dramatic talents would no longer be
exchangeable, she would no longer be able to let them out by the
evening.   We should say, therefore, that they had ceased to be a
part of her wealth.   But we are at a loss to conceive how the power
of making this distinction is an objection to the language in question.
It seems to be its principal convenience.

Again, Colonel Torrens supposes a solitary family, or a nation in
which each person should consume only his own productions, or one
in which there should be a community of goods, and urges, as a
reductio ad absurdum, that in these cases, though there might be an
abundance of commodities, as there would be no exchanges, there
would, in our sense of the term, be no wealth.   The answer is, that,
for the purposes of Political Economy, there would be no wealth ; for,
in fact, in such a state of things, supposing it possible, the Science of
Political Economy would have no application.   In such a state of
society, Agriculture, Mechanics, or any other of the Arts which are
subservient to the production of the commodities which are, with us,
the subjects of exchange, might be studied, but the Science of Political
Economy would not exist.   We may add, that if the common usage
which identifies wealth with the things which have value is a convenient
one in all the forms which human nature really exhibits, it is no
objection to it that it would not be convenient in a state of society of
which we have no experience.

STATEMENT OF THE FOUR ELEMENTARY PROPOSITIONS
OF THE SCIENCE OF POLITICAL ECONOMY

WE have already stated that the general facts on which the Science of Political Economy rests, are comprised in a few general Propositions, the result of observation or consciousness. The Propositions to which we then alluded are these:—

1. *That every man desires to obtain additional Wealth with as little sacrifice as possible.*

2. *That the Population of the world, or, in other words, the number of persons inhabiting it, is limited only by moral or physical evil, or by fear of a deficiency of those articles of wealth which the habits of the individuals of each class of its inhabitants lead them to require.*

3. *That the powers of Labour, and of the other instruments which produce wealth, may be indefinitely increased by using their Products as the means of further Production.*

4. *That, agricultural skill remaining the same, additional Labour employed on the land within a given district produces in general a less proportionate return, or, in other words, that though, with every increase of the labour bestowed, the aggregate return is increased, the increase of the return is not in proportion to the increase of the labour.*

The first of these Propositions is a matter of consciousness, the three others are matter of observation. As the first and second involve little use of the peculiar abstractions of Political Economy, except those implied in the term Wealth, and may therefore be explained with little recourse to its peculiar nomenclature, we shall consider them immediately; leaving the third and fourth for discussion in a subsequent part of this Treatise. They are, however, so nearly self-evident, that we will venture in the mean time to assume their truth. No one who reflects on the difference between the unassisted force of man, and the more than gigantic powers of capital and machinery, can doubt the former proposition; and, to convince ourselves of the other, it is necessary only to recollect that, if it were false, no land except the very best could ever be cultivated: since, if the return from a single farm were to increase in full proportion to any amount of increased labour bestowed on it, the produce of that one farm might feed the whole population of England.

DEVELOPMENT OF THE FIRST ELEMENTARY PROPOSITION OF THE SCIENCE, NAMELY, THAT ON

The General Desire for Wealth.

In stating that every man desires to cbtain additional wealth with as little sacrifice as possible, we must not be supposed to mean, that every body, or indeed any body, wishes for an indefinite quantity of every thing; still less as stating that wealth, though the universal, either is, or ought to be, the principal object of human desire. What we mean to state is, that no person feels his whole wants to be adequately supplied; that every person has some unsatisfied desires which he believes that additional wealth would gratify. The nature and the urgency of each individual's wants are as various as the differences in individual character. Some may wish for power, others for distinction, and others for leisure; some require bodily, and others mental amusement; some are anxious to produce important advantage to the public; and there are few, perhaps there are none, who, if it could be done by a wish, would not benefit their acquaintances and friends. Money seems to be the only object for which the desire is universal; and it is so, because money is abstract wealth. Its possessor may satisfy at will his ambition, or vanity, or indolence, his public spirit or his private benevolence; may multiply the means of obtaining bodily pleasure, or of avoiding bodily evil, or the still more expensive amusements of the mind. Any one of these pursuits would exhaust the largest fortune within the limits of individual acquisition; and, as all men would engage in some of them, and many in all, the desire for wealth must be insatiable, though the modes in which different individuals would employ it are infinitely diversified.

An equal diversity exists in the amount and the kind of the sacrifices which different individuals, or even the same individual, will encounter in the pursuit of wealth. And not only is the same sacrifice more severe to one than to another, as some will not give up ease or leisure for study, others good air and a country life, and others recreation and society, but the absolute desire for wealth on the one hand, and the absolute will to encounter toils or privations in its pursuit on the other, are stronger in some men than in others. These differences form some of the principal distinctions in individual and national character. Experience, however, shows, and indeed it might have been predicted *à priori*, that the greatest and longest continued sacrifices will be made in those Countries in which property is most secure, and the road to social eminence is the most open. The inhabitants of Holland and of Great Britain, and of the Countries that have derived their institutions from Great Britain, the nations which up to the present time have best enjoyed those advantages, have up to the present time been the most ardent and the most successful in the pursuit of opulence. But even the Indians of Mexico, though their indolence makes them submit to poverty under which an Englishman would feel life a burden, would willingly be rich if it cost them no trouble.

It may be necessary, however, to explain our motives for dwelling on so much that is self-evident. Our first reason is, that the proposition in question, though we are not aware that any one has thought that it required to be formally stated, is assumed in almost every process of economical reasoning. It is the corner-stone of the doctrine of wages and profits, and, generally speaking, of exchange. In short, it is in Political Economy what gravitation is in Physics, or the *dictum de omni et nullo* in Logic: the ultimate fact beyond which reasoning cannot go, and of which almost every other proposition is merely an illustration. In an attempt to state the evidence on which the Science rests, it appeared to us improper to omit its foundation, though at the hazard of appearing to take up our reader's time in defending what it may be supposed that nobody ever thought of questioning.

But, in the second place, this proposition, apparently self-evident, *has* been impliedly questioned. It is directly opposed to a doctrine of considerable popularity, and supported by great names,—we mean the doctrine of over-production or *universal* glut.

By the word glut is meant the production of a given commodity in an abundance, either absolutely beyond the desires of its intended consumers, or beyond the amount for which they are able and willing to offer in exchange equivalents sufficient to induce the producer to continue his operations. Books are, perhaps, the commodities most subject to gluts. The proportionate expenses of printing and advertising increase so rapidly, if the number of copies printed be much reduced, and authors are so little subject to underrate the probable demand for their labours, that scarcely any edition consists of less than two hundred and fifty copies, and very few of less than five hundred. But we have seen calculations showing that not in one case out of two hundred are all the copies sold off at the price at which they originally came out. In ordinary cases, from fifty to one hundred are sold in the first year, and thirty or forty in the second; by the end of which time the book has been forgotten, and the unsold copies are put up to sale at periodical auctions among the booksellers. The best that can happen to them is to be purchased on this occasion in order to be again offered to the public; but the majority of Works are found to be worth purchase not as books, but as paper. They are unsold at the trade sales, and find their way

In vicum vendentem thus et odores
Et piper, et quidquid chartis amicitur ineptis.

We have selected books as affording an illustration of a glut arising from a miscalculation not of the ability, but of the willingness of purchasers. The opening of a new trade is generally followed by gluts occasioned by miscalculations of both. Every one must recollect, when Brazil and Spanish America first became accessible, our exports of skaits, and fire-irons, and warming pans to the tropics. And, until their real poverty was known, we continued to fill their warehouses with cargoes, adapted indeed to their wants, but far beyond their means. Miscalculations of this kind must obviously be of frequent occurrence; and perhaps what ought to excite our surprise is, not the extent to which they prevail, but the degree in which they are avoided. But it appears clear that they can arise only from one or the other of two causes: either from the articles of wealth, with respect to which the glut exists, having been prepared for persons who do not want them, or from those persons not being provided with other articles of wealth, suited to the desires of the producers of the first-mentioned articles of wealth, to offer in exchange for them. Partial gluts, occasioned by the one or the other of these causes, are among the most ordinary commercial occurrences. But the opinion to which our doctrine is opposed is that which admits the possibility not only of partial but of *universal* gluts, which supposes it possible that there may be at the same time a glut of services and commodities in general,—that we may have too much of every thing; a doctrine not only of frequent occurrence in conversations on commercial subjects, but even maintained by some distinguished writers. Now as by the assumed hypothesis of a universal glut all the articles of wealth exist not only in abundance, but in superabundance, an absolute deficiency of equivalents cannot be one of its causes. And it can scarcely be supposed that there can be such a general state of commercial cross-purposes as to prevent, in the majority of cases, the proper sellers and purchasers from meeting. It can scarcely be supposed that when A has what B wants, and B what A wants, A and B should, in the majority of instances, instead of finding out and exchanging with one another, offer their respective commodities to Y and Z, who, having also each reciprocal wants and supplies, neither wish to purchase from A or B, nor have discovered the means of exchanging with one another. But if it be absurd to suppose that a general glut could be occasioned by such an universal spirit of blundering as this, the only remaining hypothesis on which the existence of a general glut can be supposed is that of a general satiety, that all men may be so fully provided with the precise articles which they desire as to afford no market for each other's superfluities. And this doctrine is opposed to the proposition with which we set out, that every man desires to obtain additional wealth.

DEVELOPMENT OF THE SECOND ELEMENTARY PROPOSITION OF THE
SCIENCE, NAMELY, THAT ON

The Causes which Limit Population.

Having explained the sense in which we use the word wealth, and stated, or rather recalled to the recollection of our readers, the general desire to obtain additional wealth with the least possible sacrifice, we now proceed to consider the second of the four elementary propositions on which the Science of Political Economy is founded; namely, that the population of the world, or, in other words, the number of persons inhabiting it, is limited only by moral or physical evil, or by fear of the deficiency of those articles of wealth which the habits of the individuals of each class of its inhabitants lead them to require.

It is now generally admitted, indeed it is strange that it should ever have required to be pointed out, that every species of plant or animal which is capable of increase, either by generation or by seed, must be capable of a constantly increasing increase; every addition to its numbers being capable of affording a source of still further additions; or, in other words, that wherever there is a capacity of increase, it must be a capacity of increase not by mere addition, but by multiplication; or, to use the short form in which the proposition is usually stated, not in an arithmetical, but in a geometrical ratio. The rate at which any species of plant or animal is capable of increasing, must depend on the average power of reproduction, and the average period of existence of the individuals of which it is constituted. Wheat, we know, is an annual, and its average power of reproduction, perhaps, about six for one; on that supposition, the produce of a single acre might cover the globe in fourteen years. The rate at which the human race is capable of increasing has been determined by observation. It has been ascertained that, for considerable periods and in extensive districts, under temperate climates, it has doubled every twenty-five years.

The power of reproduction in the human race must, under similar climates, be always the same. We say, under similar climates, because the acceleration of puberty, which has been sometimes observed in tropical climates, unless checked, as is probably the case, by an earlier cessation of child-bearing, would occasion increased fecundity. Now, the United States of America, the districts in which the rate of increase which we have mentioned has been most clearly ascertained, are not remarkable for the longevity of their inhabitants. We may infer, therefore, that such is the average power of reproduction and average duration of life in the individuals constituting the human species, that their number may double every twenty-five years. At this rate the inhabitants of every Country would, in the course of every five centuries, increase to above a million times their previous number. At this rate the population of England would, in five hundred years, exceed fifteen million millions: a population which would not allow them standing room. Such being the human powers of increase, the question is, By what checks is their expansion controlled? How comes it that the population of the world, instead of being now a million times as great as it was five hundred years ago, apparently has not doubled within that time, and certainly has not quadrupled?

Mr. Malthus has divided the checks to population into the preventive and the positive. The first are those which limit fecundity, the second those which decrease longevity. The first diminish the number of births, the second increase that of deaths. And as fecundity and longevity are the only elements of the calculation, it is clear that Mr. Malthus's division is exhaustive. The positive check to population is physical evil. The preventive checks are promiscuous intercourse and abstinence from marriage. The first is moral evil; the second is, with a very few exceptions, so few indeed that they do not affect the result, founded on an apprehended deficiency of some of the things to which we have given the general appellation of wealth. All the preventive and positive checks may therefore be distributed under prudence, moral evil, and physical evil. We will first consider the positive check.

We have seen that this check includes all the causes which tend, in any way, prematurely to shorten the duration of human existence: such as unwholesome occupations, severe labour, or exposure to the seasons, bad or insufficient food or clothing, bad nursing of children, excesses of all kinds, the corruption of the air from natural causes, or from large towns, wars, infanticide, plague, and famine. Of these, some arise from the laws of nature, and others from the crimes and follies of man: all are directly and immediately felt in the form of physical evil, though many of them are the result, more or less remotely, of moral evil.

The final and irresistible mode in which physical evil operates is the want of the necessaries of existence: death produced by hardship or starvation. This is almost the only check to the increase of the irrational animals; and as man descends towards their condition, he falls more and more under its influence. In the lowest savage state it is the principal and obvious check; in a high state of civilization it is almost imperceptible; but is unperceived only in consequence of the operation of its substitutes.

We have already stated that, as a general rule, additional labour employed in the cultivation of the land within a given district, produces a less proportionate return. And it has appeared that such is the power of reproduction and duration of life in mankind, that the population of a given district is capable of doubling itself at least every twenty-five years. It is clear, therefore, that the rate at which the production of food is capable of being increased, and that at which population, if unchecked, would increase, are totally different. Every addition made to the quantity of food periodically produced, makes in general a further periodical addition more difficult. Every addition to the existing population diffuses wider the means of still further addition. If neither evil, nor the fear of evil, checked the population of England, it would amount in a century to above two hundred millions. Suppose it possible that we might be able to raise or to import the subsistence of two hundred millions of people: is it possible that one hundred and twenty-five years hence we should be able to support four hundred millions? or, in one hundred and fifty years, eight hundred millions? It is clear, however, that long before the first century had elapsed, long before the period at which, if unchecked, we should have attained two hundred millions, no excellence in our institutions, or salubrity of climate, or unremitting industry, could have saved us from being arrested in our progress by a constantly increasing want of subsistence. If all other moral and physical checks could be got rid of, if we had neither wars nor libertinism, if our habitations, and employments, and habits were all wholesome, and no fears of indigence or loss of station prevented or retarded our marriages, famine would soon exercise her prerogative of controlling, in the last resort, the multiplication of mankind.

But though it be certain that the absence of all other checks would only give room for the irresistible influence of famine, it is equally certain that such a state of things never has existed and never will exist.

In the first place the absence of all the other moral and physical evils which retard population implies a degree of civilization not only high, but higher than mankind have as yet enjoyed. Such a society cannot be supposed to want sagacity sufficient to foresee the evils of a too rapidly increasing population, and prudence sufficient to avoid them. In such a state the preventive check would be in full operation, and its force is quite sufficient to render unnecessary even the approach of any positive check.

And, secondly, it is impossible that a positive check, so goading and so remorseless as famine, should prevail without bringing in her train all the others. Pestilence is her uniform companion, and murder and war are her followers. Whole bodies of men will not tamely lie down to die, and witness, while they are perishing, their wives, and children, and parents, starving around them. Where there is a diversity of fortunes, famine generally produces that worst form of civil war, the insurrection of the poor against the rich. Among uncivilized nations it produces those tremendous hostile migrations in which a whole people throws itself across a neighbouring frontier, and either perishes in the attempt to obtain a larger or a more fertile territory, or destroys the former possessors, or drives them out to be themselves aggressors in turn.

In fact, almost all the positive checks, by their mutual reaction, have a tendency to create and aggravate one another; and the destruction of those who perish immediately by one, may generally be found to have been remotely occasioned or promoted by one or more of the others. Among nations imperfectly civilized, the widest and the most wasting of the positive checks is predatory war. A district exposed to it is likely to suffer all the others. Mere fear of invasion must generally keep the great body of its inhabitants pent up in crowded and consequently unwholesome towns; it must confine their cultivation to the fields in the immediate neighbourhood of those towns, and, if it does not destroy, must so much impede their commerce as to render it useless as a source of subsistence; and when the invasion does come, it is often followed by the complete extirpation of the invaded community. This is the check which has kept Africa, and the central parts of Asia, in their comparatively unpeopled state.

In his journey from Abyssinia to Sennaar, Bruce crossed the territory of Atbara, subject to the incursions of the Daveina Arabs. The whole seems to have been a scene of desolation. He passed a night at Garigara, a village, of which they had destroyed the crops a year before. The inhabitants had all perished with hunger, and their remains were unburied and scattered over the ground where the village had stood. The travellers encamped among the bones: no space could be found free from them. His next stage was Teawa. "Its consequence," he observes, "was to remain only till the Daveina should resolve to attack it, when its corn fields being burnt and destroyed in a night by a multitude of horsemen, the bones of its inhabitants scattered upon the earth would be all its remains, like those of the miserable village of Garigara."

Among the positive checks to the population of uncivilized, or partially civilized, nations, the next in importance to war is famine. When a people depends principally on that subsistence which is most easily obtained, and such is the case among the nations in question, the mere variations of the seasons must, from time to time, produce destructive want. Where society is better constituted, the evil of these variations is mitigated, partly from the superfluity of the more opulent classes, partly by importation, and principally by a recurrence to a less expensive diet; but in a barbarous, and consequently a poor and non-commercial people, they are among the most frightful forms of national calamity. The histories which we possess of such Countries always particularize periods of dearth as among the most memorable events recorded. They seem in a constant oscillation between the want endured by a population that has increased to the utmost limits of subsistence, and the plenty enjoyed by the survivors after that population has been thinned by war, pestilence, or famine. The remainder of the positive checks, such as infanticide and unwholesomeness of climate, habits, or situation, appear rather to facilitate early marriages than to produce any actual diminution, or prevent any actual increase of population. Infanticide has been supposed to be rather favourable to population, by opposing to the prudential check to marriage a mode of disposing of its offspring, which may appear easy in contemplation, but from which the feelings of the parents eventually recoil. The unwholesomeness of some districts is unquestionably such as to keep them totally unpeopled, or inhabited by strangers, whose numbers must be constantly recruited. Such, for instance, appears to be the case in the most unhealthy parts of Italy. Such is the case with large manufacturing towns even in the most favourable climates, unless great skill and great care are directed towards their cleanliness and ventilation. And in a newly colonized Country like the back settlements of America, where the abundance of land and the constantly increasing means of subsistence would render any preventive check unnecessary, any cause diminishing longevity must retard increase. But with these exceptions, unhealthiness rather causes the successive generations to pass more rapidly away, than diminishes the actual number of inhabitants. In some of the healthiest districts of Switzerland, the average annual mortality does not exceed one in forty-eight. In many of the marshy villages of Holland it exceeds one in twenty-three. But it would be rash to expect the population of the former to be more dense or to increase more rapidly than that of the latter. The case is, in fact, the reverse. In the Swiss villages of which we have been speaking, the births are as rare as the deaths; the population is thin and stationary. Among the Dutch the births somewhat exceed the deaths; the population is dense and is increasing. It is obvious, indeed, that the proportion of annual births to the whole number of people being given, the rate of increase must depend on the proportion borne by the annual deaths. And again, the proportion of deaths to the whole number of people being given, it must depend on the proportion borne by the births; or, to use a shorter form of expression, given the longevity, it must depend on the fecundity, and given the fecundity it must depend on the longevity. If both are given, the rate of increase may be calculated; but from only one, the conclusion must be in the disjunctive. If the annual births bear a large proportion to the existing number of people, we may conclude either that the population is rapidly increasing, or that the positive checks are in powerful operation. On the other hand, from a small proportion of annual deaths may be inferred either a rapid increase of numbers, or a strong influence of the preventive checks. The average duration of life in England is greater than in the United States of America; but so much greater is the force of the preventive checks, that the rate of increase in America is about double that in England. Again, the average duration of life in the Swiss villages to which we have referred is the same as it is in England; but the preventive check in

England, strong as it appears when compared with its force in America, is so much weaker than it is in some districts in Switzerland, that, with the same annual mortality, the population is in the one Country stationary, in the other rapidly progressive.

But although the average longevity in a Country affords no decisive evidence as to the increasing or stationary number of its inhabitants, it is among the least deceitful tests of their prosperity; far less so than that on which legislators formerly relied, the number of births. There is not an evil, moral or physical, which has not a tendency, directly or indirectly, to shorten life, but there are many which have a direct tendency to increase fecundity. The extraordinary duration of life in Great Britain, exceeding, as it does, the average of any other equally populous district, is a convincing proof of the general excellence of our climate, our institutions, and our habits.

We now proceed to consider the preventive checks to the increase of population. We have seen that they are Promiscuous Intercourse and Abstinence from Marriage.

The first does not appear to be of sufficient importance to require much consideration. It is said to produce some effect in checking the increase of the higher classes in some of the South Sea Islands; and it appears to have produced the same effect to a considerable extent among the West Indian negroes. But the nobility of the South Seas scarcely deserve to be separately considered. And, while the other forms of moral and physical evil were accumulated, as they were among the West Indian slaves, it is probable that the removal of this evil alone would have done little to promote the increase of their population.

But, with these exceptions, there are scarcely any females whose fecundity is prevented or diminished by promiscuous intercourse, except those unhappy individuals whose only trade is prostitution. And they form so small a proportion of the population of the whole world, that the check to population, occasioned by their unfruitfulness, may safely be disregarded.

The only remaining check is Abstinence from Marriage. Our readers are of course aware that, by the word "marriage," we mean to express not the peculiar and permanent connection which alone, in a Christian Country, is entitled to that name, but any agreement between a man and woman to cohabit under circumstances likely to occasion the birth of progeny. We have already observed that abstinence from marriage is almost uniformly founded on the apprehension of a deficiency of some of the things which we have denominated by the general term Wealth, or, in other words, on Prudence. Some cases certainly occur in which men remain unmarried, although their fortunes are so ample that the expenses of a family would be unperceived. But the number of persons so situated is so small, that they create an exception which would scarcely deserve attention, even if this conduct were as common among them as it is, in fact, rare.

We shall scarcely, therefore, be led into error, if, in considering the preventive checks, we confine our attention to Prudence, and assume that, as nothing but physical evil directly and immediately diminishes the longevity of mankind, nothing but an apprehended deficiency of some of the articles of wealth prevents their fecundity.

But though an apprehended deficiency of some of the articles of wealth is substantially the only preventive check to the increase of population, it is obvious that fear of the want of different articles operates, with all men, very differently ; and even that an apprehended want of the same article will affect differently the minds of the individuals of different classes. An apprehended want of corn would produce on the minds of all Englishmen a very different effect from an apprehended want of silk. An apprehended want of butcher's meat would affect very differently the minds of Englishmen of different classes. It appears to us, therefore, convenient to divide for this purpose the articles of wealth into the three great classes of Necessaries, Decencies, and Luxuries, and to explain the different effects produced by the fear of the want of the articles of wealth falling under each class. We must begin, however, by stating, as precisely as we can, what we mean by the words *Necessaries, Decencies*, and *Luxuries;* terms which have been used ever since the Moral Sciences first attracted attention, but with little attention to precision or to consistent use.

It is scarcely necessary to remind our readers that these are relative terms, and that some person must always be assigned with reference to whom a given commodity or service is a Luxury, a Decency, or a Necessary.

By *Necessaries*, then, we express those things, the use of which is requisite to keep a given individual in the health and strength essential to his going through his habitual occupations.

By *Decencies*, we express those things which a given individual must use in order to preserve his existing rank in society.

Every thing else of which a given individual makes use, or, in other words, all that portion of his consumption which is not essential to his health and strength, or to the preservation of his existing rank in society, we term *Luxury*.

It is obvious that when consumed by the inhabitants of different Countries, or even by different individuals in the same Country, the same things may be either luxuries, decencies, or necessaries.

Shoes are necessaries to all the inhabitants of England. Our habits are such that there is not an individual whose health would not suffer from the want of them. To the lowest class of the inhabitants of Scotland they are luxuries: custom enables them to go barefoot without inconvenience and without degradation. When a Scotchman rises from the lowest to the middling classes of society, they become to him decencies. He wears them to preserve, not his feet, but his station in life. To the highest class, who have been accustomed to them from infancy, they are as much necessaries as they are to all classes in England. To the higher classes in Turkey wine is a luxury and tobacco a decency. In Europe it is the reverse. The Turk drinks and the European smokes, not in obedience, but in opposition both to the rules of health and to the forms of society. But wine in Europe and the pipe in Turkey are among the refreshments to which a guest is entitled, and which it would be as indecent to refuse in the one Country as to offer in the other.

It has been said that the coal-heavers and lightermen, and some others among the hardworking London labourers, could not support their toils without the stimulus of porter. If this be true, porter is to them a necessary. To all others it is a luxury. A carriage is a Decency to a woman of fashion, a Necessary to a physician, and a Luxury to a tradesman.

The question, whether a given commodity is to be considered as a decency or a luxury, is obviously one to which no answer can be given, unless the place, the time, and the rank of the individual using it be specified. The dress which in England was only decent a hundred years ago, would be almost extravagant now, while the house and furniture which now would afford merely decent accommodation to a gentleman, would then have been luxurious for a Peer. The causes which entitle a commodity to be called a necessary are more permanent and more general. They depend partly upon the habits in which the individual in question has been brought up, partly on the nature of his occupation, on the lightness or the severity of the labours and hardships that he has to undergo, and partly on the climate in which he lives.

Of these causes we have illustrated the two first by the familiar examples of shoes and porter. But the principal cause is climate. The fuel, shelter, and raiment, which are essential to a Laplander's existence, would be worse than useless under the Tropics. And as habits and occupations are very slowly changed, and climate suffers scarcely any alteration, the commodities which are necessary to the different classes of the inhabitants of a given district may, and generally do, remain for centuries unchanged, while their decencies and luxuries are continually varying.

Among all classes the check imposed by an apprehended deficiency of mere luxuries is but slight. The motives, perhaps we might say the instincts, that prompt the human race to marriage, are too powerful to be much restrained by the fear of losing conveniences unconnected with health or station in society. Nor is population much retarded by the fear of wanting mere necessaries. In comparatively uncivilized Countries, in which alone, as we have already seen, that want is of familiar occurrence, the preventive check has little operation. They see the danger, but want prudence and self-denial to be influenced by it. On the other hand, among nations so far advanced in civilization as to be able to act on such a motive, the danger that any given person or his future family shall actually perish from indigence, appears too remote to afford any general rule of conduct.

The great preventive check is the fear of losing decencies, or, what is nearly the same, the hope to acquire, by the accumulation of a longer celibacy, the means of purchasing the decencies which give a higher social rank. When an Englishman stands hesitating between love and prudence, a family actually starving is not among his terrors; against actual want he knows that he has the fence of the poor-laws. But, however humble his desires, he cannot contemplate without anxiety a probability that the income which supported his social rank, while single, may be insufficient to maintain it when he is married; that he may be unable to give to his children the advantages of education which he enjoyed himself; in short, that he may lose his caste. Men of more enterprise are induced to postpone marriage, not merely by the fear of sinking, but also by the hope that in an unincumbered state they may rise. As they mount the horizon of their ambition keeps receding, until sometimes the time has passed for realizing those plans of domestic happiness which probably every man has formed in his youth.

It is by this desire of decencies, as distinguished from necessaries, that long-settled civilized Countries are preserved from the evils of a population greatly exceeding the means of comfortable subsistence. There are few triter subjects of declamation than the contrast between ancient simplicity and modern luxury. Few virtues, however useful, have received more applause than the contented and dignified poverty, the indifference to display, and the abstinence from unnecessary expense, which all refined nations attribute to their ancestors. Few vices, however mischievous, have been more censured than the ostentatious expenditure which every succeeding generation seems to consider its own characteristic.

It certainly seems at first sight that habits of unnecessary expenditure, as they have a tendency to diminish the wealth of an individual, must have the same effect on the wealth of a nation. And, separately considered, it appears clear that each act of unproductive consumption, whatever gratification it may afford to the consumer, must, *pro tanto*, impoverish the community. It is so much taken from the common stock and destroyed. And as the national capital is formed from the aggregate savings of individuals, it is certain that if each individual were to expend to the utmost extent of his means, the whole capital of the Country would be gradually wasted away, and general misery would be the result. But it appears equally certain that if each individual were to confine his expenditure to mere necessaries, the result would be misery quite as general and as intense.

We have seen that the powers of population, if not restrained by prudence, must inevitably produce almost every form of moral and physical evil. In the case which we are supposing, the wants of society would be confined to the food, raiment, and shelter essential to the support of existence; and they would all consist of the cheapest materials. At present, among civilized nations, the cultivation of the land employs only a portion of its inhabitants, and, generally speaking, as a nation increases in wealth, a smaller and smaller proportion; in England not one third; and a great part of the labourers so employed are producers of luxuries. Indeed, as potatoes afford a food five or six times as abundant as corn, and more than twenty times as abundant as meat, and, as far as can be judged by the appearance and powers of the lower Irish, quite as wholesome, meat and corn may be considered luxuries, to the extent in which they are more expensive than potatoes. Nor, consistently with the existence of private property, and of the desire of wealth, can the mode of cultivation be directed to the obtaining the largest possible return. The object is to obtain the largest return that is consistent with profitable farming; but, in the pursuit of this object, quantity of produce must often be sacrificed to economy of labour or time.

If there were no desire for any thing beyond necessaries, both the existing partition of the land, and the existing division of labour, would be varied. No family would wish to occupy more land than the small plot necessary to afford them potatoes and milk. Supposing them to give to it the utmost nicety of garden cultivation, its management would still leave them time to produce the coarse manufactures necessary for their own use. The whole of the population would be agricultural. 761,348 families so employed at present in England, although their labour is far from being directed to the production of the greatest possible amount, provide, without much assistance from importation, subsistence for the whole of our 2,745,336 families. If all were so employed, and if quantity of produce were their sole object, it is probable that in ordinary seasons the soil of England, instead of fifteen millions, could feed at least sixty millions of people; and that of Europe, instead of two hundred, eight hundred millions. And that, in the absence of any checks more powerful than those experienced in the United States of America, the population of Europe might in fifty years amount to eight hundred millions. Indeed it is probable that, under the circumstances which we are supposing, the increase in Europe would be for a considerable time rather more rapid than that which has taken place in America. Preventive checks would not exist; marriages could not be hindered or even delayed by prudence, since there could be no reason to anticipate want; the habit of early marriages would put an end to profligacy; and, as all our habits would be eminently healthy, the positive checks would be reduced to their minimum.

So far the picture is rather pleasing; it exhibits a state of society, not rich certainly, nor refined, but supporting a very numerous population in health and strength, and in the full enjoyment of the many sources of happiness connected with early marriage. But it is obvious that this could not last for ever; it could not last indeed for two hundred and fifty years. By that time the population of Europe would amount to above three million millions; a number which the wildest imagination cannot conceive capable of existing simultaneously in the whole earth.

Sooner or later, therefore, the increase must be checked; and we have seen that prudence is the only check that does not involve vice or misery. But such is the force of the passions which prompt to marriage, and such is each man's reliance on his own good conduct and good fortune, that the evils, whatever they may be, the apprehension of which forms the prudential check, are frequently incurred. Where that evil is the loss of luxuries, or even of decencies, it is trifling in the first case, and bearable in the second. But, in the case which we are supposing, the only prudential check would be an apprehended deficiency of necessaries; and that deficiency, in the many instances in which it would actually be incurred, would be the positive check in its most frightful form. It would be incurred not only in consequence of that miscalculation of chances to which all men are subject, and certainly those not the least so who are anxious to marry, but through accidents against which no human prudence can guard. A *single* bad harvest may be provided against, but a succession of unfavourable seasons (and such successions do occur) must reduce such a people to absolute famine. When such seasons affect a nation indulging in considerable superfluous expenditure, they are relieved by a temporary sacrifice of that superfluity. The grain consumed in ordinary years by our breweries and distilleries is a store always at hand to supply a scarcity, and the same may be said of the large quantity of food raised for the support of domestic animals, but applicable to human subsistence. To these resources may be added the importation from abroad of necessaries instead of luxuries and the materials of luxury, of corn, for instance, instead of wine.

It may be said, however, and indeed it has been said, that while the globe remains in its present irregularly occupied and irregularly cultivated state, emigration affords to all comparatively thickly-peopled nations a resource so ample and so easy as to render every prudential check to population unnecessary.

It is obvious that if capital and skill equal to those bestowed on the best parts of Flanders, or of the Scotch Lowlands, could be applied to the whole habitable world, a population ten times, perhaps one hundred times, perhaps even five hundred times as large, could be maintained, as well, perhaps far better, than the one thousand millions now supposed to exist on its surface. It is possible, we will not say even that it is improbable, that in the course of centuries, or rather of hundreds of centuries, these splendid visions may be realized. But all experience shows, that no numerous and civilized nation, surrounded by other civilized nations, can venture to rely on emigration as a permanent and adequate check to population. We say no numerous and civilized nation surrounded by other civilized nations; for we are aware that the hordes of Central Asia and of the Northern parts of Europe, and the surplus inhabitants of some small communities, such as the petty States of ancient Greece and Phœnicia, appear to have found, the one in colonization, the others in armed migrations, a periodical outlet; and that the Americans of European descent have enjoyed for centuries, and for centuries to come may enjoy, in the immense continent behind them, room for as rapid an increase of their numbers as the most unchecked propagation can supply. But these are not examples which Europe, as now constituted, can imitate. When all the land frontier is appropriated,—when invasion for the purpose of settlement is impossible, and the solitary traveller is repelled by a different language, different laws, different arts, and often a different religion,—when the other alternative is an expensive and distant voyage, and either an unsettled, and therefore in general an unwholesome country, or equal obstacles from variations of laws, language, religion, and arts, in a previously settled district,—when these are the difficulties to be encountered, no extensive and systematic emigration will be persisted in. Even the different parts of the same empire afford little assistance to one another, if difference of language, or habits, or considerable distance be interposed. The Austrian dominions contain some of the most thinly and some of the most thickly peopled portions of Europe; but Hungary is not colonized from the plains of Lombardy. If any European nation could hope to make emigration a complete substitute for prudence, that hope might be entertained by the inhabitants of the British Islands. We have the command of unoccupied continents in each hemisphere, the largest navy that the world ever saw to convey us to them, the largest capital that ever has been accumulated, to defray the expense, and a population remarkable not merely for enterprise, but for enterprise of this particular description. These advantages we have enjoyed for centuries; almost from the times of the Tudors we have possessed a large outskirt of empire far exceeding in extent our European possessions. And yet during this long period how little effect has emigration produced on our numbers! The swarms which we have sent out, and which we now send out, seem to be instantaneously replaced. We have founded one empire, and probably shall found many; but, after once a colony has been planted, its principal increase arises, not from the comparatively scanty recruits whom it receives from home, but from the unrepressed force of human fecundity.

In a future portion of this Treatise we shall explain with more detail the causes which impede emigration; at present we shall only repeat that all experience shows its inability to keep down the population of any large, well peopled, and tolerably civilized Country, such as Europe, China, or Hindostan. It appears, therefore, that habits of prudence in contracting marriage, and of considerable superfluous expenditure, afford the only permanent protection against a population pressing so closely on the means of subsistence as to be continually incurring the misery of the positive checks. And as the former habits exist only in a civilized, and the latter only in an opulent society, it appears equally clear that, as a nation advances in civilization and opulence, the positive checks are likely to be superseded by the preventive. If this be true, the evil of a redundant population, or, to speak more intelligibly, of a population too numerous to be adequately and regularly supplied with necessaries, is likely to diminish in the progress of improvement. As wealth increases, what were the luxuries of one generation become the decencies of their successors. Not only a taste for additional comfort and convenience, but a feeling of degradation in their absence, becomes more and more widely diffused. The increase in many respects of the productive powers of labour must enable increased comforts to be enjoyed by increased numbers; and as it is the more beneficial, so it appears to be the more natural course of events that increased comfort should not only accompany but rather precede increase of numbers.

But although we believe that, as civilization advances, the pressure of population on subsistence is a decreasing evil, we are far from denying the prevalence of this pressure in all long settled-Countries; indeed in all Countries except those which are the seats of colonies applying the knowledge of an old Country to an unoccupied territory. We believe that there are few portions of Europe the inhabitants of which would not now be richer if their numbers were fewer, and would not be richer hereafter if they were now to retard the rate at which their population is increasing. No plan for social improvement can be complete unless it embrace the means both of increasing the production of wealth and of preventing population from making a proportionate advance. The former is to be effected by legislative, the latter by individual prudence and forethought. The former must be brought about by the governing classes of society; the latter depends almost entirely on the lower. As a means of improvement, the latter is, on the whole, more efficient. It may be acted upon or neglected by almost every one. But, in the present state of public opinion and of commercial and fiscal policy in Europe, perhaps a greater progress may be made by insisting on the former. The statesman who neglects either considers only a portion of the subject.

But we must admit that ours are not the received opinions; or perhaps we ought to say, that our statement is opposed, on the one side or on the other, to the language used by almost every writer who has directly treated the subject of population. Almost every Economist will be found, in that part of his writings in which what has been called *the principle of population* is the immediate and principal question considered, to range himself under one of two hostile banners, each opposed not only to the other, but also to the doctrines which we have endeavoured to explain. On one side are those who believe that an increase of numbers is necessarily accompanied, not merely by a positive, but by a relative increase of productive power; that density of population is the cause and the test of prosperity; and that, " were every nation under the sun to be released from all the natural and artificial checks on their increase, and to start off breeding at the fastest possible rate, many, very many generations must elapse before any necessary pressure could be felt." [14]

On the other side are those who maintain that population has a tendency (using the word tendency to express likelihood or probability) to increase beyond the means of subsistence; or, in other words, that, whatever be the existing means of subsistence, population is likely fully to come up to them, and even to struggle to pass beyond them, and is kept back principally by the vice and misery which that struggle must produce.

The whole of our previous remarks afford an answer to the first-mentioned class of writers. We shall not therefore recur to them. The opinions of the other class we shall consider at some length; and we will begin by the following quotations from Mr. M'Culloch, Mr. Mill, and Mr. Malthus.

Among the valuable notes which Mr. M'Culloch has appended to his edition of the *Wealth of Nations,* one of the most interesting treats of population; and one of the objects of that note is to show that the population of the United States of America cannot continue to increase for any very considerable period at the rate at which it has increased during the last hundred years. We are perfectly convinced of the correctness of this anticipation; and we make the following extract not with any intention to oppose Mr. M'Culloch's opinions as to America, but because we are anxious to express our dissent to the form in which he lays down the general doctrine of population.

" It may be said perhaps," says Mr. M'Culloch, " that allowance must be made for the effects of the improvements which may be supposed to take place in agricultural science in the progress of society, or the possible introduction, at some future period, of new and more prolific species of crops. But it is easy to see that the influence of such improvements and changes must, supposing them to be realized

[14] Scrope, *Principles of Political Economy,* 1833, p. 276.

in the fullest manner, be of very temporary duration; and that it
cannot affect the truth of the principle, *that the power of increase in
the human species must always, in the long run, prove an overmatch for
the increase in the means of subsistence.* Suppose by some extraordinary improvement the quantity of food and other articles required for
the subsistence and accommodation of man annually produced in Great
Britain were suddenly doubled; the condition of all classes being in
consequence signally improved, there would be less occasion for the
exercise of moral restraint; the period of marriage would therefore be
accelerated, and such a powerful stimulus would be given to the principle of increase, *that in a very short period the population would be
again on a level with the means of subsistence;* and there would also,
owing to the change that must have been made in the habits of the
people with respect to marriage, during the period that the population
was rising to the level of the increased supply of food, be an extreme
risk lest it should become too abundant, and produce an increased rate
of mortality. Although, therefore, it is not possible to assign any certain limits to the progress of improvement, it is notwithstanding evident that it cannot continue for any considerable period to advance in
the same proportion that population would advance supposing food
were abundantly supplied. The circumstance of inferior lands, which
require a greater outlay of capital and labour to make them yield the
same supply as those that are superior, being invariably taken into
cultivation in the progress of society, demonstrates, what is otherwise
indeed sufficiently obvious to every one, that, in despite of improvements, the difficulty of adding to the supplies of food is progressively
augmented as population becomes denser."

Mr. Mill's views are to be found in his discussion of wages. *Principles,* &c. Ch. ii. s. 2. " If it were," he observes, " the natural tendency of capital (by which term Mr. Mill designates the instruments
of labour, the materials on which they are to be employed, when produced by labour, and the subsistence of the labourer) to increase faster
than population, there would be no difficulty in preserving the prosperous condition of the people. If, on the other hand, it were the
natural tendency of population to increase faster than capital, the
difficulty would be very great. There would be a perpetual tendency
in wages to fall; the progressive fall of wages would produce a
greater and a greater degree of poverty among the people, attended
with its inevitable consequences, misery and vice. As poverty, and
its consequent misery, increased, mortality would also increase: of a
numerous family born, a certain number only, from want of the
means of well being, would be reared. By whatever proportion the
population tended to increase faster than capital, such a proportion of
those who were born would die; the ratio of increase in capital and
population would then remain the same, and the fall of wages would
proceed no further. That population *has* a tendency to increase

faster than, in most places, capital has actually increased, is proved incontestably by the condition of the population in most parts of the globe.   In almost all Countries the condition of the great body of the people is poor and miserable.   This would have been impossible, if capital had increased faster than population.   In that case wages must have risen ; and high wages would have placed the labourer above the miseries of want.   This general misery of mankind is a fact which can be accounted for upon one only of two suppositions : either that there is a natural tendency in population to increase faster than capital, or that capital has, by some means, been prevented from increasing so fast as it has a tendency to increase.   This, therefore, is an inquiry of the highest importance."

As the result of that inquiry, Mr. Mill decides the second alternative in the negative ; and consequently conceives himself to have established the former, namely, that there is a natural tendency in population to increase faster than capital.

Mr. Malthus's opinions appear to have been considerably modified during the course of his long and brilliant philosophical career.   In his first edition of his great Work, the principle of population was represented as an insurmountable obstacle to the permanent welfare of the mass of mankind.   And even in the last edition, the following passages are open to the same construction.

"There are few States in which there is not a constant effort in the population to increase beyond the means of subsistence.   This constant effort as constantly tends to subject the lower classes of society to distress, and to prevent any great permanent amelioration of their condition.   These effects, in the present state of society, seem to be produced in the following manner :—We will suppose the means of subsistence in any country to be just equal to the easy support of its inhabitants.   The constant effort towards population, which is found to act even in the most vicious societies, increases the number of people before the means of subsistence are increased.   The food, therefore, which before supported eleven millions, must now be divided between eleven millions and a-half.   The poor consequently must live much worse, and many of them be reduced to severe distress.   The number of labourers also being above the proportion of work in the market, the price of labour must tend to fall, while the price of provisions would at the same time tend to rise.   The labourer therefore must do more work to earn the same than he did before.   During this season of distress the discouragements to marriage and the difficulty of rearing a family are so great that the progress of population is retarded.   In the mean time the cheapness of labour, the plenty of labourers, and the necessity of an increased industry amongst them, encourage cultivators to employ more labour upon their land, to turn up fresh soil, and to manure and improve more completely what is already in tillage, till ultimately the means of subsistence may become in the same proportion to the population as at the period from which we set out. The situation of the labourer being then again tolerably comfortable, the restraints to population are in some degree loosened; and after a short period the same retrograde and progressive movements, with respect to happiness, are repeated." *Population*, Book i. Chap. ii. "According to the principle of population, the human race *has a tendency* to increase faster than food. It has, therefore, *a constant tendency* to people a Country fully up to the limits of subsistence; meaning, by these limits, the lowest quantity of food which will maintain a stationary population." Book iii. Chap. i. note.

But when the opposite doctrine, namely, that, in the absence of disturbing causes, subsistence is likely to increase more rapidly than population, was brought before him by Mr. Senior, he appears to have disavowed, we will not say his former expressions, but the inferences to which they lead.

"The meaning," says Mr. Malthus, "which I intended to convey by the expression to which you object" (that population has a tendency to increase faster than food) "was, that population was always ready and inclined to increase faster than food, if the checks which repressed it were removed; and that though these checks might be such as to prevent population from advancing upon subsistence, or even to keep it at a greater distance behind, yet that, whether population were actually increasing faster than food, or food faster than population, it was true that, except in new colonies, favourably circumstanced, population was always pressing against food, and was always ready to start off at a faster rate than that at which the food was actually increasing."

"We are quite agreed that, in the capacity of reason and forethought, man is endowed with a power naturally calculated to mitigate the evils occasioned by the pressure of population against food. We are further agreed that, in the progress of society, as education and knowledge are extended, the probability is that these evils will practically be mitigated, and the condition of the labouring classes be improved." [15]

So explained, Mr. Malthus's opinions are opposed to the expressions of Mr. Mill and Mr. M'Culloch; his admission that, "in the progress of society, the probability is that the evils occasioned by the pressure of population against food will be mitigated," is opposed to Mr. M'Culloch's statement, "that the power of increase in the human species must always, in the long run, prove an overmatch for the increase in the means of subsistence;" and to Mr. Mill's, "that the tendency of population to increase faster than, in most places, capital has actually increased, is proved incontestably by the condition of the

---

[15] *Appendix to* Senior's *Lectures on Population*, p. 61—82.

population in most parts of the globe." Archbishop Whately, with his usual acuteness, has in the following passage traced the question to a verbal ambiguity.

" The doctrine, that, since there is a tendency in population to increase faster than the means of subsistence, hence the pressure of population against subsistence may be expected to become greater and greater in each successive generation, (unless new and extraordinary remedies are resorted to,) and thus to produce a progressive diminution of human welfare—this doctrine, which some maintain in defiance of the fact that all civilized Countries have a greater proportionate amount of wealth now than formerly, may be traced chiefly to an undetected ambiguity in the word ' tendency,' which forms a part of the middle term of the argument. By a ' tendency' towards a certain result is sometimes meant, the existence of a cause which, operating unimpeded, would produce that result. In this sense it may be said, with truth, that the earth, or any other body moving round a centre, has a tendency to fly of at a tangent; (*i.e.*) the centrifugal force operates in that direction, though it is controlled by the centripetal ; or, again, that man has a greater tendency to fall prostrate than to stand erect; (*i.e.*) the attraction of gravitation and the position of the centre of gravity are such that the least breath of air would overset him, but for the voluntary exertion of muscular force: and, again, that population has a tendency to increase beyond subsistence; (*i.e.*) there are in man propensities which, if unrestrained, lead to that result.

" But sometimes, again, ' a tendency towards a certain result' is understood to mean ' the existence of such a state of things that that result may be expected to take place.' Now it is in these two senses that the word is used, in the two premises of the argument in question. But in this latter sense, the earth has a greater tendency to remain in its orbit than to fly off from it ; man has a greater tendency to stand erect than to fall prostrate ; and (as may be proved by comparing a more barbarous with a more civilized period in the history of any Country) in the progress of Society, subsistence has a tendency to increase at a greater rate than population. In this Country, for instance, much as our population has increased within the last five centuries, it yet bears a far less ratio to subsistence (though still a much greater than could be wished) than it did five hundred years ago." [16]

It is obvious that if the present state of the world, compared with its state at our earliest records, be one of relative poverty, the tendency of population to increase more rapidly than subsistence must be admitted. If the means of subsistence continue to bear precisely the same proportion to the number of its inhabitants, it is clear that

---

[16] Archbishop Whately, *Lectures on Political Economy*. Lecture 9.

the increase of subsistence and of numbers has been equal. If its means of subsistence have increased much more than the number of its inhabitants, it is clear not only that the proposition in question is false, but that the contrary proposition is true, and that the means of subsistence have a natural tendency (using these words as expressing what is likely to take place) to increase faster than population. Now what is the picture presented by the earliest records of those nations which are now civilized, or, which is the same, what is now the state of savage nations ?—a state of habitual poverty and occasional famine. A scanty population, but still scantier means of subsistence. Admitting, and it must be admitted, that in almost all Countries the condition of the great body of the people is poor and miserable, yet, as poverty and misery were their original inheritance, what inference can we draw from the continuance of that misery as to the tendency of their numbers to increase more rapidly than their wealth ? But if a single Country can be found in which there is now less poverty than is universal in a savage state, it must be true that, under the circumstances in which that Country has been placed, the means of subsistence have a greater tendency to increase than the population. Now this is the case in every civilized Country. Even Ireland, the Country most likely to afford an instance of what has been called the tendency of things, poor and populous as she is, suffers less from want with her eight millions of people than when her only inhabitants were a few septs of hunters and fishers. In our own early history, famines, and pestilences, the consequences of famine, constantly recur. At present, though our numbers are trebled or quadrupled, they are unheard of.

The United States of America afford the best ascertained instance of great and continued increase of numbers. They have afforded a field in which the powers of population have been allowed to exhaust their energy; but, though exerted to their utmost, they have not as yet equalled the progress of subsistence. Whole colonies of the first settlers perished from absolute want; their successors struggled long against hardship and privation; but every increase of their number seems to have been accompanied or preceded by increased means of support. It it be conceded that there exists in the human race a natural tendency to advance from barbarism to civilization, and that the means of subsistence are proportionably more abundant in a civilized than in a savage state, and neither of these propositions can be denied, it must follow that there is a natural tendency in subsistence to increase in a greater ratio than population.

But although Mr. Malthus himself, in his earlier publications, has perhaps fallen sometimes into the exaggeration which is natural to a discoverer, the error, if he has committed one, does not affect the practical conclusions which place him, as a benefactor to mankind, on a level with Adam Smith. Whether, in the absence of disturbing causes, it be the tendency of subsistence or of population to advance with greater rapidity, is a question of slight importance, if it be acknowledged that human happiness or misery depends principally on their relative advance, and that there are causes, and causes within human control, by which that advance can be regulated. These are propositions which Mr. Malthus has established by facts and reasoning which, opposed as they were to long-rooted prejudice, and assailed by every species of sophistry and clamour, are now admitted by the majority of reasoners, and even by a large majority of those who take their opinions upon trust.

To explain what are the causes of the relative increase of subsistence and population is rather the business of a writer on politics than of a Political Economist. At present we will only say that knowledge, security of property, freedom of internal and external exchange, and equal admissibility to rank and power, are the principal causes which at the same time promote the increase of subsistence, and, by elevating the character of the people, lead them to keep at a slower rate the increase of their numbers. And that restrictions on exchange and commerce, artificial barriers excluding the great majority of the community from the chance of social eminence, and, above all, ignorance, and insecurity of person and property, are the general causes which both diminish the productiveness of labour, and tend to produce that brutal state of improvidence in which the power of increase, unchecked by prudence, is always struggling to pass the limits of subsistence, and is kept down only by vice and misery. We use the expression *general* causes, to exclude those causes which, being peculiar to certain nations, require separate consideration. Such are the superstitious desire of offspring in China, the political motives which formerly occasioned the creation of freeholders in Ireland, and the administration of the poor-laws in some parts of England. But, omitting these details, it may be generally stated that all that degrades the character, or diminishes the productive power of a people, tends to diminish the proportion of subsistence to population, and *vice versâ*. And consequently that a population increasing more rapidly than the means of subsistence is, generally speaking, a symptom of misgovernment indicating deeper-seated evils, of which it is only one of the results.

And, notwithstanding the passages which we have cited, we believe these to be also the opinions of Mr. Mill and of Mr. M'Culloch. We believe that neither of these eminent writers doubts that the situation of the inhabitants of Europe has been gradually improving during the last 500 years. We believe that neither of them considers the improvement as having reached its limit, or as having any definite limit whatever. When they speak of the probable destinies of mankind, they teach the same doctrine as ourselves. It is only when separately discussing the subject of population that they have used the language to which we have ventured to object. We believe that they have used it without being misled by it themselves, and, perhaps on that very account, without perceiving its tendency to mislead others. But that those whose acquaintance with Political Economy is superficial (and they form the great mass of even the educated classes) *have* been misled by the form in which the doctrine of population has been expressed, appears to us undeniable. When such persons are told that " it is the tendency of the human race to increase faster than food "—" to people a country fully up to the means of subsistence," they infer that what *has a tendency to happen* is to be expected. Because additional population *may* bring poverty, they suppose that it necessarily *will* do so: because increased means of subsistence *may* be followed and neutralized by a proportionate increase in the number of persons to be subsisted, they suppose that such *will* necessarily be the case. And unhappily there are many whom indolence, or selfishness, or a turn to despondency, make ready recipients of such a doctrine. It furnishes an easy escape from the trouble or expense implied by every project of improvement. " What use would it be," they ask, " to promote an extensive emigration? the whole vacuum would be immediately filled up by the necessary increase of population. Why should we alter the Corn Laws? If food were for a time more abundant, *in a very short period the population would be again on a level with the means of subsistence, and we should be just as ill off as before.*"

There are many also, particularly among those who reason rather with their hearts than their heads, who are unable to assent to these doctrines, and yet believe them to be among the admitted results of Political Economy. Such persons apply to the whole Science the *argumentum ab absurdo;* and, instead of inquiring into the accuracy of the reasoning, refuse to examine the premises from which such objectionable conclusions are inferred.

It is because we believe these misconceptions to be extensively prevalent that we have ventured to detain our readers by this long discussion,—a discussion which some may think a mere dispute about the more convenient use of a word, and others an attempt to prove a self-evident fact.

Development of the Third Elementary Proposition of the Science, namely,—

That the Powers of Labour, and of the other Instruments which produce Wealth, may be indefinitely increased by using their Products as the means of further Production.

Production.—Having explained the sense in which we use the word Wealth, and given an outline of the doctrine of Population, we now proceed to consider Production, or the means by which wealth is produced. The first terms to be defined are the verb *produce*, and the substantive *product*.

Product.—*To produce*, as far as Political Economy is concerned, *is to occasion an alteration in the condition of the existing particles of matter, for the occasioning of which alteration, or for the things thence resulting, something may be obtained in exchange.* This alteration is a *product*. It is scarcely necessary to remind our readers that matter is suceptible neither of increase nor diminution, and that all which man, or any other agent of which we have experience, can effect, is to alter the condition of its existing particles. But as Political Economy treats only of wealth, and therefore only of those alterations of which wealth is the result, we are forced to exclude all other alterations from the definition of Products. The child who builds a castle with sand on the shore, and the child who kicks it down, each occasions effects the same in kind as the man who builds or pulls down a palace; but as the exertions of the latter entitle him to be paid, he is properly said to *produce*, and the result of his conduct, whether it be the covering with buildings ground previously unoccupied, or rendering vacant what was previously built over, is properly called a Product.

Products divided into Services and Commodities.—Products have been divided into material and immaterial, or, to express the same distinction in different words, into commodities and services. This distinction appears to have been suggested by Adam Smith's well known division of labour into productive and unproductive. Those who thought the principle of that division convenient, feeling at the same time the difficulty of terming unproductive the labour without which all other labour would be inefficient, invented the term services, or immaterial products, to express its results.

It appears to us, however, that the distinctions that have been attempted to be drawn between productive and unproductive labourers, or between the producers of material and immaterial products, or between commodities and services, rest on differences existing not in the things themselves, which are the objects considered, but in the modes in which they attract our attention. In those cases in which our attention is principally called, not to the act of occasioning the alteration, but to the result of that act, to the thing altered, Economists have termed the person who occasioned that alteration a productive labourer, or the producer of a *commodity* or material product. Where, on the other hand, our attention is principally called not to the thing altered, but to the act of occasioning that alteration, Economists have termed the person occasioning that alteration an unproductive labourer, and his exertions, *services*, or immaterial products. A shoemaker alters leather, and thread, and wax, into a pair of shoes. A shoeblack alters a dirty pair of shoes into a clean pair. In the first case our attention is called principally to the things as altered. The shoemaker, therefore, is said to *make* or *produce* shoes. In the case of the shoeblack, our attention is called principally to the act as performed. He is not said to make or produce the commodity, clean shoes, but to perform the service of cleaning them. In each case there is, of course, an act and a result; but in the one case our attention is called principally to the act, in the other to the result.

Among the causes which direct our attention principally to the *act*, or principally to the *result*, seem to be, first, the degree of change produced; and secondly, the mode in which the person who benefits by that change generally purchases that benefit.

1. Where the alteration is but slight, especially if the thing that has been subjected to alteration still retains the same name, our attention is directed principally to the act. A cook is not said to *make* roast beef, but to *dress* it; but he is said to make a pudding, or those more elaborate preparations which we call *made* dishes. The change of name is very material: a tailor is said to *make* cloth into a coat; a dyer is not said to *make* undyed cloth into dyed cloth. The change produced by the dyer is perhaps greater than that produced by the tailor, but the cloth in passing through the tailor's hands changes its name; in passing through the dyer's it does not: the dyer has not produced a *new name*, nor, consequently, in our minds, a *new thing*.

The principal circumstance, however, is the mode in which the payment is made. In some cases the producer is accustomed to sell, and we are accustomed to purchase, not his labour, but the subject on which that labour has been employed; as when we purchase a wig or a chest of medicine. In other cases, what we buy is not the thing altered, but the labour of altering it, as when we employ a haircutter or a physician. Our attention in all these cases naturally fixes itself on the thing which we are accustomed to purchase; and according as we are accustomed to buy the labour, or the thing on which that labour has been expended,—as we are, in fact, accustomed to purchase a commodity or a service, we consider a commodity or a service as the thing produced. The ultimate object both of painting and of acting is the pleasure derived from imitation. The means adopted by the painter and the actor are the same in kind. Each exercises his bodily organs, but the painter exercises them to distribute colours over a canvass, the actor to put himself into certain attitudes, and to utter certain sounds. The actor sells his exertions themselves. The painter sells not his exertions, but the picture on which those exertions have been employed. The mode in which their exertions are sold constitutes the only difference between menial servants and the other labouring classes: a servant who carries coal from the cellar to the drawing-room performs precisely the same operation as the miner who raises them from the bottom of the pit to its mouth. But the consumer pays for the coals themselves when raised and received into his cellar, and pays the servant for the act of bringing them up. The miner, therefore, is said to produce the material commodity, coals; the servant the immaterial product, or service. Both, in fact, produce the same thing, an alteration in the condition of the existing particles of matter; but our attention is fixed in the one case on the act, in the other on the result of that act.

In the ruder states of society almost all manufactures are domestic: the Queens and Princesses of heroic times were habitually employed in overlooking the labours of their maidens. The division of labour has banished from our halls to our manufactories the distaff and the loom; and, if the language to which we have been adverting were correct, the division of labour must be said to have turned spinners and weavers from unproductive into productive labourers; from producers of immaterial services into producers of material commodities.

Service and Commodity discriminated.—But, objecting as we do to a nomenclature which should consider producers as divided, by the nature of their products, into producers of services and producers of commodities, we are ready to admit the convenience of the distinction between services and commodities themselves, and to apply the term *service* to the act of occasioning an alteration in the existing state of things, the term *commodity* to the thing as altered; the term *product* including both commodities and services.

It is to be observed that, in ordinary language, a person is not said to produce a thing unless he has employed himself for that especial purpose. If an English oyster-fisher should meet with an oyster containing a pearl, he would be called not the producer of the pearl, but its casual finder. But a Ceylon oyster-fisher, whose trade is to fish for pearl oysters, is called a producer of pearls. The *mere existence* of the pearls is in both cases owing to the agency of nature; their existence as articles of value is in both cases owing to the agency of the fisher in removing them from a situation in which they were valueless. In the one case he did this intentionally, in the other accidentally. Attention is directed in the one case to *his* agency, and *he* is therefore called the producer of the pearl. In the other case it is directed to the agency of nature, and he is called only the appropriator. But it appears to us the more convenient classification, for scientific purposes, to term him in both cases the producer.

Consumption Defined.—Economists have in general opposed consumption to production. They have defined consumption to be the destruction wholly, or in part, of any portion of wealth. And they consider it as the ultimate object of all production.

" *Tout ce qui est produit,*"[17] says M. Say, " *est consommé; par conséquent, toute valeur créée est détruite, et n'a été créé que pour être détruite.*"

"Consumption," says Mr. Malthus, "is the great purpose and

---

[17] Say, *Principles*, Tome III. p. 276.

end of all production.''[18]   " By Consumption,'' says Mr. M'Culloch,
" is meant the annihilation of those qualities which render commodities
useful or desirable.   To consume the products of Art and Industry
is to deprive the matter of which they consist of utility, and consequently of the exchangeable value communicated to it by labour.
Consumption is, in fact, the end and object of human exertion, and
when a commodity is in a fit state to be used, if its consumption be
deferred, a loss is incurred.''[19]

That almost all that is produced is destroyed is true; but we cannot admit that it is produced for the purpose of being destroyed.   It
is produced for the purpose of being made use of.   Its destruction is
an incident to its use, not only not intended, but, as far as possible,
avoided.   In fact, there are some things which seem unsusceptible of
destruction except by accidental injury.   A statue in a gallery, or a
medal, or a gem in a cabinet, may be preserved for centuries without
apparent deterioration.   There are others, such as food and fuel,
which perish in the very act of using them, and hence, as these are
the most essential commodities, the word consumption has been
applied universally as expressing the making use of any thing.   But
the bulk of commodities are destroyed by those numerous gradual
agents which we call collectively *time*, and the action of which we strive
to retard.   If it be true that consumption is the object of all production, the inhabitant of a house must be termed its consumer, but it
would be strange to call him its destroyer; since it would unquestionably
be destroyed much sooner if uninhabited.   It would be an improvement in the language of Political Economy if the expression " to use"
could be substituted for that " to consume.''   There is, however, so
much difficulty in changing an established nomenclature, that we
shall continue to use the word consumption, premising that we use
it to signify primarily the making use of a thing; a circumstance to
which its destruction is generally, but not necessarily, incidental.

The wealth of a Country will much depend on the question, whether
the tastes of its inhabitants lead them to prefer objects of slow or of
rapid destruction.

It will depend, however, much more on their preference of productive or unproductive consumption.

Productive and Unproductive Consumption.—Productive consumption
is that use of a commodity which occasions an ulterior product.   Unproductive consumption is, of course, that use which occasions no
ulterior product.   The characteristic of unproductive consumption is,
that it adds to the enjoyment of no one but the consumer himself.
Its only effect upon the rest of the community is to diminish *pro tanto*
the mass of commodities applicable to their use.

Some commodities are unsusceptible of any but unproductive con-

----

[18] *Principles, &c.* p. 219.   [19] *Id.* p. 511—612, 2d Ed.

sumption; such are lace, embroidery, jewellery, and the other personal ornaments which are simply decorative, and afford neither warmth nor protection. Under this head may also be ranked tobacco and snuff, and the other stimulants, of which the best that can be said is, that they are not injurious. A much larger class of commodities is designed solely for productive use, and is never consumed unproductively, but by mistake. In this class are all tools, from the simplest to the most complicated; from the spade and the raft, to the steam engine and the Indiaman. But the generality of commodities may be used, according to the will of the proprietor, productively or unproductively; may be consumed so as to substitute some product in lieu of that which has been destroyed, or without any further beneficial result than the immediate pleasure which has accompanied their use. Whatever is capable of supporting human existence may be used to maintain those who are themselves producers, or those who are not. In the first case it is productively, in the second unproductively consumed.

The distinction between productive and unproductive *consumers* is less clearly marked than that between productive and unproductive *consumption*. To divide men into two classes, productive and unproductive consumers, would, in fact, be a false division, there being few who do not in some respects belong to both classes. So far as a man's consumption is essential to his production, he belongs to the first class; so far as it is not essential, to the second. Those only can be called simply unproductive who return nothing whatever for what they consume; those only simply productive who indulge in no superfluous consumption whatever.

To the first description belong those who, being provided, through their own previous exertions, or by the accidents of donation or inheritance, with a fund sufficient for their subsistence, are content to dedicate their revenue and their leisure to the purposes of mere enjoyment. This class is never large in any state of society. In an ignorant, and consequently a poor community, the number of those possessing a maintenance independent of exertion is necessarily small. Among civilized nations the love of accumulation, of power, of distinction, and of occupation, and the nobler desire of being more or less extensively useful, all powerfully counteract the slothful principles of our nature. As property becomes more secure, as the avenues to influence are opened, as merit and wealth rise in public estimation over the accidents of birth, as barbarous prejudices degrading to industry wear out, as the influence of sound religion teaches men that they were created for better purposes than selfish pleasure or useless mortification, in fact, as civilization improves, all the motives to voluntary exertion acquire force. And though the number of those who *might* live in idleness increases, the proportion of those who are unhappy enough to exercise that privilege diminishes.

Another class consists of those who derive their support solely from the spoil or the charity of others. The number of those who live by rapine has obviously a tendency to diminish in the progress of civilization. About mendicancy there may be some doubt, as some superfluous wealth seems necessary to its existence, and it may be supposed likely to increase with the superfluity on which it feeds. That laws ill framed or ill administered may allow it so to increase we know, from our own experience. But there seems to be no reason to doubt that, under a wise system of commercial and municipal legislation, the number of able-bodied paupers might be so reduced as to be practically unimportant.

The last class of unproductive consumers consists of those whom age or infirmity has rendered permanently incapable of production. We say *permanently*, to exclude children, and those suffering under temporary disability. Though a child or an invalid make no immediate return, their support is the necessary condition of their future services. This is by far the largest of the unproductive classes, and one not likely to suffer relative diminution, the same causes which tend to obviate disease and injury tending also to prolong life where their effects are incurable. But from the information collected in the House of Commons' Report on Friendly Societies, 5th July, 1825, vol. iv., we are inclined to think that in this Country the class in question cannot amount to a fortieth part, or about two-and-a-half per cent. of the whole community.

The number of absolutely productive consumers, that is, of persons who consume solely for the purpose of reproducing, is much smaller. It may be a question indeed whether in a Country free from slavery, or regulations resembling slavery, any such class is to be found. The humblest labourer has some expenses which are not essential to his health and strength. We endeavour to give to our domestic animals nothing beyond what is strictly necessary, and in the Countries where man is considered as a domestic animal it might be expected that the consumption of a slave would be equally limited. But even the slave generally acquires some peculium, which implies that his ordinary subsistence somewhat exceeds his wants.

It appears from this analysis that the bulk of the community are neither productive nor unproductive consumers, but may be referred to the one class or to the other, according to the portion of their expenses for the time being under consideration. So far as the husbandman takes just enough of the least expensive food, is just sufficiently clad with the simplest raiment, and inhabits a dwelling just sufficiently weather-tight and spacious to protect him from the seasons, he is a productive consumer. But his pipe and his gin, and generally speaking his beer, and the humble ornaments of his person and his dwelling, form his unproductive consumption.

We do not, of course, mean it to be inferred that all personal expenditure beyond mere necessaries is necessarily unproductive.   The duties of those who fill the higher ranks in society can seldom be well performed unless they conciliate the respect of the vulgar by a certain display of opulence.   If a Judge, or an Ambassador, required by his station to support an establishment costing £2000 a-year, should spend £4000, half of his consumption would be productive, and the other half unproductive.   It would be a great mistake, however, to consider the third footman behind his coach, though a mere useless weight to the horses, an unproductive consumer.   What the footman consumes are his wages, and, so far at least as he consumes them in order to enable himself to perform his services as footman, he is a productive consumer.   The things unproductively consumed are his services, and *they* are consumed by his master.   Nor is it to be supposed, on the other hand, that all consumption even of necessaries by those who are themselves producers, is a productive consumption. The half-employed pauper whose labour is worth £10 a-year, and whose consumption is £20, consumes unproductively the difference.

INSTRUMENTS OF PRODUCTION.

Having explained the nature of Production and Consumption, we now proceed to consider the Agents by whose intervention Production takes place.

I. **Labour.**—The primary Instruments of Production are Labour, and those Agents of which nature, unaided by man, affords us the assistance.

Labour is the voluntary exertion of bodily or mental faculties for the purpose of Production.   It may appear unnecessary to define a term having a meaning so precise and so generally understood. Peculiar notions respecting the causes of value have, however, led some Economists to employ the term labour in senses so different from its common acceptation, that for some time to come it will be dangerous to use the word without explanation.   We have already observed that many recent writers have considered value as solely dependent on labour.   When pressed to explain how wine in a cellar, or an oak in its progress from a sapling to a tree, could, on this principle, increase in value, they replied that they considered the improvement of the wine and the growth of the tree as so much additional labour bestowed on each.   We do not quite understand the meaning of this reply; but we have given a definition of labour, lest we should be supposed to include in it the unassisted operations of nature.   It may also be well to remind our readers that this definition excludes all those exertions which are not intended, immediately or through their products, to be made the subjects of exchange.   A hired messenger and a person walking for his amusement, a sportsman and a gamekeeper, the ladies at an English ball and a company of Natch girls in India, undergo the same fatigues; but ordinary language does not allow us to consider those as undergoing labour who exert themselves for the mere purpose of amusement.

II. **Natural Agents.**—Under the term "the Agents offered to us by nature," or, to use a shorter expression, "Natural Agents," we include every productive agent so far as it does not derive its powers from the act of man.

The term "Natural Agent" is far from being a convenient designation, but we have adopted it partly because it has been already made use of in this sense by eminent writers, and partly because we have not been able to find one less objectionable. The principal of these agents is the land, with its mines, its rivers, its natural forests with their wild inhabitants, and, in short, all its spontaneous productions. To these must be added the ocean, the atmosphere, light and heat, and even those physical laws, such as gravitation and electricity, by the knowledge of which we are able to vary the combinations of matter. All these productive agents have in general, by what appears to be an inconvenient synecdoche, been designated by the term *land;* partly because the land, as a source of profit, is the most important of those which are susceptible of appropriation, but chiefly because its possession generally carries with it the command over most of the others. And it is to be remembered that, though the powers of nature are necessary to afford a substratum for the other instruments of production to work upon, they are not of themselves, when universally accessible, causes of value. Limitation in supply is, as we have seen, a necessary constituent of value; and what is universally accessible is practically unlimited in supply.

III. **Abstinence.**—But although Human Labour, and the Agency of Nature, independently of that of man, are the primary Productive Powers, they require the concurrence of a Third Productive Principle to give to them complete efficiency. The most laborious population, inhabiting the most fertile territory, if they devoted all their labour to the production of immediate results, and consumed its produce as it arose, would soon find their utmost exertions insufficient to produce even the mere necessaries of existence.

To the Third Principle, or Instrument of Production, without which the two others are inefficient, we shall give the name of *Abstinence:* a term by which we express the conduct of a person who either abstains from the unproductive use of what he can command, or designedly prefers the production of remote to that of immediate results.

It was to the effects of this Third Instrument of Production that we adverted, when we laid down, as the third of our elementary propositions, that *the Powers of Labour and of the other Instruments which produce Wealth may be indefinitely increased by using their Products as the means of further Production.* All our subsequent remarks on abstinence are a development and illustration of this proposition; we say development and illustration, because it can scarcely be said to require formal proof.

The division of the Instruments of Production into three great branches has long been familiar to Economists. Those branches they have generally termed Labour, Land, and Capital. In the principle of this division we agree; though we have substituted different expressions for the second and third branches. We have preferred the term Natural Agents to that of Land, to avoid designating a whole genus by the name of one of its species: a practice which has occasioned the other cognate species to be generally slighted and often forgotten. We have substituted the term Abstinence for that of Capital on different grounds.

The term Capital has been so variously defined that it may be doubtful whether it have any generally received meaning. We think, however, that, in popular acceptation, and in that of Economists themselves, when they are not reminded of their definitions, that word signifies *an article of wealth, the result of human exertion, employed in the production or distribution of wealth.* We say the result of human exertion, in order to exclude those productive instruments to which we have given the name of natural agents, and which afford not profit, in the scientific sense of that word, but rent.

It is evident that Capital, thus defined, is not a simple productive instrument; it is in most cases the result of all the three productive instruments combined. Some natural agent must have afforded the material, some delay of enjoyment must in general have reserved it from unproductive use, and some labour must in general have been employed to prepare and preserve it. *By the word Abstinence, we wish to express that agent, distinct from labour and the agency of nature, the concurrence of which is necessary to the existence of Capital, and which stands in the same relation to Profit as Labour does to Wages.* We are aware that we employ the word Abstinence in a more extensive sense than is warranted by common usage. Attention is usually drawn to abstinence only when it is not united with labour. It is recognised instantly in the conduct of a man who allows a tree or a domestic animal to attain its full growth; but it is less obvious when he plants the sapling or sows the seed corn. The observer's attention is occupied by the labour, and he omits to consider the additional sacrifice made when labour is undergone for a distant object. This additional sacrifice we comprehend under the term Abstinence; not because Abstinence is an unobjectionable expression for it, but because we have not been able to find one to which there are not still greater objections. We once thought of using " providence;" but providence implies no self-denial, and has no necessary connection with profit. To take out an umbrella is provident, but not in the usual sense of the word profitable. We afterwards proposed " frugality," but frugality implies some care and attention, that is to say, some labour; and though in practice Abstinence is almost always accompanied by some degree of labour, it is obviously necessary to keep them separate in an analysis of the instruments of production.

It may be said that pure Abstinence, being a mere negation, cannot produce positive effects; the same remark might as well be applied to intrepidity, or even to liberty; but who ever objected to their being considered as equivalent to active agents? To abstain from the enjoyment which is in our power, or to seek distant rather than immediate results, are among the most painful exertions of the human will. It is true that such exertions are made, and indeed are frequent in every state of society, except perhaps in the very lowest, and have been made in the very lowest, for society could not otherwise have improved; but of all the means by which man can be raised in the scale of being, abstinence, as it is perhaps the most effective, is the slowest in its increase, and the least generally diffused. Among nations, those that are the least civilized, and among the different classes of the same nation those which are the worst educated, are always the most improvident, and consequently the least abstinent.

Capital.—We have already defined Capital to be an article of wealth, the result of human exertion, employed in the production or distribution of wealth, and we have observed that each individual article of capital is in general the result of a combination of all the three great instruments of production—labour, abstinence, and the agency of nature.

Different Modes in which Capital may be employed.—When a man has possessed himself of any article of wealth, and resolves to employ it, not for the mere purposes of enjoyment, but as Capital, or, in other words, as a means of further production, or of distribution, there appear to be eight modes in which his design may be effected.

1. He may intentionally destroy it, in order to obtain the effects which are the direct consequences of its destruction. The consumption of gunpowder in a mine, and of coals in the furnace of a steam-engine, afford instances. The food which every producer must consume in order to keep himself in the health and strength necessary to enable him to continue a producer is also thus consumed.

2. He may retain it and employ it for purposes of which its gradual destruction is the incidental but not the intended, or, in all cases, the necessary consequence. All implements and machinery are thus employed.

3. He may vary its form, as when materials are converted into finished commodities.

4. He may simply retain it until its value has been increased by changes occasioned by the lapse of time, or by an altered state of the market. The proprietor of a vineyard who, immediately after an abundant vintage, retains his wine, aims at both these advantages.

5. He may keep it ready for sale to meet the wants of his customers. A shopkeeper's finished articles or stock in trade are thus employed.

6. He may give it to the proprietor of some natural agent for the use of that agent; as when a farmer pays rent to his landlord.

7. He may give it to a labourer in exchange for his exertions; or, in other words, he may employ it in the payment of wages.

8. He may give it in exchange for some other commodity, to be itself employed as capital; or, in other words, he may use it commercially.

Most capitalists employ portions of their capital in all these eight modes.

If we suppose a wine retailer's capital to consist of the knowledge which he has acquired during his education for his business, of the warehouse and the simple machinery necessary to his trade, of the stock of commodities necessary for his own current consumption, and of one hundred pipes of wine in wood and in bottle, we shall find that his knowledge, and machinery, and necessaries are destroyed without ever being directly exchanged: the only difference being, first, that his knowledge remains unimpaired until either his death, or his retirement from business makes it suddenly valueless, while his buildings, and machinery, and clothes, furniture, and food are consumed and replaced at successive periods; and, secondly, that the destruction of his food is immediate, and that of his buildings, machinery, furniture, and clothing is gradual. We shall find that of the wine he retains a portion until it shall have been improved by age, and keeps a portion as stock in trade ready for immediate sale, but ultimately sells the whole and pays away its price, partly in rent for the land covered by his buildings, partly in wages to his clerks, porters, shopmen, and other labourers, partly in keeping up his buildings and machinery, and partly in the repurchase of wine, bottles, and corks to keep up the stock in his warehouse and shop. What remains of the price of his wine, and something must remain, or he would be in a worse situation than one of his own labourers, is generally termed his *profit*: a part of it he must employ in replacing the stock of commodities necessary to keep himself in health and strength; the remainder he may employ either in his own personal enjoyment and that of his friends, which is an unproductive use, or in the increase of his own capital, or in creating a capital for some other person, in the education, for instance, of his son, which are productive uses.

Fixed and Circulating Capital.—Adam Smith has divided Capital into fixed and circulating.

"There are two ways," he observes, "in which a capital may be employed so as to yield a revenue or profit.

"First, it may be employed in raising, manufacturing, or purchasing goods, and selling them again with a profit. The capital employed in this manner yields no revenue or profit to its employer while it either remains in his possession or continues in the same shape. The goods of the merchant yield him no revenue or profit till he sells them for money, and the money yields him as little till it is again exchanged for goods.   His capital is continually going from him in one shape, and returning to him in another, and it is only by means of such circulation, or successive exchanges, that it can yield him any profit.   Such capitals, therefore, may properly be called *circulating* capitals.

" Secondly, it may be employed in the improvement of land, in the purchase of useful machines and implements of trade, or in such like things as yield a revenue or profit without changing masters or circulating any further.   Such capitals, therefore, may properly be called *fixed* capitals.

" The capital of a merchant is altogether a circulating capital.   He has occasion for no machines or instruments of trade, unless his shop or warehouse be considered as such.

" Some part of the capital of every master artificer or manufacturer must be fixed in the instruments of his trade.   This part, however, is very small in some, and very large in others.   A master tailor requires no other instruments of trade than a parcel of needles ; those of a master shoemaker are a little, though but a little, more expensive.

" In other works a much greater fixed capital is required.   In a great iron work, for example, the furnace, the forge, the slit mill, are instruments of trade which cannot be erected without a very great expense.   That part of the capital of the farmer which is employed in the instruments of agriculture is a fixed, that which is employed in the wages and maintenance of his labouring servants is a circulating, capital.   He makes a profit of the one by keeping it in his own possession, and of the other by parting with it.   A herd of cattle, bought in to make a profit by their milk and increase, is a fixed capital ; the profit is made by keeping them.   Their maintenance is a circulating capital ; the profit is made by parting with it."   (Book II. Ch. I.)

We are not aware that the principle of Adam Smith's division has ever been directly objected to.   There may be some doubt, perhaps, whether the terms fixed and circulating are the best that could have been selected ; but Adam Smith has stamped on them the meaning which he intended, and they have passed current in that signification ever since.

Mr. Ricardo, however, with the inattention to established usage which so much diminishes the usefulness of his writings, has used the terms fixed and circulating capital in a totally different sense.   In this he has been followed by Mr. Mill ; and as neither of these writers intimates that his use of the words is not the common one, it may be well to mark the difference.

" According as capital is rapidly perishable," says Mr. Ricardo, " and requires to be frequently reproduced, or is of slow consumption, it is classed under the heads of circulating or of fixed capital : a division not essential, and in which the line of demarcation cannot be accurately drawn. A brewer, whose buildings and machinery are valuable and durable, is said to employ a large portion of fixed capital; on the contrary, a shoemaker, whose capital is chiefly employed in the payment of wages, which are expended on food and clothing, commodities more perishable than buildings and machinery, is said to employ a large proportion of capital as circulating capital." (Ch. I. sec. 4.)

Mr. Ricardo might well remark that the line of demarcation between his two sorts of capital cannot be accurately drawn; for what can be more vague, or more void of positive meaning, than such comparative terms as slow and rapid? The singular circumstance is that both he and Mr. Mill should have supposed, and it appears clear that they did suppose, that their division followed that of Adam Smith. It is obviously a cross division. The master tailor's needles which Adam Smith selects as an example of fixed capital, because the tailor retains them, would, according to Mr. Ricardo, be circulating, because they are perishable. On the other hand, the materials and stock in trade of an iron founder would be circulating capital according to Smith, and fixed according to Ricardo.

We may be able to make the nature of capital, and Adam Smith's conception of it, still clearer by quoting his subdivision of fixed and circulating capitals.

" Fixed capital," he says, " consists chiefly of the four following articles: —

" First, of all useful machines and instruments of trade which facilitate and abridge labour.

" Secondly, of all buildings used for the purpose of trade or manufacture; such as shops, warehouses, and farm-buildings, &c. They are a sort of instruments of trade, and may be considered in the same light.

" Thirdly, of the improvements of land, of what has been profitably laid out in clearing, draining, enclosing, manuring, and reducing it into the condition most proper for culture. An improved farm may be regarded in the same light as one of those useful machines which facilitate and abridge labour.

" Fourthly, of the acquired and useful abilities of all the members of the society. The acquisition of such talents by the maintenance of the acquirer during his education, study, or apprenticeship, costs an expense, which is a capital fixed and realized, as it were, in his person. The improved dexterity of a workman may be considered in the same light as a machine or instrument of trade which facilitates and abridges labour.

" The circulating capital is composed likewise of four parts:—

" First, of the money by means of which all the other three are circulated and distributed to their proper consumers.

" Secondly, of the stock of provisions in the possession of the butcher, the grazier, &c., for the purpose of sale.

" Thirdly, of the materials, whether altogether rude, or more or less manufactured, of clothes, furniture, and building, which are not yet made up, but remain in the hands of the growers, manufacturers, or merchants.

" Fourthly, of the work which is made up and completed, but is still in the hands of the merchant or manufacturer ; such as the finished work in the shops of the smith, the goldsmith, the jeweller, and the china merchant.   The circulating capital consists in this manner, of the provisions, materials, and finished work of all kinds which are in the hands of their respective dealers, and of the money that is neces- sary for circulating and distributing them to their final consumers." Book II. Ch. I.

This enumeration contains, perhaps, some useless distinctions, and, we think, two improper exclusions, but, generally speaking, it gives an excellent view of the different species of capital.

The things which appear to be improperly excluded are, first, the necessaries of life, consumed by the labourer and the capitalist for their own support : and, secondly, the houses and other commodities of slow consumption which the owner lets out to the consumer.

Adam Smith can scarcely be said to have explained his reason for excluding from the term capital the necessaries in the possession of the labourer.   He merely observes that the labourer consumes as sparingly as he can, and derives his revenue only from his labour. The attention of Mr. Malthus has been drawn to the subject ; he agrees in this respect with Adam Smith, and on the following grounds :

" The only productive consumption, properly so called, is the con- sumption or destruction of wealth by *capitalists* with a view to repro- duction.   This is the only marked line of distinction which can be drawn between productive and unproductive consumption.   The work- man whom the capitalist employs consumes that part of his wages which he does not [save, as revenue, with a view to subsistence or enjoyment ; and not as capital with a view to production." *Definitions*, p. 258.

Mr. Malthus would admit that the coals in the furnace of a steam- engine are productively employed ; because their consumption is the necessary condition to the engine's performing its work.   And in what does the consumption of food by a labourer differ from that of coals by a steam-engine ?   Simply in this, that the labourer derives pleasure from what he consumes, and the steam-engine does not.   If a labourer were so constituted as to feel no craving for food, and no gratification from eating, and were reminded of its necessity only by the debility consequent on its want, would not his meals, taken as they would be solely to enable him to undergo his fatigues, be pro- ductively consumed ?   Nature has wisely enforced an act of daily necessity by the stimulus of hunger, and the reward of enjoyment, but do that stimulus and enjoyment detract from its productiveness? Is the ploughman's dinner less the means of his toils because he considers it as their end? Is not the food of working cattle productively employed? Does not the owner of a West Indian estate consider the supplies which he sends to his slaves as a capital destined to productive consumption?

Adam Smith has stated at length his reasons for excluding from the term capital the houses and other articles which the owner lets out to the consumer.

"One portion," he states, "of the stock of a society is reserved for immediate consumption, of which the characteristic is that it affords no revenue or profit. The whole stock of mere dwelling-houses makes a part of this portion. If a house be let to a tenant, as the house itself can produce nothing, the tenant must pay the rent out of some other revenue which he derives either from labour, or stock, or land. Where masquerades are common, it is a trade to let out dresses for the night. Upholsterers frequently let furniture by the month or the year. The revenue, however, which is derived from such things must always be ultimately derived from some other source of revenue. A stock of clothes may last for several years; a stock of furniture half a century or a century; but a stock of houses, well built and properly taken care of, may last many centuries. Though the period of their total consumption, however, is more distant, they are still as really a stock reserved for immediate consumption as either clothes or furniture." Book II. Ch. I.

This language would have been consistent if Adam Smith, like most of his successors, had confined the term capital to the instruments of further consumption. But we have seen that he includes under that term things incapable of productive consumption, if they have not reached the hands of those who are finally to use them. If a diamond necklace in a jeweller's shop be correctly termed capital, and Adam Smith has expressly stated that it is so, why is not a house which has been just finished by a speculative builder? It is difficult to perceive why he should have laid so much stress on the perishableness of the things in question. Perishableness and durability are not elements in the distinction between what is and what is not to be correctly termed capital. Many of the things which are used productively are of almost evanescent existence, such as the gas which lights a manufactory. On the other hand, the jewels of a noble family are not capital, though no limits can be assigned to their duration. It is at least conceivable that a house might be built so as not to require repair, and would this circumstance affect the question? In fact, however, the perishableness of these things is unfavourable to Adam Smith's view, as it shows their resemblance to things which he has admitted to be capital. A cellar of wine at a tavern-keeper's falls under his third class of circulating capitals; gradually the cellar is emptied, and when the last bottle has been drunk the capital is at an end. A house let ready furnished, a circulating library, a job carriage, a stage coach, or a steam-packet, differs from the cellar of wine only because the progress of its consumption is less capable of being measured. Every day that it is used a portion wears away; and that portion is as much purchased and as much consumed by the hirer of the house or the carriage as the bottle of wine taken from the cellar. It is true that it may be consumed unproductively, and that in that case the hirer must pay the rent from some other revenue, as is the case with the price of *whatever* is unproductively consumed. But the portion of the house and furniture and carriage, for the time being unconsumed, is as much the capital, in the sense in which Adam Smith uses that word, of the upholsterer and the hackneyman, as the unconsumed portion of the wine is the capital of the tavern-keeper.

CAPITAL MAY AGAIN BE DIVIDED, ACCORDING TO THE PURPOSES TO WHICH IT IS APPLICABLE, INTO REPRODUCTIVE, SIMPLY PRODUCTIVE, AND UNPRODUCTIVE.

We apply the term *Reproductive* to all those articles of wealth which may be used to produce things of the same kind with themselves. All agricultural stock is reproductive; and so are all the necessaries of life.   That portion of them which is consumed by the capitalists and labourers employed in producing necessaries is one of the means by which the regular supply is kept up.   The coals in the furnace of a steam-engine used in working a coal mine, the iron instruments in an iron work, and a ship freighted with timber and naval stores are all reproductively employed.

We apply the term *Simply Productive* to those articles of wealth which, though instruments of production, cannot be employed in producing things of the same kind with themselves.   A lace machine is simply productive.   Its use is to make lace, but that lace cannot be employed to make a new machine.   All the tools and machinery employed in the production of those things which cannot be productively consumed are themselves simply productive.

We apply the term *Unproductive* or distributive capital to those commodities which are destined to unproductive use, but have not become the property of those who are to be their ultimate consumers.

A very great portion, perhaps the greater portion in value, of the commodities produced in an improved state of society, fall under this head at their first production.

We have already observed that, in every state of society, the number of absolutely unproductive *consumers* is small, and the number of absolutely productive consumers still smaller. But as wealth increases every man increases his unproductive *consumption*, until the whole amount in the whole society of such consumption may, and often does, exceed the whole amount of productive consumption. If we look through the shops of an opulent city, we shall find the commodities destined to mere enjoyment far exceeding in value those destined to be employed in further production.

Some of Adam Smith's successors have excluded the things of which we are now speaking from the term capital. We have followed his example in including them, for two reasons:—

First, because their exclusion is an unnecessary deviation from ordinary language. To say that a jeweller, with £50,000 worth of diamond ornaments in his shop, had no capital, would be an assertion of which few hearers would be able to guess the meaning.

But, in the second place, if it were possible to do, what certainly is much wanted, to form a new technical nomenclature for Political Economy, still we should include under the term capital the commodities in question. All Economists include under that term the materials and the instruments with which these commodities are formed. If the rough diamond and the gold in which it is to be set are capital while separate, it seems difficult to see what convenience there is in a nomenclature which denies them to be capital when united. Again, no Economist will doubt that a profit is received in proportion to the average time during which the commodities in question are retained by the capitalist. Why this profit is paid we shall endeavour to show hereafter, but the fact that it is paid may be assumed as unquestioned. But Economists are agreed that whatever gives a profit is properly termed capital.

Statement of Advantages derived from the Use of Capital.

The principal advantages derived from Abstinence, or, to express the same idea in more familiar language, from the Use of Capital, are two: first the Use of Implements; and second the Division of Labour.

I. **The Use of Implements.**—Implements, or tools, or machines (words which express things perhaps slightly different in some respects, but precisely similar so far as they are the subjects of Political Economy) have been divided into those which produce power, and those which transmit power. Under the first head are comprehended those which produce motion independently of human labour. Such are, for instance, those machines which are worked by the force of wind, of water, or of steam.

The second head comprises what are usually termed tools, such as the spade, the hammer, or the knife which assist the force, or save the time of the workman, but receive their impulse from his hand.

To these two classes a third must be added, including all those instruments which are not intended to produce or transmit motion, using that word in its popular sense. This class includes many things to which the name of implement, tool, or machine is not generally applied. A piece of land prepared for tillage, and the corn with

which it is to be sown, are among the implements by whose use the
harvest is produced. Books and manuscripts are implements more
productive than those invented by Arkwright or Brunel. Again,
many of the things which popularly *are* called implements, such as the
telescope, have no reference to motion ; and others, such as a chain,
or an anchor, or indeed any fastening whatever, are intended not to
produce or transmit, but to prevent it.

The instruments which derive their impulse from the person who
works them are in general of a simple description, and some of them
are to be met with in the rudest state of human society. The first
subsistence offered by nature to the savage consists of the brutes
around him ; but some instruments beyond the weapons which she
has given to him must enable him to take advantage of her bounty.

It will be observed, that we consider the use of all implements as
implying an exercise of abstinence, using that word in our extended
sense as comprehending all preference of remote to immediate results.
In civilized society this appears to be strictly true. It is obviously
true as to the *use* of all those instruments and materials which may
be used at will, either for the purpose of present enjoyment, or for
that of further production, such, for example, as the greater part of
agricultural stock. It is equally true as to the *making* of all those
implements which are incapable of any but productive use, such as
tools and machinery in the popular acceptation of those words. In
an improved state of society, the commonest tool is the result of the
labour of previous years, perhaps of previous centuries. A carpenter's tools are among the simplest that occur to us. But what a
sacrifice of present enjoyment must have been undergone by the capitalist who first opened the mine of which the carpenter's nails and
hammer are the product ! How much labour directed to distant
results must have been employed by those who formed the instruments with which that mine was worked ! In fact, when we consider
that all tools, except the rude instruments of savage life, are themselves the product of earlier tools, we may conclude that there is not
a nail, among the many millions annually fabricated in England,
which is not to a certain degree the product of some labour for the
purpose of obtaining a distant result, or, in our nomenclature, of some
abstinence undergone before the Conquest, or perhaps before the
Heptarchy.

The same remark applies to the acquired abilities which Adam
Smith has properly considered a capital fixed and realized in the
person of their possessor. In many cases they are the result of long
previous exertion and expense on his own part ; exertion and expense
which might have been directed to the obtaining objects of immediate
enjoyment, but which have, in fact, been undergone solely in the hope
of a distant reward. And in almost all cases they imply much
expense, and consequently much sacrifice of immediate enjoyment on

the part of parents or guardians. The maintenance of a boy during the first eight or nine years of his life is indeed an unavoidable burthen, and therefore cannot be considered a sacrifice. But almost all that is expended on him after that age is voluntary. At nine or ten he might earn a maintenance in an agricultural, and more than a bare maintenance in a manufacturing employment, and at twenty-one obtain better wages than at any subsequent period of his life. But even the lowest department of skilled labour is in general inaccessible except at an expense very great, when we consider by whom it is to be borne; £15 or £20 is a low apprentice fee, but amounts to half the average annual income of an agricultural family. The greater part of the remuneration for skilled labour is the reward for the abstinence implied by a considerable expenditure on the labourer's education.

We must admit, however, that this reasoning does not apply to society in that rude state which is not perhaps within the scope of Political Economy. The savage seldom employs in making his bow or his dart time which he could devote to the obtaining of any object of immediate enjoyment. He exercises, therefore, labour and providence, but not abstinence. The first step in improvement, the rise from the hunting and fishing to the pastoral state, implies an exercise of abstinence. Much more abstinence, or, in other words, a much greater use of capital, is required for the transition from the pastoral to the agricultural state; and an amount not only still greater, but constantly increasing, is necessary to the prosperity of manufactures and commerce. An agricultural Country can remain stationary; a commercial and manufacturing one cannot. The capital which fifty years ago enabled England to be the first of commercial and manufacturing nations, was probably far inferior in extent and efficiency to that now possessed by France, or even to that of the late Kingdom of the Netherlands. If our capital had remained stationary, we should have sunk to a second or third-rate power. The same consequence might now follow if commercial restraints, or the waste of a long war, should check the increase of our present capital, while that of our rivals should continue progressive.

Having shown the connection between abstinence and the employment of implements, the next thing to be considered is the advantage which the use of implements affords. This subject, however, we shall pass over very briefly; partly because an attempt to give any thing like an adequate account of it, however concise, would far exceed the limits of this Treatise; partly because the subject has been considered at some length in the Articles in this Encyclopædia on MECHANICS and MANUFACTURES; and partly because we believe all our readers to be aware that the powers of man are prodigiously increased by the use of implements, though probably no man ever had, or ever will have, sufficient knowledge of details and perception of their relations and consequences, to estimate the whole amount of that increase. A few remarks on those instruments which produce motion, or, as it is technically termed, *power*, are all that we can venture on.

The superior productiveness of modern compared with ancient labour depends, perhaps, principally on the use of these instruments. We doubt whether all the exertions of all the inhabitants of the Roman Empire, if exclusively directed to the manufacture of cotton goods, could, in a whole generation, have produced as great a quantity as is produced every year by a portion of the inhabitants of Lancashire; and we are sure that the produce would have been generally inferior in quality. The only moving powers employed by the Greeks or Romans were the lower animals, water, and wind. And even these powers they used very sparingly. They scarcely used wind except to assist their merchant vessels in a timid coasting; they used rivers as they found them, for the purposes of communication, but did not connect them by canals; they used horses only for burthen and draught, and the latter without the assistance of springs. They made little use of that powerful machine to which we give the general name of a mill, in which a single shaft, turning under the impulse of animal power, or wind, or water, or steam, enables a child to apply a force equal sometimes to that of a thousand workmen.

A ship of the line under full sail has been called the noblest exhibition of human power: it is, perhaps, the most beautiful. But if dominion over matter, if the power of directing inanimate substances, at the same time to exert the most tremendous energy, and to perform the most delicate operations, be the test, that dominion and power are no where so strikingly shown as in a large cotton manufactory. One of the most complete which we have seen is that constructed by the late Mr. Marsland at Stockport; and, as it exhibits very strikingly both the power and the manageableness of machinery, it may be worth while to give a short description of it, as we saw it in 1825.

Mr. Marsland was the proprietor of the Mersey for about a mile of its course, and of a tongue of land which two reaches of the river form into a peninsula. Through the isthmus of this peninsula he bored a tunnel sufficient to receive seven wheels of large diameter, and to give passage to enough of the river to turn them; these wheels communicated rotatory motion to perpendicular shafts; and the perpendicular shafts communicated the same motion to numerous horizontal shafts connected with them by pinions. Each horizontal shaft ran below the ceiling of a work-room more than a hundred feet long. The buildings connected with the wheels worked by the river contained six or seven stories of work-rooms, each supplied with its horizontal shaft. The rotatory motion was carried on from each horizontal shaft by means of small solid wheels called drums, affixed to the principal shaft of each detached piece of machinery, and connected with the great horizontal shaft of the work-room by a leathern strap. Many of these rooms were not occupied by Mr. Marsland himself. He let out, by the hour, the day, or the week, a certain portion of the floor of a work-room, and the liberty to make use of a certain portion of the horizontal shaft.   The tenant placed his own machinery on the floor, connected its drum with the shaft that revolved rapidly above, and instantly saw his own small mechanical world, with its system of wheels, rollers, and spindles, in full activity, performing its motions with a quickness, a regularity, and, above all, a perseverance, far beyond the exertions of man.   In the operation of machinery, power, like matter, seems susceptible of indefinite aggregation and of indefinite subdivision.   In the performance of some of its duties the machinery moved at a rate almost formidable, in others at one scarcely perceptible.   It took hold of the cotton of which a neckcloth was to be made, cleaned it, arranged its fibres longitudinally, twisted them into a strong and continuous thread, and finally wove that thread into muslin.   It took the wool of which a coat was to be made, and, after subjecting it to processes more numerous than those which cotton experiences, at last wove it into cloth.   For thousands of years, in fact from the last great convulsion which traced the course of the river, until Mr. Marsland bored his tunnel, had the Mersey been wasting all the energy that now works so obediently.

One of the most striking qualities of machinery is its susceptibility of indefinite improvement.   On looking through the instructive evidence collected by the Committee on Artisans and Machinery, (1824,) it will be found that nothing is more impressed on the minds of the witnesses than the constant tide of improvement, rendering obsolete in a very few years all that might have been supposed to be perfect.

Mr. Holdsworth, a spinner and machine-maker at Glasgow, states that the best mills at Glasgow are equal to the best mills at Manchester erected three or four years before.   Mr. Holdsworth's history of his own proceedings will illustrate many of the previous observations.

He is asked whether he got his machinery from Manchester when he first commenced business.   He replies: "I did not; I contemplated making it myself, and made the attempt, but there was so much difficulty in getting good workmen, and the expense of tools was so serious, that I desisted.   I then selected a well-qualified young mechanic, and engaged him to make it for me.   I gave over to him my patterns and my plans, and he executed well the machinery required in the first mill.   Two years after I built a second mill, the machinery of which was also executed by him.   After two years more I built a third and a larger mill, the machinery of which I made myself."

He is asked why he made the last machinery himself, and replies: "In the first place that machine maker was very busy;" (it appears, subsequently, that, at the time of the examination, that maker could not have taken an order to execute any part of it under sixteen months, and that there were then eight or nine mills waiting for machinery, some of which had been ready for twelve months, and had only a small part of their machinery, and others had been ready six months, and were empty;) " and as machine makers do not like to alter their plans, I could not prevail upon him to execute the improvements then recently made in Manchester." (Fifth Report, p. 378.)

Mr. J. Dunlop is asked (p. 473,) how far he considers the American factories behind those of Glasgow. He replies, about thirty years. He goes on to state that they are in a progressive state, and the men very active and industrious. He is then asked whether, " supposing English machinery transported to America, with the assistance of English foremen, he does not think the population of America would soon be taught to work in their factories equally to the men of this Country?" He answers, " Yes, I think they would; but before they could acquire that we should be ahead of them a long way again. I reason comparing Scotland with England. We began the business of cotton-spinning later, we were of course behind, and we have always been behind; we have never been able to get up, and I believe never will."

Sixty years form a short period in the history of a nation; yet what changes in the state of England and the Southern parts of Scotland have the steam-engine and the cotton machinery effected within the last sixty years. They have almost doubled the population, more than doubled the wages of labour, and nearly trebled the rent of land. They enabled us to endure, not certainly without inconvenience, but yet to endure, a public debt more than trebled, and a taxation more than quadrupled. They changed us from exporters to importers of raw produce, and consequently changed our corn laws from a bounty on exportation to nearly a prohibition of importation. They have clad the whole world with a light and warm clothing, and made it so easy of acquisition that we are perhaps scarcely aware of the whole enjoyment that it affords.

There appears no reason, unless that reason be to be found among our own commercial institutions, why the improvements of the next sixty years should not equal those of the preceding. The cotton machinery is far from perfection; the evidence which we have quoted shows that it receives daily improvements; and the steam-engine is in its infancy; its first application to vessels is within our recollection; its application to carriages has scarcely commenced; and it is probable that many other powers of equal efficiency lie still undiscovered among the secrets of nature, or, if known, are still unapplied. There are doubtless at this instant innumerable productive instruments known, but disregarded, because separately they are inefficient, and the effect of their combination has not been perceived. Printing and paper are both of high antiquity. Printing was probably known to the Greeks; it certainly was practised by the Romans, as loaves of bread stamped with the baker's initials have been found in Pompeii. And paper has been used in China from times immemorial. But these instruments separately were of little value. While so expensive a commodity as parchment, or so brittle a one as the papyrus, were the best materials for books, the sale of a number of good copies sufficient to pay the expense of printing could not be relied on. Paper without printing was more useful than printing without paper; but the mere labour necessary to constant transcription, even supposing the materials to be of no value, would have been such as still to leave books an expensive luxury. But the combination of these two instruments, each separately of little utility, has always been considered the most important invention in the history of man.

II. **Division of Labour.**—The second of the two principal advantages derived from Abstinence, or, in other words, from the use of Capital, is the Division of Labour.

We have already observed that Division of Production would have been a more convenient expression than division of Labour; but Adam Smith's authority has given such currency to the term Division of Labour, that we shall continue to employ it, using it, however, in the extended sense in which it appears to have been used by Adam Smith. We say *appears* to have been used, because Smith, with his habitual negligence of precision, has given no formal explanation of his meaning. But in the latter part of his celebrated first chapter, he appears to include among the advantages derived from the division of labour all those derived from internal and external commerce. It is clear, therefore, that, by Division of Labour, he meant Division of Production. or, in other words, the confining as much as possible each distinct producer and each distinct class of producers to operations of a single kind.

The advantages derived from the division of labour are attributed by Smith to three different circumstances. " First, to the increase of dexterity in every particular workman; secondly, to the saving of the time which is commonly lost in passing from one species of work to another; and lastly, to the invention of a great number of machines which facilitate and abridge labour, and enable one man to do the work of many."

Smith was the first writer who laid much stress on the division of labour. The force and the variety of the examples by which he has illustrated it make the first chapter perhaps the most amusing and the best known in his whole Work. But, like most of those who have discovered a new principle, he has in some respects overstated, and in others understated, its effects. His remark, " that the invention of all those machines by which labour is so much facilitated and abridged seems to have been originally owing to the division of labour," is too general. Many of our most useful implements have been invented by persons neither mechanics by profession, nor themselves employed in the operations which those implements facilitate. Arkwright was, as is well known, a barber; the inventor of the power-loom is a clergyman. Perhaps it would be a nearer approach to truth if we were to say that the division of labour has been occasioned by the use of implements. In a rude state of Society, every man possesses, and every man can manage, every sort of instrument. In an advanced state, when expensive machinery and an almost infinite variety of tools have superseded the few and simple implements of savage life, those only can profitably employ themselves in any branch of manufacture who can obtain the aid of the machinery, and have been trained to use the tools, by which its processes are facilitated; and the division of labour is the necessary consequence. But, in fact, the use of tools and the division of labour so act and react on one another, that their effects can seldom be separated in practice. Every great mechanical invention is followed by an increased division of labour, and every increased division of labour produces new inventions in mechanism.

——————————————Alterius sic
Altera poscit opem res et conjurat amice.

The increased dexterity of the workman, and the saving of the time which would be lost in passing from one sort of work to another, deserve the attention which they have received from Adam Smith. Both are consequences, and the first is a very important consequence of the division of labour. But he has passed by, or at least has not formally stated, other advantages derived from that principle which appear to be far more important.

One of the principal of these advantages arises from the circumstance that the same exertions which are necessary to produce a single given result are often sufficient to produce many hundred or many thousand similar results. The Post Office supplies a familiar illustration. The same exertions which are necessary to send a single letter from Falmouth to New York are sufficient to forward fifty, and nearly the same exertions will forward ten thousand. If every man were to effect the transmission of his own correspondence, the whole life of an eminent merchant might be passed in travelling, without his being able to deliver all the letters which the Post Office forwards for him in a single evening. The labour of a few individuals, devoted exclusively to the forwarding of letters, produces results which all the exertions of all the inhabitants of Europe could not effect, each person acting independently.

The utility of government depends on this principle. In the rudest state of society each man relies principally on himself for the protection both of his person and of his property. For these purposes he must be always armed, and always watchful; what little property he has must be moveable, so as never to be far distant from its owner. Defence or escape occupy almost all his thoughts, and almost all his time, and, after all these sacrifices, they are very imperfectly effected. "If ever you see an old man here," said an inhabitant of the confines of Abyssinia to Bruce, "he is a stranger; the natives all die young by the lance."

But the labour which every individual, who relies on himself for protection, must himself undergo, is more than sufficient to enable a few individuals to protect themselves, and also the whole of a numerous community. To this may be traced the origin of governments. The nucleus of every government must have been some person who offered protection in exchange for submission. On the governor and those with whom he is associated, or whom he appoints, is devolved the care of defending the community from violence and fraud. And so far as internal violence is concerned, and that is the evil most dreaded in civilized society, it is wonderful how small a number of persons can provide for the security of multitudes. About fifteen thousand soldiers, and not fifteen thousand policemen, watchmen, and officers of justice, protect the persons and property of the seventeen millions of inhabitants of Great Britain. There is scarcely a trade that does not engross the labour of a greater number of persons than are employed to perform this the most important of all services.

It is obvious, however, that the division of labour on which government is founded, is subject to peculiar evils. Those who are to afford protection must necessarily be intrusted with power; and those who rely on others for protection lose, in a great measure, the means and the will to protect themselves. Under such circumstances, the bargain, if it can be called one, between the government and its subjects, is not conducted on the principles which regulate ordinary exchanges. The government generally endeavours to extort from its subjects, not merely a fair compensation for its services, but all that force or terror can wring from them without injuring their powers of further production. In fact, it does in general extort much more; for if we look through the world we shall find few governments whose oppression does not materially injure the prosperity of their people. When we read of African and Asiatic tyrannies, where millions seem themselves to consider their own happiness as dust in the balance compared with the caprices of their despot, we are inclined to suppose the evils of misgovernment to be the worst to which man can be exposed. But they are trifles compared to those which are felt in the absence of government. The mass of the inhabitants of Egypt, Persia, and Burmah, or to go as low as perhaps it is possible, the subjects of the Kings of Dahomi and Ashantee, enjoy security, if we compare their situation with that of the ungoverned inhabitants of New Zealand. So strongly is this felt, that there is no tyranny which men will not eagerly embrace, if anarchy is to be the alternative. Almost all the differences between the different races of men, differences so great that we sometimes nearly forget that they all belong to the same species, may be traced to the degrees in which they enjoy the blessings of good government.   If the worst government be better than anarchy, the advantages of the best must be incalculable. But the best governments of which the world has had experience, those of Great Britain and of the Countries which have derived their institutions from Great Britain, are far from having attained the perfection of which they appear to be susceptible.   In these governments the subordinate duties are generally performed by persons specially educated for these purposes, the superior ones are not.   It seems to be supposed that a knowledge of politics, the most extensive and the most difficult of all Sciences, is a natural appendage to persons holding a high rank in society, or may be acquired at intervals snatched from the bustle and the occupation of laborious and engrossing professions.   In despotisms, the principal evils arise partly from the ignorance, and partly from the bad passions of the rulers.   In representative governments, they arise principally from their unskilfulness. It is to be hoped that a further application of the division of labour, the principle upon which all government is founded, by providing an appropriate education for those who are to direct the affairs of the State, may protect us as effectually against suffering under ignorance or inexperience in our governors, as we are now protected against their injustice.

Another important consequence of the division of labour, and one which Adam Smith, though he has alluded to it, has not prominently stated, is the power possessed by every nation of availing itself, to a certain extent, of the natural and acquired advantages of every other portion of the commercial world.   Colonel Torrens is the first writer who has expressly connected foreign trade with the division of labour, by designating international commerce as " the territorial division of labour."

Nature seems to have intended that mutual dependence should unite all the inhabitants of the earth into one commercial family.   For this purpose she has indefinitely diversified her own products in every climate and in almost every extensive district.   For this purpose, also, she seems to have varied so extensively the wants and the productive powers of the different races of men.   The superiority of modern over ancient wealth depends in a great measure on the greater use we make of these varieties.   We annually import into this Country about thirty million pounds of tea.   The whole expense of purchasing and importing this quantity does not exceed £2,250,000, or about 1s. 6d. a pound, a sum equal to the value of the labour of only forty-five thousand men, supposing their annual wages to amount to £50 a year. With our agricultural skill, and our coal mines, and at the expense of above 40s. a pound instead of 1s. 6d., that is, at the cost of the labour of about one million two hundred thousand men instead of forty-five thousand, we might produce our own tea, and enjoy the pride of being independent of China. But one million two hundred thousand is about the number of all the men engaged in agricultural labour throughout England. A single trade, and that not an extensive one, supplies as much tea, and that probably of a better sort, as could be obtained, if it were possible to devote every farm and every garden to its domestic production.

The greater part of the advantage of rather importing than growing and manufacturing tea arises, without doubt, from the difference between the climates of China and England. But a great part also arises from the different price of labour in the two Countries. Not only the cultivation of the tea plant, but the preparation of its leaves, requires much time and attention. The money wages of labour are so low in China, that these processes add little to the money cost of the tea. In England the expense would be intolerable. When a nation, in which the powers of production, and consequently the wages of labour, are high, employs its own members in performing duties that could be as effectually performed by the less valuable labour of less civilized nations, it is guilty of the same folly as a farmer who should plough with a race-horse.

Another important consequence of the division of labour is the existence of retailers: a class who, without being themselves employed in the direct production of raw or manufactured commodities, are, in fact, the persons who supply them to their ultimate purchasers, and that at the times and in the portions which the convenience of those purchasers requires. When we look at a map of London and its suburbs, and consider that that province covered with houses contains more than a tenth of the inhabitants of England, and consumes perhaps one-fifth in value of all that is consumed in England, and obtains what it consumes, not from its own resources, but from the whole civilized world, it seems marvellous that the daily supply of such multitudes should be apportioned with any thing like accuracy to their daily wants. It is effected principally by means of the retailers. Each retailer, the centre of his own system of purchasers, knows, by experience, the average amount of their periodical wants. The wholesale dealer, who forms the link between the actual producer or importer, and the retailer, knows also, by experience, the average amount of the demands of his own purchasers, the retailers; and is governed by that experience in his purchases from the importer or producer. And the average amount of these last purchases affords the data on which the importers and producers regulate the whole vast and multifarious supply. It can scarcely be necessary to dwell on the further advantages derived from the readiness and subdivision of the retailer's stock; or, to point out the convenience of having to buy a steak from a butcher, instead of an ox from a grazier. These are the advantages to which we formerly referred, as enabling the retailer to obtain a profit proportioned to the average time during which his stock in trade remains in his possession.

We now proceed to show that the Division of Labour is mainly dependent on Abstinence, or, in other words, on the use of Capital.

"In that rude state of society," says Adam Smith, "in which there is no division of labour, in which exchanges are seldom made, and in which every man provides every thing for himself, it is not necessary that any stock should be accumulated or stored up beforehand in order to carry on the business of the society. Every man endeavours to supply, by his own industry, his own occasional wants as they occur. When he is hungry, he goes to the forest to hunt; when his coat is worn out, he clothes himself with the skin of the first large animal he kills; and when his hut begins to go to ruin, he repairs it as well as he can with the trees and the turf that are nearest to it.

"But when the division of labour has once been thoroughly introduced, the produce of a man's own labour can supply but a very small part of his occasional wants. The far greater part of them are supplied by the produce of other men's labour, which he purchases with the produce, or, what is the same thing, with the price of the produce of his own. But his purchase cannot be made until such time as the produce of his own labour has not only been completed, but sold. A stock of goods of different kinds, therefore, must be stored up somewhere, sufficient to maintain him, and to supply him with the materials and tools of his work, till such time, at least, as both these events can be brought about. A weaver cannot apply himself entirely to his peculiar business, unless there is beforehand stored up somewhere, either in his own possession, or in that of some other person, a stock sufficient to maintain him, and to supply him with the materials and tools of his work, till he has not only completed, but sold his web. This accumulation must evidently be previous to his applying his industry for so long a time to such a peculiar business." *Wealth of Nations*, Book II. *Introduction*.

Perhaps this is inaccurately expressed; there are numerous cases in which production and sale are contemporaneous. The most important divisions of labour are those which allot to a few members of the community the task of protecting and instructing the remainder. But their services are sold as they are performed. And the same remark applies to almost all those products to which we give the name of services. Nor is it absolutely necessary in any case, though, if Adam Smith's words were taken literally, such a necessity might be inferred, that, before a man dedicates himself to a peculiar branch of production, a stock of goods should be stored up to supply him with subsistence, materials, and tools, till his own product has been completed and sold. That he must be kept supplied with those articles is true; but they need not have been stored up before he first sets to work, they may have been produced while his work was in progress. Years must often elapse between the commencement and sale of a picture. But the painter's subsistence, tools, and materials for those years are not stored up before he sets to work: they are produced from time to time during the course of his labour. It is probable, however, that Adam Smith's real meaning was, not that the identical supplies which will be wanted in a course of progressive industry must be already collected when the process which they are to assist or remunerate is about to be begun, but that a fund or source must then exist from which they may be drawn as they are required. That fund must comprise in specie some of the things wanted. The painter must have his canvass, the weaver his loom, and materials, not enough, perhaps, to complete his web, but to commence it. As to those commodities, however, which the workman subsequently requires, it is enough if the fund on which he relies is a productive fund, keeping pace with his wants, and virtually set apart to answer them.

But if the employment of capital is required for the purpose of allowing a single workman to dedicate himself to one pursuit, it is still more obviously necessary in order to enable aggregations, or classes of producers, to concur, each by his separate exertions, in one production. In such cases even the mere matter of distribution, the mere apportionment of the price of the finished commodity among the different producers requires the employment of a considerable capital, and for a considerable time, or, in other words, a considerable exertion of abstinence. The produce of independent labour belongs by nature to its producer. But where there has been a considerable division of labour, the product has no *one* natural owner. If we were to attempt to reckon up the number of persons engaged in producing a single neckcloth, or a single piece of lace, we should find the number amount to many thousands; in fact, to many tens of thousands. It is obviously impossible that all these persons, even if they could ascertain their respective rights as producers, should act as owners of the neckcloth or the lace, and sell it for their common benefit.

This difficulty is got over by distinguishing those who assist in production by advancing capital, from those who contribute only labour—a distinction often marked by the terms master and workman; and by arranging into separate groups the different capitalists and workmen engaged in distinct processes, and letting each capitalist, as he passes on the commodity, receive from his immediate successor the price both of his own abstinence and of his workmen's labour.

It may be interesting to trace this process in the history of a coloured neckcloth or a piece of lace. The cotton of which it is formed may be supposed to have been grown by some Tenessee or Louisiana planter. For this purpose he must have employed labourers

in preparing the soil and planting and attending to the shrub for more
than a year before its pod ripened.   When the pod became ripe, considerable labour, assisted by ingenious machinery, was necessary to
extricate the seeds from the wool.   The fleece thus cleaned was
carried down the Mississippi to New Orleans, and there sold to a
cotton factor.   The price at which it was sold must have been sufficient,
in the first place, to repay to the planter the wages which had been
paid by him to all those employed in its production and carriage; and,
secondly, to pay him a profit proportioned to the time which had
elapsed between the payment of those wages and the sale of the
cotton; or, in other words, to remunerate him for his abstinence in
having so long deprived himself of the use of his money, or of the
pleasure which he might have received from the labour of his work-
people, if, instead of cultivating cotton, he had employed them in
contributing to his own immediate enjoyment.   The New Orleans
factor, after keeping it perhaps five or six months, sold it to a Liverpool
merchant.   Scarcely any labour could have been expended on it at
New Orleans, and, in the absence of accidental circumstances, its
price was increased only by the profit of the cotton factor.   A profit
which was the remuneration of his abstinence in delaying, for five or
six months, the gratification which he might have obtained by the
expenditure on himself of the price paid by him to the planter.   The
Liverpool merchant brought it to England and sold it to a Manchester
spinner.   He must have sold it at a price which would repay, in the
first place, the price at which it was bought from the factor at New
Orleans; in the second place, the freight from thence to Liverpool;
(which freight includes a portion of the wages of the seamen, and of
the wages of those who built the vessel, of the profits of those who
advanced those wages before the vessel was completed, of the wages
and profits of those who imported the materials of which that vessel
was built, and, in fact, of a chain of wages and profits extending to
the earliest dawn of civilization;) and, thirdly, the merchant's profit
for the time that these payments were made before his sale to the
manufacturer was completed.

The spinner subjected it to the action of his work-people and
machinery, until he reduced part of it into the thread applicable to
weaving muslin, and part into the still finer thread that can be formed
into lace.

The thread thus produced he sold to the weaver and to the lacemaker; at a price repaying, in addition to the price that was paid to
the merchant, first, the wages of the work-people immediately engaged
in the manufacture; secondly, the wages and profits of all those who
supplied, by the labour of previous years, the buildings and machinery;
and, thirdly, the profit of the master spinner.   It would be tedious to
trace the transmission of the thread from the weaver to the bleacher,
from the bleacher to the printer, from the printer to the wholesale

warehouseman, from him to the retailer, and thence to the ultimate purchaser; or even its shorter progress from the lacemaker to the embroiderer, and thence to the ultimate purchaser. At every step a fresh capitalist repays all the previous advances, subjects the article, if unfinished, to further processes, advances the wages of those engaged in its further manufacture and transport, and is ultimately repaid, by the capitalist next in order, all his own advances, and a profit proportioned to the time during which he has abstained from the unproductive enjoyment of the capital thus employed.

It will be observed, that we have not mentioned the Taxation that must have been incurred throughout the whole process which we have described, or the Rent that must have been paid for the use of the various appropriated natural agents whose services were requisite or beneficial. We have left rent unnoticed, because its amount depends so much on accident, that any further allusion to it would have much increased the complexity of the subject. We have not expressly mentioned taxation, because it is included under the heads which we have enumerated. The money raised by taxation is employed in paying the wages and profits of those who perform, or cause to be performed, the most important of all services, the protecting the community from fraud and violence. Those who are thus employed afford precisely the same assistance to the merchant or the manufacturer, as the private watchman who protects the warehouse, or the smith who fortifies it with bars and padlocks.

Our limits prohibit our attempting to trace the gradual increase of the value of a pound of cotton from the time it was gathered on the banks of the Mississippi, till it appears in a Bond-Street window as a piece of elaborate lace. We should probably be understating the difference if we were to say that the last price was a thousand times the first. The price of a pound of the finest cotton wool, as it is gathered, is less than two shillings. A pound of the finest cotton lace might easily be worth more than a hundred guineas. No means, except the separation of the functions of the capitalist from those of the labourer, and the constant advance of capital from one capitalist to another, could enable so many thousand producers to direct their efforts to one object, to continue them for so long a period, and to adjust the reward for their respective sacrifices.

DEVELOPMENT OF THE FOURTH ELEMENTARY PROPOSITION OF THE
SCIENCE, NAMELY,

That Agricultural Skill remaining the same, Additional Labour employed on the Land within a given district, produces in general a Less Proportionate Return.

Additional Labour when employed in Manufactures is MORE, when employed in Agriculture is LESS, efficient in proportion.—Before we quit the subject of Production, it is necessary to explain an important difference between the efficiency of the different productive instruments when employed in cultivating the earth, and their efficiency when employed in preparing for human use the raw produce obtained by agriculture : or, in other words, between the efficiency of Agricultural and Manufacturing Industry. In the course of this discussion we shall illustrate the last of the four elementary propositions on which we believe the Science of Political Economy to rest; namely, that, *agricultural skill remaining the same, additional labour employed on the land within a given district produces in general a less proportionate return.*

The difference between the efficiency of agricultural and of manufacturing industry which we have now to consider, consists in the power which agricultural industry possesses, and manufacturing industry does not possess, of obtaining an additional product from the same materials. We have seen that the use of implements and the division of labour assist the exertions of man to an extent quite incalculable at present, and apparently capable of indefinite increase. But manufacturing improvements, though they enable one man to do the work of hundreds or of thousands,—though they enable the same amount of labour employed on the same materials to produce a more and more useful commodity, cannot enable the same amount of labour, or even increased labour, employed on the same quantity of *materials*, to produce a much larger amount of finished work of the same quality, than could have been produced before. If the labour and the skill now employed throughout England on the manufacture of cotton were doubled, but the quantity of raw materials remained the same, the quantity of manufactured produce could not be sensibly increased. The value of that produce might perhaps be much increased, it might be made much finer, and consequently of greater length or breadth ; but supposing the quality of the produce unaltered, its quantity could be increased only by the saving which might be made of that small portion of the raw material which now is wasted.

The case of agriculture is different. Those regions, indeed, which lie within the limits of perennial snow, or consist of rock or loose sand, or precipitous mountain, are unsusceptible of improvement. But with these exceptions, the produce of every extensive district seems capable of being almost indefinitely increased by constantly increasing the labour bestowed on it. Nothing appears more hopelessly barren than an extensive bog with its black-looking pools and rushy vegetation. But, by draining, by burning the limestone on which, in Ireland at least, it generally rests, and by employing the lime to convert the matted fibres of the turf into a vegetable mould, the bog may be made not only productive but fertile. There are about thirty-seven millions of acres in England and Wales. Of these it has been calculated that not eighty-five thousand, less in fact than one four-hundredth part, are in a state of high cultivation, as hop grounds, nursery grounds, and fruit and kitchen gardens ; and that five millions are waste. All that is not waste is productively employed, but how small is its produce compared to the amount to which unlimited labour and abstinence might raise it! If the utmost use were made of lime, and marl, and the other mineral manures; if by a perfect system of drainage and irrigation water were nowhere allowed to be excessive or deficient; if all our wastes were protected by enclosures and planting; if all the land in tillage, instead of being scratched by the plough, were deeply and repeatedly trenched by manual labour; if minute care were employed in the selecting and planting of every seed or root, and watchfulness sufficient to prevent the appearance of a weed; if all live stock, instead of being pastured, had their food cut and brought to them; in short, if the whole Country were subjected to the labour which a rich citizen lavishes on his patch of suburban garden; if it were possible that all this should be effected, the agricultural produce of the Country might be raised to ten times, or indeed to much more than ten times, its present amount. No additional labour or machinery can work up a pound of raw cotton into more than a pound of manufactured cotton; but the same bushel of seed-corn, and the same rood of land, according to the labour and skill with which they are treated, may produce four bushels, or eight bushels, or sixteen.

But although the land in England is capable of producing ten times, or more than ten times as much as it now produces, it is probable that its present produce will never be quadrupled, and almost certain that it will never be decupled.

On the other hand, unless our manufactures be checked by war, or by the continuance or introduction of legislative enactments unfavourable to their progress, their produce may increase during the next century at the same rate, or at a still greater rate, than it increased during the last century. It may be quadrupled, or much more than quadrupled.

The advantage possessed by land in repaying increased labour, though employed on the same materials, with a constantly increasing produce, is overbalanced by the diminishing proportion which the increase of the produce generally bears to the increase of the labour. And the disadvantage of manufactures in requiring for every increase of produce an equal increase of materials, is overbalanced by the constantly increasing facility with which the increased quantity of materials is worked up.

A century ago the average annual import of cotton wool into Great Britain was about one million two hundred thousand pounds. The amount now annually manufactured in Great Britain exceeds two hundred and forty millions of pounds. But though the materials now manufactured are increased at least two hundred times, it is obvious that the labour necessary to manufacture them has not increased two hundred times. It may be doubted whether it has increased thirty times. The whole number of families in Great Britain, exclusively of those employed in agriculture, amounted, at the enumeration in 1831, to 2,453,041; if we suppose the transport, manufacture, and sale of cotton to employ about one-eighth of them, or about 300,000 families, it is a large allowance.   But with the inefficient machinery in use a century ago, the annual manufacture of one million two hundred thousand pounds of cotton could not have required the annual labour of less than ten thousand families.   It probably required many more. The result has been that, although we now require two hundred times as much of the raw material as was required a century ago, and although that additional quantity of raw material is probably obtained from the soil by more than two hundred times the labour that was necessary to obtain the smaller quantity, yet, in consequence of the diminution of the labour necessary to manufacture a given amount, the price of the manufactured commodity, (a price which exhibits the sum of the labour necessary for both obtaining the materials and working them up) has constantly diminished.   In 1786, when our annual import was about twenty millions of pounds of cotton wool, the price of the yarn denominated No. 100 was 38s. a pound.   In 1792, when the import amounted to thirty-four millions of pounds, the price of the same yarn was 16s. a pound.   In 1806, when the import amounted to sixty millions, the price of the yarn had fallen to 7s. 2d. a pound ; and with the increased quantity manufactured, it has now fallen below 3s. a pound.   Every increase in the quantity manufactured has been accompanied by improvements in machinery, and an increased division of labour, and their effects have much more than balanced any increase which may have taken place in the proportionate labour necessary to produce the raw material.

The proposition that, in agriculture, additional labour generally produces a less proportionate result, or, in other words, that the labour of twenty men employed on the land within a given district, though it will certainly produce more than that of ten men, will seldom produce twice as much, will be best illustrated by confining our attention to a single example.

We will suppose a farm consisting of one thousand acres, two hundred very good land, three hundred merely tolerable, and the remainder barren down, affording only a scanty sheep walk.   We will suppose the farmer to employ upon it twenty men, and to obtain an average annual product, which, to reduce it to a single denomination, we will call six hundred quarters of wheat.   We will suppose him now to double the number of his labourers, and we shall see what probability there is that the produce will consequently be doubled.   If the twenty additional labourers are employed in cultivating the down land, they must necessarily produce a less return than that which is produced on the other land by the previous twenty, as the land is supposed to be worse.   It is equally clear that their labour, if applied to the land already in cultivation, will be less productive than the labour previously applied to it ; or, in other words, that the produce of that land, though increased, will not be doubled, since on no other principle can we account for any land except the very best having been ever cultivated. For if the farmer could have gone on applying additional labour to land already in cultivation without any diminution in the proportionate return, it is clear that he never would have cultivated the three hundred acres of inferior land. In fact, if this were the case, if additional labour employed in agriculture gave a proportionate return, he never need have cultivated more than a single acre, or even a single rood. It is probable that in the supposed case he would employ some of his additional labourers in breaking up a portion of the down, and some of them in cultivating more highly the land already in tillage. So employed, they might produce an additional crop of four hundred, or five hundred, or five hundred and fifty quarters, but it is certain that the additional crop would not be equal to the whole six hundred previously obtained: the produce would be increased, but would not be doubled.

This imaginary farm is a miniature of the whole Kingdom. We have in England large tracks of barren waste, and we have under cultivation soil of every description of fertility, from that which produces forty bushels of wheat an acre, to that which produces, with the same labour, and on the same extent of land, only twelve or thirteen. If additional produce is to be raised, the resource, generally speaking, must be either the cultivation of what has been as yet untilled on account of its barrenness, or the employment of additional labour on what is now in cultivation. That in either case the additional produce is not likely to be in the proportion of the additional labour, is as obvious in the case of the whole Kingdom, as it has appeared to be in that of a single farm.

But the proposition which we have been endeavouring to illustrate, though general, is not universal; it is subject to material exceptions. In the first place, the negligence or ignorance of the occupier, or proprietor, or obstacles of ownership, often prevent for a long time particular portions of land from being subjected to the average degree of labour bestowed on land of equal capability. Increased labour, when at length bestowed on land so circumstanced, may fairly be expected to be as productive, indeed more productive, than the average of agricultural labour. Advantages of this kind have sometimes been derived from extensive operations of drainage and embankment; but the chances of great profit are so apt to blind men to the amount of physical obstacles, that projects of this kind are perhaps more frequently attempted prematurely, than deferred till after the time when an increased demand for raw produce first rendered them fair speculations. Undertakings which have been postponed in consequence of obstacles arising from ownership, are far more frequently productive. The enclosure of a common often subjects to the plough land of which the former unproductiveness was not owing to deficient fertility. Effects similar in kind, though not in degree, often take place when an estate becomes unfettered, after the title has been long so circumstanced that the farmers could not rely on the duration or renewal of their leases.   In these cases considerable additional produce may often be obtained by a comparatively small addition of labour.

But the most important exception to the general rule takes place when increase of labour is accompanied by increase of skill.   More efficient implements, a better rotation of crops, a greater division of labour, in short, improvements in the art of agriculture, generally accompany the increase of agricultural labour.   They always accompany that increase when it is accompanied by an increase of the capital as well as of the population of a Country; and they always counteract, and often outweigh, the inferiority or diminished proportional powers of the soil to which they are applied.

The total amount of the annual agricultural produce of Great Britain has much more than doubled during the last hundred years; but it is highly improbable that the amount of labour annually employed in agriculture has also doubled.   It is not supposed that during that period the population of Great Britain has more than doubled; and the principal increase has till lately been in the manufacturing districts. The last hundred years, with all their misfortunes, form the most prosperous period of our History.   We owe to them the enclosure of millions of acres formerly almost useless common field; we owe to them almost all that we possess that deserves the name of Agricultural Science; and we owe to them also all the canals, and almost all the roads, which, by obviating in a great measure the accidents of situation, enable the amount of labour to bear throughout the Kingdom something like an average proportion to the quality of the soil on which it is employed.   It is possible, though certainly not probable, that our progress may be equal during the next hundred years; but though indefinite, it certainly cannot be infinite.   It is obviously impossible that the produce of the soil of a given district can increase geometrically for ever, whatever be the amount of the labour employed on it.

On the other hand, every increase in the number of manufacturing labourers is accompanied not merely by a corresponding, but by an increased productive power.   If three hundred thousand families are now employed in Great Britain to manufacture and transport two hundred and forty millions of pounds of cotton, it is absolutely certain that six hundred thousand families could manufacture and transport four hundred and eighty millions of pounds of cotton.   It is, in fact, certain that they could do much more.   It is not improbable that they could manufacture and transport seven hundred and twenty millions.   The only check by which we can predict that the progress of our manufactures will in time be retarded, is the increasing difficulty of importing materials and food.   If the importation of raw produce could keep pace with the power of working it up, there would be no limit to the increase of wealth and population.

DISTRIBUTION OF WEALTH

OF the three great branches of Political Economy, the Nature, the Production, and the Distribution of Wealth, we have now considered the two former, and we proceed to treat of the last, namely, of the laws according to which all that is produced is *Distributed* among those who become its ultimate consumers. In that state of society which is presupposed by the Political Economist, this is principally effected by means of Exchange. We may indeed conceive a state of human existence admitting of this distribution without the intervention of Exchanges. But such a situation of society, if it can be called society, neither deserves nor requires scientific investigation. Political Economy considers men in that more advanced state, which may fairly be called their natural state, since it is the state to which they are impelled by the provisions of nature, in which each individual relies on his fellows for the greater part, in many cases for the whole of what he consumes, and supplies his own wants principally or wholly by the Exchanges in which he contributes to theirs.

But we must admit that we use each of the words Production and Exchange in a sense rather more extensive than is usual. We have already stated that we apply the word Production to much that would commonly be called appropriation, and that we include under Exchanges what are usually termed public burdens. We consider all that is received by the officers of Government as given in Exchange for Services affording protection, more or less complete, against foreign or domestic violence or fraud. It is true, as we have already remarked, that this Exchange is conducted on peculiar principles. In those governments which are not democratic or representative, the rulers themselves assess the amount which they are to receive, and generally assess it at the utmost which, under such circumstances, can be extorted from their subjects. And even under representative or democratic institutions, no individual inhabitant is permitted to refuse his share of the general contribution, though he should disclaim his share in the general protection. But the transaction, though often involuntary, and still more often inequitable, is still an Exchange, and on the whole a beneficial exchange. The worst and most inefficient Government affords to its subjects a cheaper and a more effectual Protection than they could obtain by their individual and unaided exertions.

The laws by which Exchanges are regulated may be divided into two great branches. The one comprises those laws which apply generally to all Exchanges; the other those which apply specifically to the respective kinds of Exchanges in which the owners of the different Productive Instruments exchange specifically with one another the Produce of those Instruments.

In treating of the one, we have to consider the general laws which regulate Exchanges; in treating of the other, the relative proportions in which different classes of the community benefit by those laws. The things exchanged will be the principal subjects of the one discussion, the exchanging parties of the other.

One of the greatest difficulties to which a writer on Political Economy is exposed, arises from the mutual dependence of the different propositions constituting the Science; a dependence which makes it difficult to explain any one without a frequent allusion to many others. And this is particularly the case with respect to distribution. The proportions in which different classes of the community are entitled to the things that are produced, cannot be explained without a constant reference to the general Laws of Exchange; and, on the other hand, those Laws cannot be discussed without a constant reference to the exchanging parties. Admitting, as we are forced to do, that no arrangement can be free from objection, we have thought that the least objectionable mode of presenting the subject of distribution will be to begin by a general classification of the parties among whom the results of the different instruments of production are divided; then to proceed to state the general laws of exchange; and, lastly, to point out the general circumstances which decide in what proportions the different classes of the community share in the general distribution.

Society divided into Three Classes—Labourers, Capitalists, and Proprietors of Natural Agents.

According to the usual language of Political Economists, Labour, Capital, and Land are the three Instruments of Production; Labourers, Capitalists, and Landlords are the three classes of Producers; and the whole Produce is divided into Wages, Profit, and Rent: the first designating the Labourer's share, the second that of the Capitalist, and the third that of the Landlord. We approve, on the whole, of the principles on which this classification is founded, but we have been forced, much against our will, to make considerable alterations in the language in which it has been usually expressed; to add some new terms, and to enlarge or contract the signification of some others.

It appears to us that, to have a nomenclature which should fully and precisely indicate the facts of the case, not less than *twelve* distinct terms would be necessary. For each class there ought to be a name for the *Instrument* employed or exercised, a name for the *Class of persons* who employ or exercise it, a name for the *Act* of employing or exercising it, and a name for the *Share* of the produce by which that act is remunerated. Of these terms we have not much more than half, as will appear if we examine each class separately.

Nomenclature applicable to the First Class, the Labourers.—For the first class we have the terms "to Labour," "a Labourer," and "Wages." Neither of these terms expresses the instruments of production: the substantive "labour," and the verb "to labour," express merely an act. "A labourer" is an agent, and wages are a result: but what is the thing employed? what is it that the labourer exerts? Clearly his mental or bodily faculties. With the addition of this term the nomenclature of the first class will be complete. To Labour is to employ strength of body or mind for the purpose of Production; the person who does so is a Labourer, and Wages are his remuneration.

Nomenclature applicable to the Second Class, the Capitalists.—In the second class we have the words Capital, Capitalist, and Profit. These terms express the instrument, the person who employs or exercises it, and his remuneration; but there is no familiar term to express the act, the conduct of which profit is the reward, and which bears the same relation to profit which labour does to wages. To this conduct we have already given the name of Abstinence. The addition of this term will complete the nomenclature of the second class. Capital is an article of wealth, the result of human exertion, employed in the production or distribution of Wealth. Abstinence expresses both the act of abstaining from the unproductive use of capital, and also the similar conduct of the man who devotes his labour to the production of remote rather than of immediate results. The person who so acts is a Capitalist, the reward of his conduct is Profit.

Nomenclature applicable to the Third Class, the Proprietors of Natural Agents.—The defectiveness of the established nomenclature is more striking when we come to the third class. Wages and Profits are the creation of man. They are the recompense for the sacrifice made in the one case, of ease, in the other, of immediate enjoyment. But a considerable part of the produce of every country is the recompense of no sacrifice whatever; is received by those who neither labour nor put by, but merely hold out their hands to accept the offerings of the rest of the community.

The powers of nature, as distinguished from those of man, are necessary to afford a field for the exercise of human abstinence and labour. Of these, some from their abundance and the notoriety of the means of employing them, are incapable of appropriation. Being universally accessible, they bear no price notwithstanding their utility; and what has been produced with their assistance has no value beyond that of the labour and abstinence which it has cost. It sells therefore for a price equal to, but not exceeding, the sum of the wages and

profits which must be paid if the production is to be continued.   The
agency of nature is equally essential to the production of timber in the
forests of Upper Canada and in England.   But the supply of timber
in the forests of Upper Canada is practically unlimited.   No portion
of the price of a Canadian hut is paid for the agency of nature in
producing the logs of which it is constructed.   The pine while
standing was valueless.   The purchaser pays only for the labour and
abstinence necessary to fell and to fashion it.

But the assistance of an *Appropriated* Natural Agent may render
possible the production of a commodity more valuable than the result
of equal labour and abstinence without such assistance.   Such a
commodity sells for a price exceeding the sum of the wages and profits
which are sufficient to repay the capitalist and the labourer who have
been employed on it.   The surplus is taken by the proprietor of the
natural agent, and is his reward, not for having laboured or abstained,
but simply for not having withheld what he was able to withhold; for
having permitted the gifts of nature to be accepted.

If we subtract from the price of an English oak what must be paid
for the labour of him who planted the sapling, and for the abstinence
of those who allowed it to grow for a century, still something is to be
paid for the use of the land by which it was nourished.   And that is
the price of the agency not of man but of nature.

Of the Agents afforded by nature, the principal is the Land, with its
Rivers, Ports, and Mines.   In the rare cases in which the quantity of
useful land is practically unlimited, a state of things which occurs
only in the early stages of colonization, Land is an agent universally
accessible, and, as nothing is paid for its use, the whole produce
belongs to the cultivators, and is divided, under the names of wages
and profit, between the capitalists and the labourers, of whose
abstinence and industry it is the result.

But in all old Countries, and even in colonies within a very few
years after their foundation, certain Lands, from peculiar advantages
of soil or situation, are found to make more than the average return
to a given expenditure of capital and industry.   The proprietor of such
lands, if he cultivate them himself, receives a surplus after having paid
the wages of his labourers and deducted the profit to which he is
entitled on his capital.   He of course receives the same surplus if,
instead of cultivating them himself, he lets them out to some other
capitalist.   The tenant receives the same profit, and the labourers
receive the same wages as if they were employed on land possessing
merely average natural advantages; the surplus forms the rent of the
proprietor, or, as we usually term him, the landlord.   The whole
produce, instead of two, is divided into three shares—Rent, Profit, and
Wages.   If the owner is also the capitalist or farmer, he receives two
of these shares, both the profit and the rent.   If he allow it to be
cultivated by the capital of another, he receives only rent.   But rent

with or without profit, he necessarily receives. And when the whole of a Country has been appropriated, though it be true, as will be shown hereafter, that some of the produce is raised by the application of additional capital without payment of additional rent, and may therefore be said to be raised rent free, yet it is equally true that a rent is received from every cultivated acre; a rent rising or falling according to the accidents of soil and situation, but the necessary result of limited extent and productive power.

It is obvious, however, as we have already stated, that land, though the principal, is not the only natural agent that can be appropriated. The mere knowledge of the operations of nature, as long as the use of that knowledge can be confined either by secrecy or by law, creates a revenue to its possessor analogous to the rent of land. The knowledge of the effect on the fibres of cotton of rollers moving with different velocities, enabled a village barber to found in a very few years a more than aristocratic fortune. Still greater wealth might probably have been acquired by Dr. Jenner, if he could have borne somewhat to limit the benefits which he has conferred on mankind.

When the author of a useful discovery puts it himself in practice, he is like a proprietor farming his own property; the produce, after paying average wages for the labour, and average profits for the capital, employed, affords a still further revenue, the effect not of that capital or of that labour, but of the discovery, the creation not of man but of nature. If, instead of using it himself, he let out to another the privilege of using it, he obtains a revenue so precisely resembling the rent of land, that it often receives the same name. The payment made by a manufacturer to a patentee for the privilege of using the patent process, is usually termed, in commercial language, a RENT; and under the same head must be ranked all the peculiar advantages of situation or connection, and all extraordinary qualities of body and mind. The surplus revenue which they occasion beyond average wages and profits is a revenue for which no additional sacrifice has been made. The proprietor of these advantages differs from a landlord only in the circumstance that he cannot in general let them out to be used by another, and must consequently either allow them to be useless or turn them to account himself. He is forced, therefore, always to employ on them his own industry, and generally his own capital, and receives not only rent, but wages and profit. If, therefore, the established division is adhered to, and all that is produced is to be divided into rent, profit, and wages,—and certainly that appears to be the most convenient classification; and if wages and profit are to be considered as the rewards of peculiar sacrifices, the former the remuneration for labour, and the latter for abstinence from immediate enjoyment, it is clear that under the term "rent" must be included all that is obtained without any sacrifice; or, which is the same thing, beyond the remuneration for that sacrifice; all that nature or fortune bestows either without any exertion on the part of the recipient, or in addition to the average remuneration for the exercise of industry or the employment of capital.

But though we see no objection to this extension of the word rent, the terms land and landlord are too precise to admit of being equally extended. It would be too great an innovation to include under the term land every natural agent which is capable of appropriation, or under the term landlord every proprietor of such an agent. For these terms we must substitute those of *natural agent,* and *proprietor of a natural agent.* And the third class will then have a term for the third instrument of production, a term for the owner of that instrument, and a term for the share which he receives of the produce: terms corresponding with the terms faculties of body and mind, labourer, and wages, as applied to the first class, and with capital, capitalist, and profit, as applied to the second. We shall still want a term corresponding with labour and abstinence,—a term indicating the *conduct* which enables the proprietor of a natural agent to receive a rent. But as this conduct implies no sacrifice,—as it consists merely in not suffering the instrument of which he is the owner to be useless, it perhaps does not require a distinct designation. When a man possesses an estate, we take it for granted that he does not allow it to lie waste, but either uses it himself, or lets it to a tenant. In ordinary language the receipt of rent is included under the term ownership. There will therefore be little danger of obscurity if we consider the word "possess," when applied to the proprietor of a natural agent, as implying the receipt of the advantages afforded by that agent, or, in other words, of rent. Talents, indeed, often lie idle, but in that case they may be considered for economical purposes as not possessed. In fact, unaccompanied by the will to use them, they are useless.

But though the whole produce may be considered as divided into three shares, one of which is taken by the capitalists, another by the labourers, and another by the proprietors of the natural agents which have concurred in the production, it is very seldom that any given commodity, or the produce of any one productive exertion, is thus actually divided. The nearest approach to it takes place in those cases in which producers belonging to different classes become partners, and agree that the produce of their joint exertions shall be sold and the price divided between them. Such a partnership is often formed between a capitalist and his labourers when the success of the enterprise depends much on the zeal of the labourers, and the capitalist is unable to overlook them. Such is the case in the Greenland fishery. The men seldom receive preascertained wages, but, on the termination of the voyage, the blubber is sold, and the price divided between the owners and the crew. The practice is the same in privateering, and probably in many other maritime speculations. Somewhat similar is the mode of letting land called the métayer system. Under that system, which is still common on the Continent of Europe, and probably is always to be found in a certain state of society, the landlord supplies the capital as well as the land, and receives half the crop, the remainder forming the wages of the tenant or head labourer, and of the inferior work-people in his employ. But these are exceptions occasioned by the peculiarities of the adventure, or by the poverty or ignorance of imperfect civilization. The usual practice is to consider one of the parties as entitled to the whole product, paying to the others a price for their co-operation. The person so entitled is uniformly the capitalist: the sums which he pays for wages and rent are the purchase-money for the services of the labourer, and for the use of the natural agent employed.

In most cases a considerable interval elapses between the period at which the natural agent and the labourer are first employed, and the completion of the product. In this climate the harvest is seldom reaped until nearly a year after it has been sown; a still longer time is required for the maturity of oxen; and a longer still for that of a horse; and sixty or seventy years may pass between the commencement of a plantation, and the time at which the timber is saleable. It is obvious that neither the landlord nor the labourer, as such, can wait during all this interval for their remuneration. The doing so would, in fact, be an act of abstinence. It would be the employment of land and labour in order to obtain remote results. This sacrifice is made by the capitalist, and he is repaid for it by his appropriate remuneration, profit. He advances to the landlord and the labourer, and in most cases to some previous capitalist, the price of their respective assistance; or, in other words, the hire of the land and capital belonging to one, and of the mental and bodily powers of another, and becomes solely entitled to the whole of the product. The success of his operations depends on the proportion which the value of that produce, (or, in commercial language, the value of his returns,) bears to the value of his advances, taking into consideration the time for which those advances have been made. If the value of the return is inferior to that of the advance, he is obviously a loser; he is a loser if it be merely equal, as he has incurred abstinence without profit, or, in ordinary language, has lost the interest on his capital. He is a loser even if the value of his returns do not exceed that of his advances by an amount equal to the current rate of profit for the period during which the advance has been made. In any of these cases the product is sold, so far as the capitalist is concerned, for less than the cost of its production. The employment of capital, therefore, is necessarily a speculation; it is the purchase of so much productive power which may or may not occasion a remunerative return.

The common language of Economists, therefore, which describes the landlord, the capitalist, and the labourer as sharers of the produce, is a fiction. Almost all that is produced is in the first instance the property of the capitalist; he has purchased it by having previously paid the rent and wages, and incurred or paid for the abstinence, which were necessary to its production. A portion of it, but generally a small portion, he consumes himself in the state in which he receives it; the remainder he sells. He may, if he think fit, employ the price of all that he sells in purchases for his own gratification; but he cannot remain a capitalist unless he consent to employ some portion of it in the hire of the land and labour, by the assistance of which the process of production is to be continued or recommenced. He cannot, generally speaking, fully retain his situation as a capitalist unless he employ enough to hire as much land and labour as before; and if he wish to raise himself in the world, he must, generally speaking, not merely keep up, but increase the sum which he devotes to the purchase of productive force. If, for instance, he has hired the use of a farm for a year for £1000, and has paid £2000 more as wages to his labourers, and has expended £1000 in the purchase, from other capitalists, of Agricultural stock, and at the end of the year has sold the produce for £4400, he may, if he like, spend on his own gratification the whole of that £4400; or he may so spend only £400, and employ the rest in hiring the farm and the labourers, and purchasing stock for another year; or he may spend on himself only £200, and by employing productively £4200 instead of £4000, hire more land, or more labourers, or purchase more stock and provide for the increase of his capital and his profit. But in whatever way he employ his £4400, he still must pay it to landlords, (using that word to comprise all proprietors of natural agents,) capitalists, and labourers.

It has been objected, however, that this nomenclature is incomplete. Rent, profit, and wages, it has been said, designate only those portions of the annual produce which the producers consume for their own gratification. They form the *revenue* of a nation. A further portion, and a very large one, must be employed, not as revenue, but as capital; not in directly supplying the wants or directly ministering to the enjoyments of either landlords, labourers, or capitalists, but merely in keeping up the instruments of production. Thus of the farmer's whole return, which we have supposed to be of the value of £4400, we may suppose a portion, amounting in value to £200, to have consisted of corn which he returned to the earth as seed, and another portion, amounting to the same value, to have consisted of the forage which he gave to his working cattle. It has been said that neither this seed nor this forage was rent, profit, or wages.

The answer to this objection is, that the seed-corn and forage in question were the result of land, labour, and abstinence; they were entitled, therefore, when produced, to be denominated rent, wages, or profit, and the circumstance that they were employed to produce future instead of immediate gratification, does not vary their character. When produced, they were revenue: their *conversion* into capital was a subsequent accident.   No one would except against the expression that such and such a labourer has *saved part of his wages* and employed them in stocking his garden.   If the words revenue and income were co-extensive with expenditure, the common statement, that a man is living within his income, would be a contradiction in terms.

Perhaps this may be made clearer if we retrace the history of capital.

The primary instruments of production were labour, and those productive agents which are spontaneously afforded by nature.   The first dwellers on the earth had only rent and wages.   The savage who, instead of devouring the animals which he had entrapped, reserved them to become the origin of a domesticated flock, and he who reserved, to be employed as seed, some of the grains which he had gathered, laid the foundation of capital.   The produce of that flock and of that seed was partly rent, partly wages, and partly profit.   And it did not cease to be so, although he refused to employ the whole of it on his immediate gratification.

It must be admitted, however, that the portion of the annual produce which is employed in the production or the support of brute or inanimate capital is not usually termed rent, wages, or profit.   It has not, in fact, any specific name.   But it appears to us to be the most philosophical arrangement to consider it as rent, wages, or profit, according to the character of its proprietor, without regard to its subsequent destination.

EXCHANGE.

Having made this general classification of the parties among whom the results of the different productive instruments are divided, we now proceed to consider the general laws which regulate the proportions in which those results are exchanged for one another.   To a certain degree this question was considered when we treated of value; but not having at that time explained the words production, wages, profit, or rent, we were unable to do more than to state and illustrate the following propositions:—

First, that all those things, and those things only, are susceptible of exchange, which, being transferable, are limited in supply, and are capable, directly or indirectly, of affording pleasure or preventing pain; a capacity to which we have affixed the name of utility. Secondly, that the reciprocal values of any two things, or, in other words, the quantity of the one which will exchange for a given quantity of the other, depend on two sets of causes; those which occasion the utility and limit the supply of the one, and those which limit the supply and occasion the utility of the other. The causes which occasion the utility and limit the supply of any given commodity or service, we denominated the *intrinsic* causes of its value. Those which limit the supply and occasion the utility of the commodities or services for which it is capable of being exchanged, we denominated the *extrinsic* causes of its value. And, thirdly, that comparative limitation of supply, or, to speak more familiarly, though less philosophically, comparative scarcity, though not sufficient to constitute value, is by far its most important element; utility, or, in other words, demand, being mainly dependent on it. We had not then shown the means by which supply is effected. Having done this, having shown that human Labour and Abstinence, and the spontaneous agency of Nature, are the three instruments of production, we are at liberty to explain what are the obstacles which limit the supply of all that is produced, and the mode in which those obstacles affect the reciprocal values of the different subjects of exchange.

Price.—In the following discussion, however, we shall in general substitute *price* or value in money for general value.

The general value of any commodity, that is, the quantity of all the other subjects of exchange which might be obtained in return for a given quantity of it, is incapable of being ascertained. Its specific value in any other commodity may be ascertained by the experiment of an exchange; the anxiety of each party in the exchange to give as little, and obtain as much as possible, leading him to investigate, as accurately as he can, the intrinsic causes giving value to each of the articles to be exchanged. This is, however, a troublesome operation, and many expedients are used to diminish its frequency. The most obvious one is to consider a single exchange, or the mean of a few exchanges, as a model for subsequent exchanges of a similar nature. By an extension of this expedient it may become a model for exchanges not of a similar nature. If given quantities of two different articles are each found by experience to exchange for a given quantity of a third article, the proportionate value of the two first-mentioned articles may, of course, be inferred. It is *measured* by the third. Hence arise the advantages of selecting, as one of the subjects of every exchange, a single commodity, or, more correctly, a species of commodities constituted of individuals of precisely similar qualities. In the first place, all persons can ascertain, with tolerable accuracy, the intrinsic causes which give value to the selected commodity, so that one half the trouble of an exchange is ready performed. And, secondly, if an exchange is to be effected between any other two commodities, the quantity of each that is usually exchanged for a given quantity of the third commodity is ascertained, and their relative value is inferred. The commodity thus selected as the general instrument of exchange, whatever be its substance, whether salt, as in Abyssinia, cowries, on the Coast of Guinea, or the precious metals, as in Europe, is *money*.

When the use of such a commodity, or, in other words, of money, has become established, value in money, or *price*, is the only value familiarly contemplated. The scarcity and durability of gold and silver (the substances used as money by all civilized nations) make them peculiarly unsusceptible of alteration in value from intrinsic causes. On these accounts we think it better, in the following discussoin, to refer rather to *price* than to general value, and to consider the value of money, so far as it depends on intrinsic causes, to be unvarying.

We must preface our explanation of the effect on price of the causes limiting supply, by a remark which may appear self-evident, but which must always be kept in recollection, namely, that *where the only natural agents employed are those which are universally accessible, and therefore are practically unlimited in supply, the utility of the produce, or, in other words, its power, directly or indirectly, of producing gratification, or preventing pain, must be in proportion to the sacrifices made to produce it, unless the producer has misapplied his exertions; since no man would willingly employ a given amount of labour or abstinence in producing one commodity, if he could obtain more gratification by devoting them to the production of another.*

We now revert to the causes which limit supply.

There are some commodities the results of agents no longer in existence, or acting at remote and uncertain periods, the supply of which cannot be increased, or cannot be reckoned upon. Antiques and relics belong to the first class, and all the very rare productions of Nature or Art, such as diamonds of extraordinary size, or pictures, or statues of extraordinary beauty, to the second. The values of such commodities are subject to no definite rules, and depend altogether on the wealth and taste of the community. In common language, they are said to bear a fancy price, that is, a price depending principally on the caprice or fashion of the day. The Boccaccio, which a few years ago sold for £2000, and after a year or two's interval for £700, may, perhaps, fifty years hence, be purchased for a shilling. Relics which, in the ninth century, were thought too valuable to admit of a definite price, would now be thought equally incapable of price in consequence of their utter worthlessness. In the following discussion we shall altogether omit such commodities, and confine our attention to those of which the supply is capable of increase, either regular, or sufficiently approaching to regularity, to admit of calculation.

The obstacle to the supply of those commodities which are produced by labour and abstinence, with that assistance only from nature which every one can command, consists solely in the difficulty of finding persons ready to submit to the labour and abstinence necessary to their production. In other words, their supply is limited by the cost of their production.

Cost of Production.—The term " cost of production " must be familiar to those who are acquainted with the writings of modern Economists; but, like most terms in Political Economy, though currently used, it has never been accurately defined; and it appears to us impossible that it should have been defined without the assistance of the term " abstinence," or of some equivalent expression.

Mr. Ricardo, who originally introduced the term " cost of production," uses as an equivalent expression, " the quantity of labour which has been bestowed on the production of a commodity." Mr. Mill (Ch. III. sec. 2,) appears to consider cost of production as equivalent to "quantity of labour." Mr. Malthus more elaborately defines it as " the advance of the quantity of accumulated and immediate labour necessary to production, with such a per centage upon the whole of the advances for the time they have been employed as is equivalent to ordinary profits." (*Definitions*, p. 242.)

In a note to the third edition, page 46, Mr. Ricardo admits that profit also forms a part of the cost of production. Mr. Mill, by a stretch of language, in the convenience of which we cannot concur, includes profit under the term labour. The definitions of Mr. Ricardo and Mr. Mill appear, therefore, to coincide. And that adopted by Mr. Malthus only differs from them in referring, not to the labour that *has* been employed, but to that which must be employed if the production must be continued. In this respect the language of Mr. Malthus is undoubtedly the most correct. The sacrifices that *have* been made to produce a given commodity have no effect on its value. All that the purchaser considers is the amount of sacrifice that its production would require at the time of the exchange. If the expense of producing a pair of stockings were suddenly to fall or to rise by one half, a rise or fall in the value of the existing stockings would be the consequence, although the labour that *has* been employed on them is of course unalterable. And when Mr. Ricardo and Mr. Mill speak of the labour which *has* been employed on a commodity as affecting its value, they must be understood as implying that the circumstances of production remain unchanged.

Colonel Torrens considers cost of production as equivalent to " the amount of capital expended on production," and refuses to consider profit as forming one of its elements. His remarks throw so much light on the whole subject, that we will venture to extract them at some length.

" Those writers who contend for the general equality of market and natural price, include the customary rate of profit under the term natural price, or cost of production. But this classification is highly unphilosophical and incorrect. The profits of stock never make any part of the expense of production; they are, on the contrary, a new creation brought into existence in consequence of this expense. The farmer, we will suppose, expends one hundred quarters of corn in cultivating his fields, and obtains in return one hundred and twenty quarters. In this case twenty quarters, being the excess of produce above expenditure, constitute the farmer's profit, but it would be absurd to call this excess or profit a part of the expenditure. The expenditure or cost of production was one hundred quarters. It has been now repaid with a surplus of twenty quarters; and, unless the surplus which remains after the expenditure is replaced, be a part of the expenditure, unless, in fact, one hundred and twenty quarters be equal to a hundred, it is impossible that market price should be equivalent to natural. Supposing that corn is £3 per quarter, then, in the case we have stated, the natural price of the farmer's produce, or the one hundred quarters expended upon production, will be equivalent to £300; while the produce of one hundred and twenty quarters obtained in return will be equivalent to £360. The excess of market above natural price, or cost of production, is profit; and to contend that this profit is included in the cost of production, is the same thing as contending that the hundred quarters, or £300 laid out in cultivation, are equal to the one hundred and twenty quarters, or £360 thereby obtained.

" In manufacturing, as well as in agricultural industry, the profit of stock is distinct from the cost of production. The master manufacturer expends a certain quantity of raw material, of tools and implements of trade, and of subsistence for labourers, and obtains in return a given quantity of finished work. This finished work must possess a higher exchangeable value than the materials, tools, and subsistence, by the advance of which it was obtained; otherwise the master could have no inducement to continue his business. Manufacturing industry would cease, if the value produced did not exceed the value expended. But it is the excess of value which the finished work possesses above the value of the materials, implements, and subsistence expended, that constitutes the master's profit; and therefore we cannot assert that the profit of his stock is included in the cost of production without affirming the gross absurdity, that the excess of value above expenditure constitutes a part of expenditure. Supposing that the materials, tools, and subsistence cost £300, and that the finished work is worth £360, then the difference will be the master's profit; and we cannot maintain that the annual profit is included in the amount of expenditure, or cost of production, without urging the contradiction that £300 are equal to £360.

" The profit of stock, so far from forming any part of the cost of production, is a surplus remaining after this cost has been completely replaced. In carrying on their business, the farmer and manufacturer do not expend their profit, they create it. It forms no part of their first advances; on the contrary, it forms a part of their subsequent returns. It could not have been employed in carrying on the work of production, because, until this work was completed, it had no existence. It is essentially a surplus, a new creation, over and above all that is necessary to replace the cost of production, or, in other words, the capital advanced. It is hoped that enough has been said to convince the reader of the nature of the error into which those Economists fall who maintain that the profit of stock is included in the expense of production, and that natural and market price tend to an equality. Market price is that which we give in order to obtain a commodity by exchange in the market: natural price is that which we give to effect a purchase at the great storehouse of nature: it consists of the several articles of capital employed in production, and cannot by possibility include the surplus or profit created during the progress of production.'' [20]

Colonel Torrens's remarks are just, so far as they apply to the mere expressions which he is criticising. Profit is certainly not a means, but a result. It is true that unless that result were expected, production would not be continued. Neither the farmer nor the manufacturer could be induced by any other motive to abstain from the unproductive enjoyment of his capital; so food would not be produced unless its consumption were necessary or agreeable. But the obtaining a profit is no more a part of the cost of producing a harvest than the gratification of appetite is a part of the cost of producing a dinner, or protection from cold part of the cost of producing a coat.

Want of the term abstinence, or of some equivalent expression, has led Mr. Malthus into inaccuracy of language. He seems to have felt that something besides mere labour is essential to production. He felt that simple industry would not convert a naked heath into a valuable wood; that the planter, in addition to the labour of inserting and protecting the saplings, incurred the additional *sacrifice* of directing his labour to the production of remote results; and that the successive generations of proprietors, in suffering the young plantation to become mature, sacrificed their own emolument to that of their successors. He seems to have felt that these sacrifices were part of the cost of producing the wood, and, having no term to express them, he denominated them by the name of their reward. When he termed profit a part of the cost of production, he appears to us to have meant not profit, but that conduct which is repaid by profit: an inaccuracy precisely similar to that committed by those who term wages a part of the cost of production; meaning not wages, which are a result, but the labour for which wages are the remuneration.

Colonel Torrens's error is an error of omission. He refuses to consider profit as part of the cost of production, but he does not substitute for it abstinence or any equivalent expression. Although he admits that where equal capitals are employed the value of the products may differ if the one be brought to market sooner than the other, he has not stated the principle on which this difference depends. That prin-

[20] Torrens, *On the Production of Wealth*, 51—55.

ciple is that, though in both cases the labour employed is the same, more abstinence is necessary in the one case than in the other.

Cost of Production Defined.—By *Cost of Production*, then, we mean the sum of the labour and abstinence necessary to production. But Cost of Production, thus defined, must be divided into the cost of production on the part of the producer or seller, and the cost of production on the part of the consumer or purchaser. The first is of course the amount of the labour and abstinence which must be undergone by him who offers for sale a given class of commodities or services in order to enable him to continue to produce them. The second is, the amount of the labour and abstinence which must be undergone by those to whom a given commodity or service is offered for sale, if, instead of purchasing, they themselves, or some of them on the behalf of themselves and the others, were to produce it. The first is equal to the minimum, the second to the maximum, of price. For, on the one hand, no man would continue to produce, for the purpose of sale, what should sell for less than it cost him to produce it. And, on the other hand, no men would continue to buy what they themselves, or some of them on the behalf of themselves and the others, could produce at less expense. With respect to those commodities, or, to speak more accurately, with respect to the value of those parts or attributes of commodities, which are the subjects of equal competition, which may be produced by all persons with equal advantages, the cost of production to the producer and the cost of production to the consumer are the same. Their price, therefore, represents the aggregate amount of the labour and abstinence necessary to continue their production. If their price should fall lower, the wages or the profits of those employed in their production must fall below the average remuneration of the labour and abstinence that must be undergone if their production is to be continued. In time, therefore, it is discontinued or diminished, until the value of the product has been raised by the diminution of the supply. If the price should rise beyond the cost of their production, the producers must receive more than an average remuneration for their sacrifices. As soon as this has been discovered, capital and industry flow towards the employment which, by this supposition, offers extraordinary advantages. Those who formerly were purchasers, or persons on their behalf, turn producers themselves, until the increased supply has equalized the price with the cost of production.

Some years ago London depended for water on the New River Company. As the quantity which they can supply is limited, the price rose with the extension of buildings, until it so far exceeded the cost of production as to induce some of the consumers to become producers. Three new Water Companies were established, and the price fell as the supply increased, until the shares in the New River Company fell to nearly one-fourth of their former value; from £15,000

to £4000.   If the metropolis should continue to increase, these transactions will recur.   The price of water will increase and exceed the
cost at which it could be afforded.   New Companies will arise, and,
unless the additional supply is checked by greater natural obstacles
than those which the existing Companies have to surmount, the price
will again fall to its present level.

But though, under free competition, cost of production is the regu-
lator of price, its influence is subject to much occasional interruption.
Its operation can be supposed to be perfect only if we suppose that
there are no disturbing causes, that capital and labour can be at once
transferred, and without loss, from one employment to another, and
that every producer has full information of the profit to be derived
from every mode of production.   But it is obvious that these suppositions have no resemblance to the truth.   A large portion of the capital
essential to production consists of buildings, machinery, and other
implements, the results of much time and labour, and of little service
for any except their existing purposes.   A still larger portion consists
of knowledge and of intellectual and bodily dexterity, applicable only
to the processes in which those qualities were originally acquired.
Again, the advantage derived from any given business depends so
much upon the dexterity and the judgment with which it is managed,
that few capitalists can estimate, except upon an average of some
years, the amount of their own profits, and still fewer can estimate
those of their neighbours.   Established businesses, therefore, may
survive the causes in which they originated, and become gradually
extinguished as their comparative unprofitableness is discovered, and
the labourers and capital engaged in them wear away without being
replaced; and, on the other hand, other employments are inadequately
supplied with the capital and industry which they could profitably
absorb.   During the interval, the products of the one sell for less, and
those of the others for more, than their cost of production.   Political
Economy does not deal with particular facts but with general tenden-
cies, and when we assign to cost of production the power of regulating
price in cases of equal competition, we mean to describe it not as a
point to which price is attached, but as a centre of oscillation which it
is always endeavouring to approach.

We have seen that, under circumstances of equal competition, or,
in other words, where all persons can become producers, and that with
equal advantages, the cost of production on the part of the producer
or seller, and the cost of production on the part of the consumer or
purchaser, are the same, and that the commodity thus produced sells
for its cost of production; or, in other words, at a price equal to the
sum of the labour and abstinence which its production requires; or,
to use a more familiar expression, at a price equal to the amount of
the wages and profits which must be paid to induce the producers to
continue their exertions.   It has lately been a general opinion that

the bulk of commodities is produced under circumstances of equal competition. "By far the greater part of those goods," says Mr. Ricardo, (*Principles*, &c. p. 3,) "which are the objects of desire, are produced by labour, and may be multiplied almost without any assignable limit, if we are disposed to bestow the labour necessary to obtain them. In speaking then of commodities, of their exchangeable value, and of the laws which regulate their relative prices, we always mean such commodities only as can be increased in quantity by the exertion of human industry, and in the production of which competition operates without restraint."

Now it is clear that the production in which no appropriated natural agent has concurred, is the only production which has been made under circumstances of perfectly equal competition. And how few are the commodities of which the production has in no stage been assisted by peculiar advantages of soil, or situation, or by extraordinary talent of body or mind, or by processes generally unknown, or protected by law from imitation. Where the assistance of these agents, to which we have given the general name of natural agents, has been obtained, the result is more valuable than the result of equal labour and abstinence unassisted by similar aids. A commodity thus produced is called the subject of a *monopoly;* and the person who has appropriated such a natural agent, a *monopolist.*

MONOPOLIES.

Monopolies may be divided into four kinds.

1. *Where the monopolist has not the exclusive power of producing, but only certain exclusive facilities as a producer, and can increase, with undiminished, or even increased facility, the amount of his produce.*

The value of a commodity produced under such circumstances approaches more nearly to the cost of production on the part of the seller, than that of any other monopolised commodity. It is obvious that its price can never permanently fall below the value of the sacrifices which must be made by the producer, and, on the other hand, that it never can permanently rise above the value of the sacrifices which must be made by the consumers, if, instead of purchasing, they, or some persons in their behalf, were to turn producers. Sir R. Arkwright's yarn could not sell for more than yarn of an equal quality produced without the aid of his patent machinery ; nor would Arkwright have sold it for less than the value of the labour and abstinence employed in its production. The first was the cost of production to the consumer, the second the cost of production to the producer. But the difference between the two was enormous; the cost to Arkwright was not one-fifth of what it would have been to his customers.

His inventions enabled him to produce a greater quantity, but not a better quality. The finger and thumb constitute an instrument more delicate than any system of rollers, and the muslin formed by the comparatively unassisted labour of the Hindoo is finer and more durable than the produce of our elaborate manufactories. The price which Arkwright *could* exact was therefore limited, as we have seen, by the competition of other productive instruments, more expensive but quite as efficient. The price which he *did* exact was still further limited by a regard to his own interest. He had discovered an instrument of which the powers, instead of being exhausted, increased with every increase in its application. To erect a mill for the purpose of spinning annually a hundred or a thousand pounds of cotton would be madness. The expense of spinning ten thousand pounds very little exceeds the expense of spinning one thousand, and forty thousand might probably be spun at less than double the expense of ten thousand. As the quantity produced is increased, the relative cost of production is diminished. If, therefore, on the sale of ten thousand pounds weight of yarn at a given price, which we will call £10,000, his profit amounted to £5000, the profit of selling one hundred thousand weight at the same price might have amounted to £90,000, and his profit on selling one million pounds weight to £900,000. But to effect this was obviously impossible. As value depends mainly on limitation of supply, he could not have at once offered a large quantity for sale without diminishing the price, if he left that price to be fixed by the competition of the purchasers, or without having a large portion unsold, if he refused to submit to that diminution. His only mode of stimulating a constant increase of consumption was to submit to such a constant lowering of price as should constantly widen the circle of those able and willing to purchase. As is usually the case, his own interest and that of the public coincided, and led him to accept a price far exceeding indeed the cost of production to himself, but falling short by a still wider interval of what would have been the cost of production to them.

Sir R. Arkwright's monopoly, therefore, was of the most limited kind. His remuneration was bounded, and it was not his interest even to approach that boundary.

2. A second kind of monopoly is in the opposite extreme. *It exists where price is checked neither by the hopes nor by the fears of the producer, where no competition is dreaded, and no increased supply can be effected.* The owners of some vineyards have such a monopoly. Constantia owes its peculiar flavour to the agency of a few acres of ground, and that flavour would be destroyed if high cultivation were employed to force from that ground a larger quantity of wine. As no person but the proprietor of the Constantia farm can be a producer, the price is not checked by any cost of production to the consumer. It is not checked by any wish of the proprietor to increase the consumption, since the quantity produced, and consequently the quantity

consumed, is incapable of increase. The price cannot of course fall below the cost of production, but may indefinitely exceed it. It is limited solely by the will and the ability of the consumers. And if fashion were to make it an object of intense desire among the opulent, a pipe of Constantia, produced perhaps at the expense of £20, might sell for £20,000.

3. A third and more frequent kind of monopoly lies between these two extremes, and is neither so strict as the last, nor so comparatively open as the first. *This comprises those cases in which the monopolist is the only producer, but, by the application of additional labour and abstinence, can indefinitely increase his production.* The book trade affords an illustration. While a work is protected by copyright, no person but the proprietor of that copyright can produce copies; and he may multiply them indefinitely by the application of additional labour and abstinence. There is here no cost of production on the part of the purchaser, and, as far as he is concerned, the price is limited only by his will and ability. The efficient check arises from the interest of the publisher. As is the case with manufactures generally, the relative expense of publication diminishes as the number of copies published increases. It is his interest, therefore, to encourage a large sale by affixing a price but slightly exceeding the cost of production, diminished as that cost is by the magnitude of the produce. A hundred copies of *Waverley* might, perhaps, have been sold at ten guineas a copy; but there can be no doubt that a larger aggregate profit was obtained by selling ten thousand at a guinea and a half.

4. *The fourth and last class of monopolies exists where production must be assisted by natural agents, limited in number, and varying in power, and repaying with less and less relative assistance every increase in the amount of the labour and abstinence bestowed on them.* It is under these circumstances that the greater part of the raw produce, whatever it be, which is the staple food of the inhabitants in every Country, potatoes in Ireland, wheat in England, or rice in India, is produced. It is, in fact, THE GREAT MONOPOLY OF LAND; and as there are scarcely any commodities of which the supply is not in some measure limited by the limited extent of the land essential or serviceable to some process in their production, all general theories as to value must be subject to error until the general laws regulating the value of the assistance to be derived from land have been ascertained. It will be necessary, therefore, to examine them at some length.

Land.—The soil of every extensive district is of different degrees of fertility and convenience of situation, and the soils of each degree constitute a distinct class of natural agents, affording each a distinct amount of assistance to the cultivator. And we have seen that each portion of soil, whatever be its fertility, agricultural skill remaining the same, generally gives a less and less proportionate return to each additional quantity of labour and abstinence bestowed on its cultivation, and may be said, therefore, to comprise within itself a system of natural agents of different powers.   The different classes of natural agents will be successively employed, in proportion to their efficiency; an inferior class being never resorted to while a superior one is equally accessible: and each class, until it has been completely appropriated, may be considered as practically unlimited in supply, since it is universally accessible.   What shall be the worst natural agent employed, or, in other words, to what extent inferior soils shall be cultivated, or additional labour and abstinence employed at a comparative disadvantage on the cultivation of those which are more fertile or better situated, must always be determined by the wealth and wants of the community; by the quantity of agricultural produce which they have the power and the desire to purchase.   While those wants can be satisfied by slightly cultivating only a portion of the most fertile and best situated land, that land, though highly productive, indeed more productive in proportion to the labour and abstinence bestowed on it than at any subsequent stage, cannot be a separate and independent source of value.   It is then a natural agent universally accessible, and its produce, however large, will exchange only for the value of the labour and abstinence employed on its production.   In short, the cost of production to the producer, and the cost of production to the consumer, are, under such circumstances, the same.   This is the state of some of the fertile and thinly-peopled districts of the tropics.   The inhabitants of the greater part of the Tierra Caliente, of Mexico, appropriate at will from the fertile wilderness over which they are scattered the small patches which afford them the materials of lodging, food, and raiment.   We are told that in these districts the labour of a week will provide subsistence for a year, but even this vast productive power, or even any conceivable increase in it, is incapable of giving value to the assistance afforded as long as the supply of that assistance remains unlimited.

It becomes limited, however, in the very earliest stages of improvement.   Both the causes and the consequences of this event may be illustrated by tracing the progress of a Colony.

When a body of emigrants arrives on the coast of an unoccupied district, their first operation must be to fix the situation of their future metropolis; the seat of government, of law, of foreign trade, and of those manufactures which require the congregation of numerous workmen.   We may suppose their numbers and the local advantages to be such as to enable them to occupy, within such a distance from their infant town as to render the expense of carriage immaterial, as much land of the highest fertility as each agricultural family may wish to cultivate.   The agricultural produce thus obtained must sell for its cost of production to the producer; every consumer being able at will to turn a producer, with advantages equal to those enjoyed by the existing producers, and being unwilling to give for the result of a given amount of labour and abstinence on their part more than the result of an equal amount of labour and abstinence on his own part. Such a community rapidly increases in numbers and in wealth, and that increase is accompanied by an increased desire and ability to purchase agricultural produce. Until the supply of raw produce has been increased, the price must now rise above the cost of production. But when the most fertile lands within a given distance of the town have been occupied, there remain only three modes of increasing the supply: either 1. by cultivating the fertile lands at a greater distance from the town; or, 2. by cultivating the inferior land in its neighbourhood; or, 3. by employing additional labour and abstinence in the cultivation of the lands already occupied. Whichever of these plans be adopted, and probably they will all be adopted, the additional quantity must be supplied at an increased expense. The first is loaded with the expenses of carriage; and we know that a given amount of labour and abstinence is employed to comparative disadvantage, when applied either to the cultivation of inferior land, or to the further improvement of the best land.

The immediate consequence of the increase of supply must be a fall of price, but a fall not equal to the previous rise. The additional supply is produced under circumstances of equal competition, every consumer having it in his power to turn producer by occupying the more distant or less fertile territory; it sells, therefore, for the cost of production to the producer. But commodities of precisely the same qualities cannot sell in the same market for different prices. The purchaser of a bushel of wheat does not inquire whether it was grown within a furlong or at ten miles from the place of sale. The produce, therefore, of the fertile lands in the immediate vicinity of the market, sells at the same price as that of the distant or inferior land.

That price, as it is equal to the cost of production of what is produced at the greatest expense, must exceed the cost of production of what is produced at the least expense. The proprietor of the most fertile and best situated land has no motive to take less, as he cannot, like the owner of a patent, increase the amount of what he produces and continue to produce at equal advantage; and the purchaser cannot support an offer of less, as he cannot turn producer but by submitting to disadvantages which equalize the current price and the cost of production.

As the Colony grows into a People and an Empire, the same processes are repeated. Every increase of wealth and population raises the price of raw produce. Increase of price occasions an increase of supply, raised at a comparatively greater expense. The price falls in consequence of the increased supply, but is prevented from falling to its former level by the increase which has taken place in the cost of producing that part of the whole supply which is brought to market at the greatest expense.

The effect will be the same whether we select for the scene a continent or an island; a district containing soils of every degree of fertility, or of precisely uniform quality.   The Anglo-Americans have supplied their constantly increasing wants chiefly by spreading themselves backwards over their unbounded Western territory, and have made little use of inferior soils, or of high cultivation, except in the immediate vicinity of their cities.   In Malta, a single acre receives more labour than would be devoted to a square mile in the Illinois; but precisely the same motives impel the Maltese to terrace his mountains into gardens, and the American to reclaim the prairies of the Missouri.

It may be inferred, from the picture which we have given of the progress of society, that we believe an increased difficulty of obtaining raw produce to be the natural incident to an increase of population. In the absence of counteracting causes it certainly would be so; but those causes are so powerful, that, unless checked by legislation, they in many respects balance the causes which we have been considering.   In a colony, the counteracting causes appear likely to preponderate for a period, the duration of which must of course depend in part on the quantity of fertile and unoccupied land in its vicinity.   As the circle of appropriated land expands, and the expense of bringing food to the consumers becomes more oppressive, there is a tendency in the consumers to follow the food.   The colonial capital, now turned into a metropolis, may continue to send out portion after portion of her increased inhabitants, until the whole territory acquires something approaching to an average amount of cultivation.   Again, in every Country increased wealth and numbers are accompanied by increased agricultural skill and improved means of transport.   The use of implements, the division of labour, and physical knowledge are powerful aids to the agriculturist, though they do not afford to him the almost magical increase of power which they give to the manufacturer.   The improvements in carriage are still more important: a given amount of labour applied for twenty years to a given piece of land, would probably now produce a return four or five times as great as would have been obtained at the Conquest.   But the labour necessary to transport that produce one hundred miles is probably now not one one-hundreth of what it was then.   No improvements in husbandry instruments, or in breeding, or in the rotation of crops, have been so efficient as the substitution of the waggon, the Macadamized road, the canal, the navigable river, and the railway, for the pack-horse of our ancestors and the dangerous tracks through which they beat out and picked their way.   The intervention of a hill or a morass was then an obstacle sufficient to allow the price of corn on one side to be double that on the other; and London was so dependent on the immediately adjacent Counties, that the landlords of those Counties petitioned against the opening of roads, as interfering with their vested right to a monopoly of the metropolitan supply; a petition which failed because the immediate interests of other land-lords opposed it.

But the principal means by which a Country, when increasing in wealth and population, may avoid the necessity of raising its raw produce at a constantly increasing disadvantage, is by importation.

We have seen that additional labour employed in manufactures produces an increasing proportionate effect; that if one thousand men can in a given time work up one million of pounds of cotton, two thousand men would be able to work up in the same time more than two millions of pounds, and four thousand men, much more than twice as much as two thousand. As a nation increases in opulence and population, it becomes the interest, therefore, of the community to devote their additional population rather to manu-factures, in which they have a constantly increasing advantage, than to agriculture, at a constantly increasing disadvantage. As their industry becomes more and more efficient, they are in general able to purchase with the produce of a given amount of labour and abstinence a larger and larger amount of the produce of the industry of their less advanced contemporaries. The produce of the labour of a single Englishman employed for a given time in fabricating cotton, will pur-chase the cotton grown by the labour of five, or perhaps ten, Hindoos, or the wheat grown by three, or perhaps five, Lithuanians or Poles.

It must be recollected, indeed, that a nation, while extending its manufactures, must increase its importation of raw produce; and we have already stated that the increased labour at which the additional produce must be obtained would retard the progress of such a com-munity. But though this is unquestionable, though it is even certain that, if sufficient time be allowed, this obstacle is able, not merely to retard, but almost to arrest, the advance of manufactures, there seems to be little to fear from it within any of those periods within which calculations for practical purposes are generally confined. In the first place, the stimulus of an advantageous trade must tend to increase the agricultural skill of the exporting nations, and increase the facilities of transport; causes which, especially in the earlier stages of a nation's improvement, often enable it, and for considerable periods, to bring to market an increased quantity of raw produce with the same or even less proportionate labour. And, secondly, even if we suppose the manufacturing nation to be supplied by its agricultural customers at an increased proportionate expense to *them*, it does not follow that the proportionate expense to *her* need be increased. The increased difficulty on the one side may be balanced by the increased facility on the other. We will suppose that at present one hundred thousand yards of muslin, fabricated by twelve Englishmen, can be exchanged for one hundred and fifty quarters of wheat, raised by thirty-six Poles; that an increase in population of one-third makes it necessary to import two hundred instead of one hundred and fifty quarters, and that the two hundred quarters are raised, not by forty-eight, the former proportion, but by sixty Poles. If the increase in our skill has kept pace with our increase of numbers, it is probable that eighteen Englishmen would be able to fabricate at least two hundred thousand yards of muslin, instead of one hundred and fifty thousand, the former proportion. The exchange under such circumstances, instead of being less, would be more beneficial than before. England would purchase more corn, and Poland more muslin, at a less proportionate amount of labour.

It must be carefully remembered that the preceding remarks apply not to the higher or lower *price* of raw produce, but to the greater or less difficulty in obtaining it; things which have no necessary connection; one of them depending on the causes which affect the general value of raw produce, the other on the causes which affect the general value of money. At the same time, and in the same place, the prices of articles exactly measure the difficulty of obtaining them. It is exactly half as difficult to get a commodity that costs one sovereign as to get a commodity that costs two. But this is only true at the same time and in the same place. Though in England a quarter of corn now costs about fifty shillings, and in the reign of Henry VIII. cost about twenty, it is probable that it was then more difficult to obtain one than it is now. This must have been the case if it was then more difficult to obtain twenty shillings than it is now to obtain fifty. It is equally clear that, although a quarter of wheat now costs in England about ten ounces of silver, and about six ounces in Poland, yet, if it is easier in England to obtain ten ounces of silver than in Poland to obtain six ounces, it is easier in England to obtain a quarter of wheat than it is in Poland. Experience shows that wealth and population almost always increase together, though not in equal ratios, the increase of wealth being, as we have already stated, generally greater than the increase of population. The increased capital and labour of an increasing population are naturally directed to manufactures, in which, as we have already seen, every increased production is more easily effected. As their labour becomes more productive, the value of the products of a given quantity of that labour rises in the general market of the world; or, in other words, they obtain in return for it a greater amount of the precious metals; or, in other words, a higher price. Therefore, although they may have to pay a higher price for a given quantity of raw produce, whether of home growth or imported, it does not follow that the difficulty of obtaining that given quantity has increased; it is possible, and not improbable, that it may have diminished. A nation so situated may be compared to an individual whose income happens to be rising at the same time when the price of corn is rising. If the rise of his income more than counterbalances the rise of corn, he finds it every year more easy to purchase a given quantity, though he may have to give a higher and higher price for it.

Effects of the Cost of Production on Price.—We have seen that production may take place under five different circumstances.

1. Absence of monopoly; all persons being capable of producing with equal advantage.

2. A monopoly under which the monopolist has not the exclusive power of producing, but exclusive facilities as a producer, which may be employed indefinitely with equal or increasing advantage.

3. A monopoly under which the monopolist is the only producer, and cannot increase the amount of his produce.

4. A monopoly under which the monopolist is the only producer, and can increase indefinitely, with equal or increasing advantage, the amount of his produce.

5. A monopoly under which the monopolist is not the only producer, but has peculiar facilities which diminish and ultimately disappear as he increases the amount of his produce.

The price of those commodities which are comprehended in the first class appears to be subject to laws capable of accurate investigation. Where labour alone has been employed, the price must be equal to the wages of that labour. Where that labour has been assisted by abstinence, or, in other words, where a period has elapsed between the employment of the labour and the sale of its produce, the price must be equal to the amount of the wages of that labour and the remuneration to be paid either to the labourer for having suffered the payment of his wages to be deferred, or to the capitalist who has paid those wages in advance.

There are, however, very few commodities of which the whole price can be resolved into the remuneration for the labour, or the abstinence, or both, which must be bestowed on their production.

Mere abstinence can produce nothing. Labour, or the agency of nature, must afford the subject with respect to which it is to be exercised. It is possible, indeed, that a natural agent universally accessible may sometimes afford a product of no value at first, but capable of becoming valuable by mere keeping; but no instance of the kind occurs to us, and some little trouble is generally requisite for the mere safe custody of any article.

Mere labour *does* produce a very few articles. The laver collected and sold on the coast of Devonshire is an example. It grows naturally on the unappropriated rocks within the influence of the tide, and in abundance practically unlimited. No instruments are necessary to gather or prepare it, and, as it will not keep, it is sold as soon as it has been collected and washed. The price of a given quantity consists, therefore, merely of the wages of those who gather, wash, and bring it to market.

A class of commodities, perhaps rather larger, but still inconsiderable when compared with the general mass, is produced by labour and abstinence, assisted only by those natural agents which are universally accessible. It is difficult, however, to point out an article, however simple, that can be exposed to sale without the concurrence, direct or indirect, of many hundred, or, more frequently, of many thousand different producers; almost every one of whom will be found to have been aided by some monopolized agent.

There are few things of which the price seems to consist more exclusively of wages and profits than a watch; [21] but if we trace it from the mine to the pocket of the purchaser, we shall be struck by the payment of rent (the invariable sign of the agency of some instrument not universally accessible) at every stage of its progress. Rent was paid for the privilege of extracting from the mines the metals of which it is composed; for the land which afforded the materials of the ships in which those metals were transported to an English port; for the wharfs at which they were landed, and the warehouses where they were exposed to sale; the watchmaker pays a rent for the land covered by his manufactories, and the retailer for that on which his shop is situated. The miner, the shipwright, the house-builder, and the watchmaker, all use implements formed of materials produced by the same processes as the materials of the watch, and subject also in their different stages to similar payments of rent. The whole amount of all these different payments forms probably a very small portion of the value of the watch; but if we were to attempt to enumerate them, they would be found subdivided into ramifications too minute for calculation. What remains consists of the wages of the workmen, and the profits of the capitalists who paid those wages in advance. The attempt to trace back these wages and profits to their earliest beginnings, would be as vain as the attempt to enumerate all the payments of rent. In estimating, therefore, the value of a manufactured commodity, we seldom go further back than to the price paid by the manufacturer for his materials and implements, a price which must have included all previous payments of rent, wages, and profits.

We will now trace the causes which increase the value of those materials after they have been the property of the manufacturer. We will suppose a watchmaker's capital to consist of materials worth £500, that he has bought the land covered by his buildings for £500, and has expended £900 in erecting them, that his tools have cost him £100, and that an annual expense of £100 is necessary to keep his buildings and tools in repair. We will suppose him to employ ten workmen, each receiving at an average £100 a-year, and that one year is the average period from the commencement to the sale of a watch. We will suppose that his ten workmen can annually convert his £500 worth of materials into five hundred watches, and that the

---

[21] It has been used by M. Canard, M. Flores Estrada, and Mr. M'Culloch, as an example of the value derived from labour alone.

average rate of profit in his business amounts to ten per centum per annum.   To give him this profit it is clear that his watches must sell for

Value of materials,...	£500
Wages for a year,...	1000
Repairs for a year,...	100
	1600
Profit on the advance of these sums, and on the value of the land, and buildings, and tools, for half-a-year, at 10 per cent. per annum, ...	155
	£1755

It will be observed that, although a year is supposed to elapse between the commencement and the sale of a watch, we suppose the cost of its production to have been advanced for only half-a-year.   The fact is that some part of the advances must have been made for more, and some for less than half-a-year.   Supposing a workman to have been employed on the watch for a year, and paid daily, he received his first day's wages one year before the watch was sold, but his last day's wages on the very day of the sale; six months, therefore, is the average period for which the whole were advanced before the sale; just as large a proportion having been advanced for a shorter as for a longer period.

It will be observed, too, that we suppose the whole value of the materials, repairs, and wages to be repaid, but only a profit on the value of the land, buildings, and tools.   The first are annually expended by the capitalist, the second remain to be used as instruments of further production.   The land is indestructible, and the damage done to the buildings and tools is paid for by the £100 supposed to be expended in repairs.

But the whole cost of production has not yet been enumerated.

In the first place, some wages must be allowed to the master watch-maker himself for his labour in superintending his business; and, secondly, some profit on the expense of his education.   And as his knowledge and habits, which form his mental capital, will not survive him, something more than the average rate of profit is necessary to replace their value.

If we suppose the expense of his education to have amounted to £1000, and that it will be replaced with average profit by an annual return of £15 per cent., and the average wages of labour to be £30 a-year, we have £180 to add to the price of the watches, and £9 more for the advance of this sum for half-a-year, making £1944.

The last source of expense is taxation, or, in other words, the wages and profits of those who have protected all the different producers of the watches from foreign and domestic violence and fraud.

A considerable portion of the price paid by the watchmaker for his materials, tools, and buildings, probably consisted of the taxation to which those commodities had been previously subjected; but the taxation which we are now considering is that which he incurs during the year supposed to be employed in manufacturing the watch.

This is an expense little capable of previous estimation; partly because the expenses of government are subject to constant variation, and partly because no general principle regulates the proportions in which those expenses are divided among the contributors. In England they are in general imposed upon the persons using or producing certain commodities; upon the use, for instance, of a carriage or window, and upon the production of candles or glass. We will suppose the annual taxation imposed on the shop and other instruments of production used by the watchmaker to amount to £53 7s., the profit on the advance of this sum far half-a-year would exceed by a slight fraction £2 13s., together £56, making with the £1944, the amount of our previous calculation, the sum of £2000, the whole cost of production of the five hundred watches, or £4 a-piece.

The different sums in this example have of course been taken at random; but we have thought it worth while to go through it partly as an instance of the calculations on which every manufacturer must found his estimate of the profit or loss likely to follow any given undertaking; and partly to show in how many shapes, labour, abstinence, and the agency of nature, or in other words, rent, profits, and wages, are constantly re-appearing in every productive process.

When we speak, therefore, of a class of commodities as produced under circumstances of equal competition, or as the result of labour and abstinence unassisted by any other appropriated agent, and consider their price as equal to the sum of the wages and profits that must be paid for their production, we do not mean to state that any such commodities exist, but that, if they did exist, such would be the laws by which their price would be regulated; and that so far as labour or abstinence, or both, are conducive to the production of any given commodity, it is to be considered as produced under circumstances of equal competition, and as worth the wages or profits, or both, with which that labour or abstinence, or both, must be remunerated.

Effects of Monopolies on Price.—The prices of the commodities comprised in the second, third, and fourth classes, are but little governed by any general rules. The prices of those comprised in the second class, cannot rise above the cost of production when unassisted by the monopolized agent, but have a tendency to approach the cost of production to the monopolist. The prices of those comprised in the third and fourth classes have no necessary limits, but approach much more nearly to the cost of production in the fourth class, where the monopolist can increase his produce, than in the third class, where nature strictly limits the amount that can be produced.

Rent.—The price of the commodities comprised in the fifth and last class, those which are produced under what may be called unequal competition or qualified monopoly, where all persons may become producers, but every additional quantity is obtained at a greater proportionate expense, has a constant tendency to coincide with the cost of production of that portion which is continued to be produced at the greatest expense. The annual supply of London requires about one million five hundred thousand quarters of wheat. Of this quantity, perhaps fifty thousand can be obtained only by means of high cultivation, or very distant carriage, at an expense of about 50s. a quarter. While the wants and the wealth of the inhabitants of London are such as to make them require, and enable them to purchase, one million five hundred thousand quarters, and the expenses of carriage and cultivation remain unaltered, it is clear that the whole quantity, supposing it to be of uniform quality, must sell at the rate of 50s. a quarter. If it were to sell for less, the last fifty thousand quarters would cease to be produced, and the price would again rise in consequence of the deficiency of the supply. But of the whole one million five hundred thousand quarters, a portion, perhaps fifty thousand, might be produced by slightly cultivating the most fertile and best situated land, at the expense of 10s. a quarter. A hundred thousand may cost the producer 20s. a quarter, two hundred thousand 25s., two hundred thousand more 30s. a quarter, and the cost of production of all, except the last fifty thousand, must have been less than the 50s. for which they are sold. The difference between the price and the cost of production is *Rent*. It is an advantage derived from the use of a natural agent not universally accessible. It is taken, therefore, by the owner of the agent by whose assistance it was obtained.

A portion of the whole supply, however, that portion which is produced at the greatest expense, is produced without any payment of rent. If the cost of producing and sending to market from a given farm be in the following proportions: for one hundred quarters £100, for ninety more £100, for eighty more £100, for seventy more £100, for sixty more £100, for fifty more £100, for forty more £100, and for thirty-three and one-third of a quarter more £100, and the price per quarter is 60s., it is clear that the landlord's rent will be in the following proportions:—

On the first	£100 expended,	£200
On the second	100	170
On the third	100	140
On the fourth	100	110
On the fifth	100	80
On the sixth,	100	50
On the seventh	100	20
In all,		£770

And it is equally clear that no rent can be paid by the farmer for the privilege of producing the last thirty-three one-third quarters, as the whole £100 for which it sells is absorbed by the cost of production. The last thirty-three one-third quarters will continue to be produced as long as the wants and the wealth of the purchasers render them willing and able to purchase a quantity of corn, the whole of which cannot be supplied unless this last and most expensive portion is produced. If those wants and wealth should increase, it might become necessary to raise an additional supply at a still further additional expense, at the cost, we will say, of £100 for only twenty quarters. But it is clear that this could not be done unless the price should be £5 a quarter, since that is the lowest price at which the cost of producing the last supply would be repaid. The price, indeed, would probably have previously risen to above £5 a quarter, since an interval must have elapsed between the increased demand occasioned by the increased wants and wealth of the purchasers and the increase of the supply. During that interval the price must have risen somewhat above the price at which it would settle when the additional supply had been obtained. The appearance of that additional supply would sink it to £5 a quarter, the cost at which that supply is produced, but it could not permanently fall below that price unless a diminution should take place either in the wants or wealth of the purchasers, or in the expenses of cultivation or conveyance.

All this appears almost too plain for formal statement. It is however one of the most recent discoveries in Political Science: so recent that it can scarcely be said to be universally admitted even in this Country, and abroad it does not seem to be even comprehended. If any writer could be expected to be fully master of it, it would be Say, the most distinguished of the Continental Economists, and the annotator on Ricardo. In his notes to the French translation of the *Principles of Political Economy and Taxation*, he constantly objects to Mr. Ricardo's Reasonings, the fact that all cultivated land pays rent; as if such a fact were inconsistent with the existence of corn raised without the payment of rent. He repeats this objection in a note to a passage in which Ricardo has demonstrated its falsity. In the twenty-fourth chapter of the *Principles*, Mr. Ricardo examines Adam Smith's opinions on rent.

" Adam Smith," observes Mr. Ricardo, " had adopted the notion that there were some parts of the produce of land for which the demand must always be such as to afford a greater price than what is sufficient to bring them to market; and he considered food as one of those parts.

" He says that ' land in almost every situation produces a greater quantity of food than what is sufficient to maintain all the labour necessary for bringing it to market, in the most liberal way in which labour is ever maintained. The surplus, too, is always more than sufficient to replace the stock which employed that labour, together with its profits. Something, therefore, always remains for a rent to the landlord.'

"But what proof does he give of this? No other than the assertion that ' the most desert moors in Norway and Scotland produce some sort of pasture for cattle, of which the milk and the increase are always more than sufficient not only to maintain all the labour necessary for tending them, and to pay the ordinary profit to the farmer or owner of the herd or flock, but to afford some small rent to the landlord.' Now of this I may be permitted to entertain a doubt. I believe that as yet in every Country, from the rudest to the most refined, there is land of such a quality that it cannot yield a produce more than sufficiently valuable to replace the stock employed on it, together with the profits ordinary and usual in that Country. In America we all know that this is the case, and yet no one maintains that the principles which regulate rent are different in that Country and in Europe. But if it were true that England had so far advanced in cultivation, that at this time there were no lands remaining which did not afford a rent, it would be equally true, that there formerly must have been such lands ; *and that whether there be or not, is of no importance to this question, for it is the same thing if there be any capital employed in Great Britain on land which yields only the return of stock with its ordinary profits, whether it be employed on new or old land.* If a farmer agrees for land on a lease for seven or fourteen years, he may propose to employ on it a capital of £10,000, knowing that at the existing price of grain and raw produce he can replace that part of his stock which he is obliged to expend, pay his rent, and obtain the general rate of profit. He will not employ £11,000 unless the last £1000 can be employed so productively as to afford him the usual profits of stock. In his calculation whether he shall employ it or not, he considers only whether the price of raw produce is sufficient to replace his expenses and profits, for he knows that he shall have no additional rent to pay. Even at the expiration of his lease his rent will not be raised ; for if his landlord should require rent, because this additional £1000 was employed, he would withdraw it, since by employing it he gets by the supposition, only the ordinary and usual profits which he may obtain by any other employment of stock." *Principles, &c.*, 389—391.

To this passage, M. Say affixes the following note : " This is precisely what Adam Smith does not admit, since he says that the worst land in Scotland gives to its proprietor a rent." We answer to M. Say : " This is precisely what Mr. Ricardo declares to be immaterial, since a portion of what is produced on a farm giving a rent of ten guineas an acre, may be produced without any rent being paid for the privilege of producing it."

It must be admitted, however, that the doctrine in question has often been stated in a form likely to confuse the dull or inattentive, and liable to the cavils of the uncandid.   Mr. Ricardo, who, though not its discoverer, is its best known expositor, was led, both by his merits and his deficiencies, into frequent inaccuracy of language. He was not enough master of logic to obtain precision, or even to estimate its importance.   His sagacity prevented his making sufficient allowance for the stupidity or carelessness of his readers; and he was too earnest a lover of truth to anticipate wilful misconstruction.

Under the influence of these causes he is, perhaps, the most incorrect writer who ever attained philosophical eminence; and there are few subjects on which he has been guilty of more faults of expression than on rent.

He perceived that an increased will and power on the part of the community to purchase raw produce, and the impossibility of increasing the supply but at an increased expense, must necessarily raise rents, and must also occasion an extension of cultivation.   Associating, therefore, in his own mind the ideas of the rise of rents and of the extension of cultivation, he has often spoken of them as if they stood in the relation of cause and effect: as if the extension of cultivation were a cause of the rise of rent, instead of being, as it obviously is, a means by which that rise is counteracted.   The inaccuracy is so obvious that we can scarcely suppose it to have misled any reader of tolerable care and acuteness.

He has also too frequently used the expression "the corn raised *on land* paying no rent," as an equivalent for "the corn raised without the payment of rent."   And when his opponents reply, as is true, that "in old Countries all land pays a rent," he has sometimes denied the truth of the reply, instead of showing, as he has done in the passage which we have quoted, that the doctrine is just as true when applied to a small district in which all the land is highly rented, as when applied to a colony where rent is the exception and freedom from it the rule.

Again, he has often spoken of the existence of rent as dependent on the cultivation of land of different degrees of fertility, or on the fact that the same land repays, with a proportionably smaller return, the application of additional capital.   And yet it is clear that if we suppose the existence of a populous and opulent district of great but uniform fertility, giving a large return to a given expenditure of capital, but incapable of giving any return whatever on a less expenditure, or any greater return on a larger expenditure, such a district would afford a high rent though every rood of land and every portion of the capital applied to it would be equally productive.

Consequences of the Proposition that Additional Labour, when employed in Manufactures is MORE, and when employed in Agriculture is LESS, efficient in proportion.—We now proceed to consider some remarkable consequences of the proposition [see page 81,] that additional labour when employed in Manufactures is *more*, and when employed in Agriculture *less*, efficient in proportion; or, in other words, that the efficiency of labour increases in Manufactures in an increasing ratio, and in Agriculture in a decreasing ratio. And, consequently, that every additional quantity of manufactured produce is obtained, so far as the manufacturing of it is alone concerned, at a less proportionate cost, and every additional quantity of agricultural produce is obtained, generally speaking, at a greater proportionate cost.

I. **Different effects of increased demand on Manufactured and Raw Produce.**—So far as the price of any commodity is affected by the value of the raw material of which it is formed, it has a tendency to rise, so far as the price consists of the remuneration to be paid for the labour and abstinence of those employed in manufacturing it, it has a tendency to fall, with the increase of population.

It is obvious that commodities of rude or simple workmanship are subject to the first rule, and the finer manufactures to the second. Bread may afford an instance of the first kind, and lace of the second. The average price in England of a half-peck loaf is now about 1s. 3d. Of this sum 10d., at least, may be assumed to be the price of the wheat; the wages and profit of the miller, baker, and retailer absorbing the remainder. If circumstances should arise, requiring the present supply of bread to be immediately doubled from our home-produce, it is obvious that the increased supply of wheat could not be obtained by merely doubling the amount of labour now employed in its production. It is impossible to say to what amount the increased difficulty of production would raise the price of wheat; we will, however, suppose it to be doubled, and the price of the wheat necessary to make a half-peck loaf to be 1s. 8d. instead of 10d.: at the same time the increased labour employed in its manufacture and sale would become more efficient. The miller and the baker would employ better instruments and a greater division of labour, and the retailer would be able to double his sales at little additional expense. The price of bread, so far only as its manufacture and retail is concerned, would be reduced perhaps one-fourth, or from 5d to 3¾d. In which case, the whole result of the increased production would be that the half-peck loaf would sell for 1s. 11¾d. instead of 1s. 3d.

We will now see what would be the effect of an increased use of lace. At the present price of lace and cotton, a pound of cotton worth, in the Liverpool market, 2s., may be converted into a piece of lace worth 100 guineas. Suppose the consumption of lace to double, and the increased difficulty of producing the additional quantity of the cotton fit for lacemaking to raise its price from 2s. to 4s. a pound; the price of the lace, supposing it still to be manufactured at the same expense, would be raised one thousand-and-fiftieth part, or from £105 to £105 2s. But it is impossible to doubt that the stimulus thus applied to the production of lace would improve every process of the manufacture. We should probably much underrate the amount of that improvement if we were to estimate the consequent saving of expense at one fourth; in which case the whole result of the increased production would be that the lace would sell for £78 17s. instead of £105; the same circumstances which would nearly double the price of bread would reduce by one-fourth the price of lace.

II. **Different effects of Taxation on the Prices of Manufactured and Raw Produce.**—Another inference from the proposition in question is the difference between the effects of taxation when imposed on raw produce and when imposed on manufactured produce.

Taxes on manufactured commodities ultimately raise the price, and that by an amount exceeding the amount of the tax. Taxes on agricultural produce in its unmanufactured state do not necessarily occasion any ultimate rise of price, and raise it, if at all, by an amount less than that of the tax.

EFFECT OF TAXATION ON MANUFACTURED PRODUCE.—The first proposition may be easily illustrated.

We will suppose a tax on watches of twenty-five per cent. on their value to have existed from the commencement of that trade. As there is no reason to suppose that the profits or the wages of master watchmakers or their workmen are, under present circumstances, above the average wages and profits of persons similarly employed, it is clear that, if such a tax had always existed, the price for the time being of watches must always have been one-fourth higher than it has been, or the trade of watchmaking would have been followed neither by labourers nor capitalists. It is clear also that such an increase of price must always have diminished or retarded in its increase the sale, and, consequently, the production of watches. But if fewer watches had been made, the smaller number would have been made at a greater proportionate expense. And the price of watches must have been higher than it actually has been, first by the amount of the tax, and secondly by the greater expensiveness of the more limited manufacture. It is equally clear that, after the removal of such a tax, the price of watches would sink, first by the amount of the tax removed, and secondly by the improvement in the manufacture consequent on an increased production. It is equally clear that, if such a tax were now for the first time to be imposed, the price of watches must rise, first by the amount of the tax, and secondly by the amount of the increased proportionate expense of making and selling the diminished quantity sold, or watchmaking would cease to be as profitable as the average of trades. It is clear, too, that the more the use of watches diminished, the higher the price must eventually rise. If only ten new watches were made every year, they would probably cost £500 a-piece. If only one were made, it would probably cost little less than the whole price of the ten. It is true that these effects would not immediately follow either the imposition or the removal of the tax: an interval must in either case elapse, during which, the existing capital in the watchmaking trade continuing the same, the supply of watches would be neither increased nor diminished, and, consequently, the price but little affected. During this interval, both the wages and the profits of those engaged in that business would be unnaturally high, or unnaturally low, and they would not acquire their natural level until, in the case of the removal of the tax, a sufficient number of persons were educated to the business, or, in the case of the imposition of the tax, the number of persons educated to the business had been sufficiently diminished, to enable the supply of watches to be proportioned to the demand, at a price giving average profits and wages to the capitalists and labourers employed in their manufacture and sale.

EFFECT OF TAXATION ON AGRICULTURAL PRODUCE.—But if agricultural produce were subjected to such a tax, relief would be afforded by precisely the same conduct which in manufactures aggravates the pressure, namely, by a diminution of production.

It may be assumed that capital is fairly distributed among the various channels for its employment, and that, in the absence of peculiar disturbing causes, agriculture, the most agreeable of all occupations, has not less than an average share of it. It may therefore be assumed, generally speaking, that capital is employed on land until its produce repays, but does not more than repay, the expense of cultivation; or, in other words, that the occupier of land pushes its cultivation until the additional produce obtained by means of the last labourers employed is just sufficient, at the existing price, to pay their wages, and average profits to himself, for the time during which those wages must be paid in advance. On the imposition of a tax, either the price of what he produces must rise by the amount of the tax, or the farmer must discontinue the production of that portion of his crop which is raised at the greatest expense.

We will suppose a farmer to occupy a farm containing six hundred acres of arable land of different degrees of fertility; one hundred acres of which, with the labour of ten men directly and indirectly employed on them, would give a return which, in order to reduce it to one denomination, we will call six quarters of wheat an acre; one hundred others capable of giving with an equal number of men only five quarters per acre; one hundred others, four quarters per acre; one hundred others, three quarters per acre; one hundred others, two quarters per acre; and the last and worst one hundred acres, only one quarter per acre. We will suppose, also, that the wages of ten men for a year amount at an average to £400, or £40 a man; that the farmer has to advance these wages for a year before the produce is sold; and that the average rate of profit in similar occupations, is ten per cent. per annum. Under such circumstances, when wheat was £2 4s. a quarter it would be worth his while to employ every man whose labour produced twenty quarters, the price of which would amount to £44, being £40 for the labourer's wages, and £4 for the farmer's profit. The forty men supposed to be employed on the four best qualities of soil produce each this amount and more; the ten men employed on the fifth quality of soil produce each precisely this amount, namely, a return of two hundred quarters, worth £440. The sixth and last quality of soil, on which one man could produce only ten quarters, would not repay the cultivation of wheat. Now, if a tax were laid on raw produce, which, to make the illustrations less complex, we will call a tax of 14s. 8d. on every quarter of wheat, and no rise of price should take place, it is obvious that it would no longer be worth his while to cultivate any land of worse quality than that in which the labour of ten men could produce three hundred quarters of corn; a return which, at the existing price of £2 4s. a quarter, would procure £660, being £220 for the tax, and £440 as before for wages and profits. But it would obviously be worth his while to cultivate land of that quality, and also to employ labour in the cultivation of his superior land up to the point at which the labour of an additional man would no longer produce an additional product of thirty quarters. Nothing but a tax so great as absolutely to prohibit agriculture, such a tax as never has existed, and which would, in fact, be rather a penalty than a tax, could induce him to discharge all his labourers, and leave his best land uncultivated. We do not deny that he would be a loser, even by the conduct which we have supposed him to adopt. We do not deny that he would much have preferred a rise in the price of corn equal to the tax,—a rise which would have enabled him to continue in its existing investment all his agricultural capital. But we deny that any imposition to which the name of a tax can fairly be applied, though unaccompanied by a rise of price, would induce him altogether to discontinue production. And we wish to draw the attention of our readers to the contrast between his situation and that of the manufacturer, whom any tax, however slight, if unaccompanied by a rise of price, must in time force to discontinue manufacturing. What is a remedy to the agriculturist is an aggravation of evil to the manufacturer; a diminution of capital makes what remains in agriculture more productive, and makes what remains in manufactures less so.

It has been supposed, however, that the price of agricultural produce would rise to the full amount of the tax, and that the whole amount of that tax would consequently fall on the consumer. This is the opinion of Mr. Ricardo and of Mr. Mill. And it is on this ground that they both maintain that the effect of tithes is to produce a rise in the price of raw produce equal to the whole value of the tithe, and affecting equally all classes so far as they are consumers of raw produce. We believe that the *immediate* effect of a general tax on raw produce is to raise its price, but to an amount not equal to that of the tax; but that its *ultimate* effect is to diminish the consumption and production of raw produce, but to leave its price unaffected.

To prove our first proposition we need only show that the rise of price, which we admit to be the immediate consequence of the imposition of the tax, would diminish the consumption, and consequently the production of the taxed commodity. It has been shown already that, as production is diminished; the expense of producing the quantity still produced is diminished: and that the price of agricultural produce depends on the expense of producing that portion of it which is produced at the greatest expense, or, in other words, under circumstances of equal competition. That no person would diminish his consumption of corn in consequence of the rise of its price, is therefore a premise necessary to the conclusion which we are combating. This is true as respects that portion of the population of England which is dependent on parochial relief. In those districts in which the amount of that relief is calculated with reference to the price of bread, their means of purchasing are unconnected with price, and neither rise with its fall nor sink with its rise. It is true, also, as respects the families of those opulent individuals (a prominent, but in fact a small portion of society) whose direct expenditure in bread and flour bears a small proportion to their general expenses. But the bulk of the community, consisting of the labourers who receive no parish assistance, and happily they are now the majority, and we trust will soon be the great majority; and the smaller shopkeepers and farmers, unquestionably regulate, in a great measure, their purchases of wheat by its price. Much of their consumption, when it is comparatively cheap, consists of puddings and pies, articles of mere luxury, which, on the slightest rise, are immediately discontinued. If the rise continue, they turn from wheaten bread to cheaper subsistence: in the North to oatmeal, in the South to potatoes. And, indeed, without recurring to details, it may be laid down as a principle of universal application, that, in the absence of disturbing causes, every increase in the price of a commodity must diminish both the ability and the will to purchase it.

We now proceed to prove our second proposition, namely, that the ultimate effect of a tax on raw produce is not to raise its price, but to diminish the quantity produced. It will be at once admitted that the price of raw produce, in any Country, does not depend on the positive extent, or on the positive fertility of that Country, but, all the other things remaining the same, on the proportion which that extent, or that fertility bears to the number and wealth of the existing inhabitants. It may be low in a barren territory, if that territory be thinly peopled, just as it may be high in a fertile and populous one. It is high in the rich Lowlands of Scotland, and low in the sandy plains of Poland. And it will also be admitted that, all other things remaining the same, the population of a Country is in proportion to its extent and its fertility. Now, the ultimate effect of tithes, or of any other tax, on the cultivation of land, is precisely the same as if the Country in which they have long prevailed were thereby rendered rather less extensive, or rather less fertile, and consequently, rather less populous, and probably also rather poorer than it otherwise would have been.

Tithes.—If England, from time immemorial, had been rather more extensive, or rather more fertile than it now is, no one will suppose that the price of provisions would have been lower than it now is. We should have had rather more corn, and a rather greater population to eat that corn, than we now have. The increase would have been positive, not relative. So if Devonshire or Lincolnshire had never existed, the agricultural produce and the population of England would each have been positively diminished; but, as they would have borne the same proportion to one another as they do now, the price of the existing quantity of corn could not have been higher than it is now. So if tithes had never existed, we should have had rather more corn, and a rather larger and probably a rather richer population; every thing else would have been as it is. It is true that, if a new Devonshire, or a new Lincolnshire, fit for immediate cultivation, were now suddenly added to our shores, the immediate consequences would be, an increased supply of provisions, and a fall in their price. But it is also true that, if this accession to our territory were followed by no change in our habits and institutions, the comparative cheapness, which would be its immediate consequence, would gradually disappear as our population rose with the increased supply of subsistence, and, ultimately, we should be just where we are now, excepting that we should be rather more numerous. So, if tithes were suddenly commuted, and their interference, such as it is, with agricultural improvement, got rid of, the same consequences would follow as if the extent of our territory, or its fertility, were suddenly augmented. And, supposing no improvement to take place in our institutions and habits, the consequent increase of our population would bring us back, as far as the price of provisions is concerned, to the point at which we are now.

It is probable, indeed, that the ultimate effect of the abolition of tithes would be not a lowering but an increase of the price of raw produce. A denser population cultivating a territory, the productiveness of which had increased in proportion to the increased number of its inhabitants, would probably advance in opulence. The productiveness of the soil of a Country in proportion to its population

being given, or, in other words, the amount of raw produce and the
number of people being ascertained, the smaller the extent of the
land from which that amount is obtained the better.   The expenses of
transport, and the trouble and loss of time in journeys, are material
elements of the cost of production both in agriculture and in manufactures, and the amount of these expenses depends principally on
the extent of Country affording a given return.   As our industry
became more efficient the value of our labour would rise in the
general market of the world, and the consequence would be a general
rise of prices, in which agricultural produce would participate.   But
these statements form no part of our argument.   We believe, indeed,
that the ultimate effect of tithes is to lower the price of raw produce:
but all that we have undertaken to show is, that they do not raise it.

From these premises follow very important practical inferences.   If
we lay a tax on the production at home of any manufactured commodity which is produced with the same, or nearly the same, facility
abroad, it is absolutely necessary that a duty of the same, or a rather
greater amount, should be imposed on the importation of that commodity.   On the imposition of the tax the cost of production at home is
increased, first by the tax, and secondly by the increased expense of
producing the smaller quantity which, when the price becomes higher,
continues to be demanded.   But if importation were untaxed, the
cost of production abroad would be diminished in consequence of the
diminished proportionate expense of producing the larger quantity
demanded.   The domestic production, and with the domestic production the tax, would not be merely diminished, but absolutely destroyed,
and the whole result would be gratuitous evil.   But when a tax,
unbalanced by any countervailing duty on importation, is imposed on
any agricultural produce for which a foreign substitute can be obtained,
the only result is to stop *that portion which is most expensive* of the
domestic production.   The least productive part of the existing agricultural capital is withdrawn, or worn out without being replaced.
The deficiency is attempted to be supplied by importation; but the
increased demand, instead of lowering, as would be the case with
manufactures, raises the cost of production abroad, just as the diminished demand, instead of raising, lowers the cost of production at
home.   The price of agricultural produce rises until the state of the
population has accommodated itself to the change, and then falls to
its former level.   If our present heavy tax on the domestic production
of glass were unbalanced by any duty on importation, all the English
glass-works would in time be abandoned.   Or, if some of our glass-
works were free from the tax, and others subject to it, all those which
were taxed would be ruined.   But the lands in England which are
subject to the payment of tithes are not thrown out of cultivation by
the competition of those which are free from that burden, or by the
importation of the tithe-free corn and cattle of Scotland, or of the

comparatively tithe-free produce of Ireland. The estates which are subject to tithes continue to be productive, they continue even to afford a rent, though the burden diminishes the productiveness, and diminishes in a still greater degree the rent.

Before we quit the subject of tithes, it may be worth while to expose another error connected with them, namely, the popular opinion that their tendency to increase in amount is greater than that of rent. We believe the fact to be just the reverse.

Tithes are a definite, rent is an indefinite, share of the produce. Tithes can never exceed a tenth; rent need not be a tenth, or even a hundredth, but may amount to a fourth, a third, a half, or even more than a half. Tithes, therefore, can be exacted, where rent cannot be; but when once any spot of land can afford to pay both rent and tithes, there is no comparison between their respective powers of increase. This will immediately appear on a reference to the familiar illustration of the progress of rent.

If we suppose a Country to be divided into ten districts designated by the numbers from 1 to 10, each of equal extent, but each of a different degree of fertility, No. 1 producing, at a given expense, two hundred quarters of corn, and the amount of the produce, at the same expense, of each quality of land, diminishing by ten quarters until we come to No. 10, which produces only one hundred quarters, we shall find that when No. 1 only will pay for cultivation, it affords twenty quarters for tithes, and no rent. When the price of corn has risen sufficiently to enable No. 2 to be cultivated, there will be on Nos. 1 and 2 thirty-nine quarters for tithes, and on No. 1 ten for rent. When No. 3 has become worth cultivation, there will be on Nos. 1, 2, and 3, fifty-seven for tithes, and on Nos. 1 and 2 thirty for rent. When No. 4 has become worth cultivating, there will be on Nos. 1, 2, 3, and 4, seventy-four for tithes, and on Nos. 1, 2, and 3, sixty for rent. When No. 5 has become worth cultivating, there will be on Nos. 1, 2, 3, 4, and 5, ninety for tithes, and on Nos. 1, 2, 3, and 4, one hundred for rent. Rent has now passed tithes, and its subsequent superiority is very striking. When No. 6 has become worth cultivating, there will be one hundred and five for tithes, and one hundred and fifty for rent. When No. 7 has become worth cultivating, there will be one hundred and nineteen for tithes, and two hundred and ten for rent. When No. 8 has become worth cultivating, tithes will be one hundred and thirty-two, and rent two hundred and eighty. When No. 9 has become worth cultivating, tithes will be one hundred and forty-four, and rent three hundred and sixty. And when No. 10 has become worth cultivating, tithes will be one hundred and fifty-five, and rent four hundred and fifty. And the same results will follow if, instead of supposing fresh land of a regularly decreasing fertility to be taken into cultivation, we suppose further capital to be applied to the same land, with a regularly decreasing proportionate return. Of course we do not mean that either of these suppositions represents what actually takes place, but they each represent the course of events to which there is a natural tendency. They represent the relative ratio at which rent and tithes would increase in the absence of disturbing causes. It must be recollected, however, that these events would not take place in the regular order in which we have placed them, except on the supposition of each different district which we have supposed to be successively cultivated being of the same extent, and of each successive application of capital being of the same value. If, for instance, No. 10 were ten times as large as any one of the other districts, and received ten times as much capital, it would increase the whole amount of titheable produce by one thousand quarters instead of by one hundred quarters, and tithes would be raised from one hundred and forty-four quarters to two hundred and forty-four quarters, while rent would have risen only from three hundred and sixty quarters to four hundred and fifty. In such an event, therefore, tithes would rise more than rent. And it must also be recollected that tithes and rent do not rise at precisely the same period. The highest amount of rent must be just *before* the land producing the additional supply has been cultivated. The increased demand is then in full operation, and has not been counteracted by the increased supply. But the amount of tithes is not increased until *after* the additional supply has been produced. Their increase, therefore, is generally contemporaneous with a temporary fall of rent: which is probably one of the causes of the popular opinion that their general tendency to increase is greater than that of rent. Another source of that opinion is, that in England the land has been for centuries subject to a constant process of subdivision, while tithes, except the comparatively small part which belongs to laymen, have not. The incumbent of a given benefice receives the tithes of the same quantity of land which was tithed by his predecessor three hundred years ago. But that land three hundred years ago may have belonged to one or two persons, and may now be divided between ten or twenty. The present incumbent's income may bear a higher proportion than his predecessors did to the average income of a single landlord, though it bears a lower proportion to the aggregate income of all the landlords of the parish. And as a general proposition, we have no doubt that, in a progressive Country, the value of tithes will seldom increase in proportion to the increasing value of the land out of which they issue.

It appears, therefore, that in a new or ill-peopled Country where the abundance of land and the want of agricultural capital almost prevent the existence of rent, in the economical sense of the word, tithes are the only endowment which a Clergy can receive from the soil. We see, therefore, why they were adopted for the Israelites, who, in fact, were colonists, and by our Danish and Saxon ancestors.

We see too why the attempt to endow with lands the Canadian Church has so signally failed. Tithes would not, perhaps, have been a politic, but they would have been an actual endowment. The reserves stand so many desert spots in the midst of improvements retarding the settlement, interrupting the communications, and injuring the wealth and civilization of all that is round them. Five centuries hence they might afford an ample provision.

RELATIVE PROPORTIONS OF RENT, PROFIT, AND WAGES.

Having given a general outline of the three great classes among whom all that is produced is distributed, and of the general laws which regulate the comparative values of different products, we now proceed to consider the general laws which regulate the proportions in which Landlords, Capitalists, and Labourers share in the general distribution, or, in other words, which regulate the proportions which Rent, Profit, and Wages bear to one another.

Nomenclature.—We have followed the established nomenclature which divides society into Landlords, Capitalists, and Labourers ; and revenue into Rent, Wages, and Profit. And we have defined RENT to be *the revenue spontaneously offered by nature or accident ;* WAGES, *the reward of labour ;* and PROFIT, *that of abstinence.* At a distance these divisions appear clearly marked, but when we look into the details, we find them so intermingled that it is scarcely possible to subject them to a classification which shall not sometimes appear to be inconsistent, and still more frequently to be arbitrary. But it must be remembered that questions of classification relate rather to language than to facts; and that our object will have been effected if we can assist the memory by supplying a precise and consistent nomenclature.

We will begin by recurring to a subject to which we have already alluded, the frequent difficulty of deciding whether a given revenue ought or ought not to be called Rent. When an estate has been for some time leased to a careful tenant, it generally receives permanent ameliorations, which enable the owner, at the expiration of the lease, to obtain a higher rent. A bog worth 2s. annually an acre may be converted into arable or pasture worth annually £2. Is the increase of revenue rent or profit ? It arises from an additional fertility, now inseparably attached to the land. It is received by the owner without sacrifice on his part. It is, in fact, undistinguishable from the previous rent. On the other hand, its existence is owing to the abstinence of the farmer, who devoted to a distant object, the amelioration of the land, labour which he might have employed in producing immediate enjoyment for himself. If the owner of the estate had farmed it himself, and had directed labour to be employed on its permanent improvement, the additional produce occasioned by those improvements would clearly have been termed profit. It appears, therefore, most convenient to term it profit when occasioned by the improvements made by a tenant. In fact, these improvements are as consistently to be termed capital as a dock or a cotton-mill. Whose capital are they then? During the lease the capital of the tenant; when it has fallen in, the capital of the landlord, who has purchased them by engaging not to raise the rent during the currency of the lease.

We may be asked, then, whether the improvements which form the greater part of the value of the soil of every well-cultivated district are all, and for ever, to be termed capital? Whether the payments received from his tenants by the present owner of a Lincolnshire estate, reclaimed by the Romans from the sea, are to be termed, not rent but profit on the capital which was expended fifteen centuries ago? The answer is that, for all useful purposes, the distinction of profit from rent ceases as soon as the capital, from which a given revenue arises, has become, whether by gift or by inheritance, the property of a person to whose abstinence and exertions it did not owe its creation. The revenue arising from a dock, or a wharf, or a canal, is profit in the hands of the *original constructor*. It is the reward of *his* abstinence in having employed capital for the purposes of production instead of for those of enjoyment. But in the hands of his heir it has all the attributes of rent. It is to him the gift of fortune, not the result of a sacrifice. It may be said, indeed, that such a revenue is the reward for the owner's abstinence in not selling the dock or the canal and spending its price in enjoyment. But the same remark applies to every species of transferable property. Every estate may be sold, and th purchase money wasted. If the last basis of classification were adopted, the greater part of what every Political Economist has termed rent must be called profit.

Again, there are few employments in which extraordinary powers of body or mind do not receive an extraordinary remuneration. It is the privilege of talent to work not only better but more easily. It will generally be found, therefore, that the commodity or service produced by a first-rate workman, while it sells for more than an average price, has cost less than an average amount of labour. Sir Walter Scott could write a volume with the labour of about three hours a-day for a month, and for so doing received £500 or £1000. An ordinary writer, with equal application, would find it difficult to produce a volume in three months, and still more difficult to sell it for £50.

Is then the extraordinary remuneration of the labourer, which is assisted by extraordinary talents, to be termed Rent or Wages? It originates in the bounty of nature; so far it seems to be rent. It is to be obtained only on the condition of undergoing labour; so far it seems to be wages. It might be termed, with equal correctness, rent, which can be received only by a labourer, or wages, which can be received only by the proprietor of a natural agent. But as it is clearly a surplus, the labour having been previously paid for by average wages, and that surplus the spontaneous gift of nature, we have thought it most convenient to term it rent. And for the same reason we term *rent* what might, with equal correctness, be termed fortuitous profit. We mean the surplus advantages which are sometimes derived from the employment of capital after making full compensation for all the risk that has been encountered, and all the sacrifices which have been made, by the capitalist. Such are the fortuitous profits of the holders of warlike stores on the breaking out of unexpected hostilities; or of the holders of black cloth on the sudden death of one of the Royal family. Such would be the additional revenue of an Anglesea miner, if, instead of copper, he should come on an equally fertile vein of silver. The silver would, without doubt, be obtained by means of labour and abstinence; but *they* would have been repaid by an equal amount of copper. The extra value of the silver would be the gift of nature, and therefore rent.

Secondly. It is still more difficult to draw the line between Profit and Wages. There are, perhaps, a few cases in which capital may improve in value, without superintendence or change, simply by being preserved from consumption. Wine and timber, perhaps, afford instances. But even a wine-cellar or a plantation, if totally neglected, would probably deteriorate. And, as a general rule, it may be laid down that capital is an instrument which, to be productive of profit, must be employed, and that the person who directs its employment must *labour*, that is, must to a certain degree conquer his indolence, sacrifice his favourite pursuits, and often incur other inconveniences from his residence, from the persons to whose contact he is exposed, from confinement or from exposure to the weather, and must also often submit to some inferiority of rank. If labour be in general necessary to the use of material capital, it is universally necessary to the use of that immaterial capital which consists of appropriate knowledge, and of moral and intellectual habits and reputation,—a capital created and kept up at more expense, and productive of a greater return than that which is material, but which, from the impossibility of actually transferring it, or implanting in one man the ability of another, can never be productive but through the labour of its possessor.

Is then the remuneration of this labour to be termed Wages or Profit? A certain portion of it, that portion which would be sufficient to repay equal exertions and hardships endured by an ordinary labourer, unprovided with capital, must, without doubt, be termed wages. And where extraordinary natural talents or favourable accidents have occasioned the exertions of the capitalist to obtain more than an average remuneration, that excess is, as we have already seen, rent. But the revenue to which our present question applies is the revenue

obtained from the employment of capital, after deducting ordinary
interest on the capital, as the remuneration for the abstinence of the
capitalist, ordinary wages, as the remuneration for his labour, and any
extraordinary advantages which may have been the result of accident.

The subject may be made clearer by a few examples; and we have
endeavoured to find some in which the remuneration for the capitalist's
trouble, instead of being, as is usually the case, mixed up with the
gross amount of his returns, appears as a separate item.   The trade
of bill-broking affords an instance.   The business of a bill-broker is
to advance, before it becomes due, the money for which bills of
exchange are drawn, deducting, under the name of discount, interest
at the rate of not more than five per cent. per annum on the sum
secured by the bill.   In time of peace, and in the ordinary state of
the money-market, the rate of discount varies from four to three per
cent. per annum.   It has been sometimes as low as two and-a-half.   It
appears at first strange that such a trade should exist, since the money
capital employed in it does not return even so high a profit as may
often be obtained from the public funds, leaving the additional risk
and labour uncompensated.   It is, in fact, a trade which no one *would*
carry on if he employed in it his own money.

The commercial inhabitants of a great trading city have from time
to time under their control considerable sums of money for short
periods.   Scarcely a single estate in this Country is mortgaged or
sold without the price or the mortgage-money being placed for some
days at a banker's or agent's until the "more last words" of the
lawyers have been said.   These sums cannot in the mean time be
employed in any permanent investment; but they can be lent from
day to day, or, in some cases, from week to week, and it is better to
lend them at the lowest rate of interest than to suffer them to lie
perfectly idle.   The bill-broker's trade is to borrow these sums from
week to week, or even from day to day, at one rate of interest, and
to lend them from month to month, or for two or three months, at a
higher.   To borrow, for instance, at two per cent., and to lend at three.

It is obvious that these operations require much knowledge, industry,
and skill.   The broker must be well acquainted with the circumstances
of almost every eminent commercial man in order to estimate the
value of his acceptance or indorsement.   He must keep up his knowledge by unremitting observation, and by inferences drawn from very
slight hints and appearances.   He must also have the skill so to
manage his concerns as to have his receipts always falling in to correspond with his engagements.   This knowledge, and the moral and
intellectual habits which enable him to apply it, form his personal or
immaterial capital.   But he must also have a material capital, not
for the purpose of being employed in his business, for no one would
so employ money of his own, but as the means of obtaining confidence.
The interest paid by a broker is so trifling, that no one would lend to

him if it implied the slightest risk; and the best pledge which he can give is the notoriety of his possessing a large capital, which could at any time make good an unforeseen interruption in his regular receipts. This capital he must not waste, but he may employ it productively, and may consume on himself the annual profit derived from it. The confidence which it enables him to enjoy is a distinct advantage.

We will suppose a bill-broker to possess £100,000 in the Four per Cents.; and to have sufficient knowledge, skill, and character as a man of business and of wealth, to be able, at an average throughout the year, to borrow £400,000 at two per cent., and to lend the same sum at three per cent. Is the £4000 a-year which his business would give him wages or profit?

Again, a capital which in this Country would enable its employer to obtain ten per cent., would often, if he were to employ it in Jamaica or Calcutta, produce fifteen or twenty. If the capitalist with £50,000 encounter the climate and the society of Jamaica, and is rewarded by his annual returns being raised from £5000 to £7500, is his additional income of £2500 a-year wages or profit?

There is no doubt that a sufficient portion of it to purchase the same services from a person unprovided with capital, must be considered as wages: £500 a-year, however, would considerably exceed this sum. The remaining £2000 a-year may be considered, with equal correctness, either wages which can be received only by the possessor of £50,000, or profit which can be received only by a person willing to labour in Jamaica.

Adam Smith considers it as profit. "The profits of stock," he observes,[22] "it may, perhaps, be thought, are only a different name for the wages of a particular sort of labour, the labour of inspection or direction. They are, however, altogether different, are regulated by quite different principles, and bear no proportion to the quantity, the hardship, or the ingenuity of this supposed labour of inspection and direction. They are regulated altogether by the value of the stock employed, and are greater or smaller in proportion to this stock. If we suppose two manufacturers, the one employing a capital of £1000, and the other one of £7300, in a place where the common profits of manufacturing stock are ten per cent., the one will expect a profit of about £100 a-year, while the other will expect about £730. Yet their labour of inspection may be very nearly or altogether the same. In many great works, almost the whole labour of this kind is committed to some principal clerk. His wages properly express the value of this labour of inspection and direction. Though in settling them some regard is commonly had, not only to his labour and skill, but to the trust which is reposed in him, yet they never bear any regular proportion to the capital of which he oversees the manage-

[22] Book I. Ch. VI.

ment. And the owner of this capital, though he is thus discharged of almost all labour, still expects that his profits should bear a regular proportion to his capital."

After much hesitation, we have resolved to adopt this as the most convenient classification, and to confine the term wages to the remuneration for simple labour; including under the word labour the endurance of all its attendant hardships, but excluding from the word wages the additional revenue which the labourer often receives because he happens to be also a capitalist. We have done so on the grounds which are so ably stated in the passage which we lastly quoted.

To revert to our supposition of a capitalist with £50,000 repaid by an extra revenue of £2500 a-year for living in Jamaica: it is clear that another capitalist taking there 100,000 would, *cæteris paribus*, obtain an extra revenue of £5000 a-year, and *that* notwithstanding his labour would not necessarily be greater than that of the first-mentioned capitalist, or notwithstanding it might in fact be much less. Perhaps the best plan might appear to be, to apply the term *wages* to the remuneration of mere labour, the term *interest* to the remuneration of mere abstinence, and the term *profit* to the combination of wages and interest, to the remuneration of abstinence and labour combined. This would make it necessary to subdivide capitalists into two classes, the inactive and the active: the first receiving mere interest, the second obtaining profit.

In this, however, as in many other cases, the inconveniences occasioned by a departure from an established nomenclature and an established classification are so great, that we do not think that they will be compensated by the nearer approach to precision. We shall continue, therefore, to include under the term profit the whole revenue that is obtained from the possession or employment of capital, after deducting those accidental advantages which we have termed rent, and also deducting a sufficient sum to pay to the capitalist, if actively employed, the wages which would purchase an equal amount of labour from a person unpossessed of capital. In one respect, however, we are forced to differ from Adam Smith. Although he considers the useful, acquired knowledge and abilities of all the inhabitants of a Country as part of the national fortune, as a capital fixed and realized in the persons of their possessors, yet he generally terms the revenue derived from this capital *wages*. " The average and ordinary rates of profit in the different employments of stock are," he observes, " more nearly on a level than the wages of the different sorts of labour. The difference between the earnings of a common labourer and those of a well-employed lawyer or physician, is evidently much greater than that between the ordinary profits in any two different branches of trade." Book I. Ch. X.

According to our nomenclature (and indeed according to that of Smith, if the produce of capital is to be termed profit) a very small portion of the earnings of the lawyer or of the physician can be called wages. Forty pounds a-year would probably pay all the labour that either of them undergoes, in order to make, we will say, £4000 a-year. Of the remaining £3960, probably £3000 may in each case be considered as rent, as the result of extraordinary talent or good fortune. The rest is profit on their respective capitals; capitals partly consisting of knowledge, and of moral and intellectual habits acquired by much previous expense and labour, and partly of connection and reputation acquired during years of probation while their fees were inadequate to their support.

Under this view of the case, the revenue which consists of profit will in the progress of improvement bear a constantly increasing proportion to that which consists of wages. There appears no reason to doubt that, as civilization advances, every person will receive an education which will materially increase his power of production. Brutes and machinery can effect almost every thing that is to be effected by mere bodily exertion. Whatever requires mind, will be done better in proportion as the mind has received earlier or more judicious cultivation. We have heard it made a subject of complaint, that the uneducated Irish have dispossessed the English of the lowest employments in London and its neighbourhood. We rather rejoice that the English are sufficiently educated to be fit for better things. If they had remained as ignorant as their rivals, many who are now earning 40s. a-week as mechanics, might have been breaking stones and carrying hods at 2s. a-day. Even in our present state of civilization, which, high as it appears by comparison, is far short of what may easily be conceived, or even of what may confidently be expected, the intellectual and moral capital of Great Britain far exceeds all her material capital, not only in importance, but even in productiveness. The families that receive mere wages probably do not form a fourth of the community; and the comparatively large amount of the wages even of these is principally owing to the capital and skill with which their efforts are assisted and directed by the more educated members of the society. Those who receive mere rent, even using that word in its largest sense, are still fewer: and the amount of rent, like that of wages, principally depends on the knowledge by which the gifts of nature are directed and employed. The bulk of the national revenue is profit; and of that profit the portion which is mere interest on material capital probably does not amount to one-third. The rest is the result of personal capital, or, in other words, of education.

It is not on the accidents of soil or climate, or on the existing accumulation of the material instruments of production, but on the quantity and the diffusion of this immaterial capital, that the wealth of a Country depends. The climate, the soil, and the situation of Ireland have been described as superior, and certainly are not much inferior, to our own. Her poverty has been attributed to the want of material capital; but were Ireland now to exchange her native population for seven millions of our English North Countrymen, they would quickly create the capital that is wanted. And were England, North of Trent, to be peopled exclusively by a million of families from the West of Ireland, Lancashire and Yorkshire would still more rapidly resemble Connaught. Ireland is physically poor because she is morally and intellectually poor, because she is morally and intellectually uneducated. And while she continues uneducated, while the ignorance and violence of her population render persons and property insecure, and prevent the accumulation and prohibit the introduction of capital, legislative measures, intended solely and directly to relieve her poverty, may not indeed be ineffectual, for they may aggravate the disease, the symptoms of which they are meant to palliate, but undoubtedly will be productive of no permanent benefit. Knowledge has been called power; it is far more certainly wealth. Asia Minor, Syria, Egypt, and the Northern coast of Africa, were once among the richest, and are now among the most miserable Countries in the world, simply because they have fallen into the hands of a people without a sufficiency of the immaterial sources of wealth to keep up the material ones. "In what way," asks Adam Smith, "has Europe contributed to the grandeur of the colonies of America? In one way, and in one way only, she has contributed a great deal. *Magna virum mater*. She bred and formed the men who were capable of achieving such great actions, and of laying the foundation of so great an empire; and there is no other quarter of the world of which the policy is capable of forming, or has ever actually and in fact formed such men. The colonies owe to Europe the education and great views of their active and enterprising founders, and some of the greatest and most important of them owe to her scarce any thing else."

CAUSES ON WHICH THE PROPORTIONATE AMOUNT OF RENT DEPENDS.

We have already defined Rent to be the revenue spontaneously offered by nature or accident, or, in other words, to be the price paid for the assistance of an appropriated natural agent. It might with equal propriety be defined the surplus produce arising from the use of an appropriated natural agent, or the amount by which the price of the produce of an appropriated natural agent exceeds the costs of its production.

The nature and the progress of the Rent of Land have usually been illustrated by supposing lands of different fertility to be successively taken into cultivation. Thus the land No. 1 is supposed to afford, in return for the application of a given amount of labour and capital, one hundred quarters; No. 2, ninety quarters; No. 3, eighty quarters; No. 4, seventy quarters; No. 5, sixty quarters; and so on. While any portion of the most fertile lands is unappropriated, No. 1 only is cultivated, and no rent is paid. Before it has become necessary to cultivate No. 2, No. 1 must have become an appropriated agent, affording a larger return than can be obtained without its assistance. Its owner, or, as he is termed, the landlord, obtains, therefore, the value of that assistance, being ten quarters, or the difference between one hundred quarters and ninety quarters; and receives it himself, in kind, if he himself is the cultivator, or is paid for it the remuneration termed "rent," if he allows another person to be the cultivator. Before it has become necessary to cultivate No. 3, the rent of No. 1 must have risen from ten quarters to twenty, and No. 2, from giving no rent, must have given a rent of ten quarters; and so on until the point is reached at which the labour and capital employed will produce a return only sufficient to give a bare subsistence to the labourer and average profits to the capitalist: the highest extreme to which cultivation can be intentionally pushed, and one indeed beyond which it is seldom carried.

It is obvious, therefore, that the amount of rent depends on two causes: 1. the positive productiveness of the natural agent by which it is afforded; 2. the comparative productiveness of that agent, or the degree in which it exceeds those agents which are universally accessible. If the supply of natural agents were unlimited, or if their power of affording assistance were to cease, in either case rent would be at an end. Rent is the value of their assistance, and that value, like all others, depends partly on their utility, and partly on their limitation of supply. Much error has arisen from attending to only one of these causes.

The French Economists[22] perceived that the produce of fertile land,

[22] *Le laboureur est le seul dont le travail produisse au delà du salaire du travail. Il est donc l'unique source de toute richesse.*

La terre, indépendamment de tout autre homme et de toute convention, lui paie immédiatement le prix de son travail. La nature ne marchande point avec lui pour l'obliger à se contenter du nécessaire absolu. —Ce qu'elle donne n'est proportionnée ni à ses besoins ni à une évaluation conventionnelle du prix de ses journées. C'est le résultat physique de la fertilité du sol, et de la justesse, bien plus que de la difficulté des moyens, qu'il a employés pour le rendre fécond. Dès que le travail du laboureur produit au delà de ses besoins, il peut, avec ce superflu que la nature lui accorde en pur don, au delà du salaire de ses peines, acheter le travail des autres membres de la société. Ceux-ci en le lui vendant ne gagnent que leur vie, mais le laboureur recueille outre sa subsistence une richesse disponible; qu'il n'a point achetée, et qu'il vend. Il est donc l'unique source des richesses, qui, par leur circulation, animent tous les travaux de la société; parcequ'il est le seul dont le travail produisse au delà du salaire du travail.

Il reste donc constant qu'il n'y a de revenu que le produit net des terres, et que tout autre profit annuel, ou est payé par le revenu, ou fait partie des frais qui servent à produire le revenu.—Turgot, vol. v. pp. 8—9—126.

Vous ne pouvez trouver le meilleur état possible d'une nation, que dans la plus grande richesse possible. J'entends ici par le terme de richesse, une masse de valeurs disponibles, de valeurs qu'on puisse consommer au gré de ses désirs, sans s'appauvrir, sans altérer le principe qui les reproduit sans cesse.

Le meilleur état possible est évidemment celui auquel est attachée la plus grande sûreté; il consiste donc dans la plus grande masse possible de valeurs disponibles: car ce sont les seules dont nous puissions toujours jouir, et sur lesquelles la sûreté puisse s'établir.

Je voudrois bien que mes lecteurs donnassent à cette vérité toute l'attention qu'elle mérite, je voudrois bien qu'ils saisissent que la richesse ne consiste que dans les valeurs disponibles, qu'on peut consommer sans aucun inconvénient; par conséquent, qu'il n'y a que le produit net des cultures qui soit richesse, parcequ'il est dans la masse des reproductions, la seule partie dont nous puissions disposer pour nos jouissances; le surplus de cette masse n'est pas disponible pour nous, il appartient à la culture, c'est elle qui tous les ans doit le consommer; nous ne pouvons le lui dérober, que nous n'en soyons punis par l'extinction de nos richesses. —L'Ordre Naturel, &c. pp. 379—381.

the most important of all appropriated natural agents, sells for a price exceeding the expense of its cultivation.   This excess of price, or *produit net*, as they termed it, they conceived to be the only source of wealth.   All other commodities appeared to them merely to represent the toil employed in their acquisition.   They believed, therefore, a community to be rich in proportion to the amount of rent received by the proprietors of its land; and consequently that production enriches only so far as it is subservient to the creation of rent.

It is impossible that they could have maintained this doctrine, if they had perceived that abundance is an element in wealth, and that high rents and the greatest abundance are incompatible; or if they had recollected that, according to their views, a community possessing the highest skill and exerting the utmost diligence, but scattered over a territory of unbounded extent and fertility, as they might be even unacquainted with the existence of such a thing as rent, must be totally without riches, must be poor from the mere prodigality of their resources.

In the following passage Mr. Ricardo seems to have fallen into an opposite error.

" Nothing is more common than to hear of the advantages which the land possesses over every other source of useful produce, on account of the surplus which it yields in the form of rent.   Yet, when land is most abundant, when most productive, and most fertile, it yields no rent; and it is only when its powers decay, and less is yielded in return for labour, that a share of the original produce of the more fertile portions is set apart for rent.   It is singular that this quality in the land, which should have been noticed as an imperfection, compared with the natural agents by which manufactures are assisted, should have been pointed out as constituting its peculiar pre-eminence.   If air, water, the elasticity of steam, and the pressure of the atmosphere, were of various qualities, if they could have been appropriated, and each quality existed only in moderate abundance, they, as well as the land, would afford a rent, as the successive qualities were brought into use.   With every worse quality employed, the value of the commodities in the manufacture of which they were used would rise, because equal quantities of labour would be less productive.   Man would do more with the sweat of his brow, and nature would perform less; and the land would be no longer pre-eminent for its limited powers.

" If the surplus produce which the land affords in the form of rent be an advantage, it is desirable that every year the machinery newly constructed should be less efficient than the old, as that would undoubtedly give a greater exchangeable value to the goods manufactured, not only by that machinery, but by all other machinery in the Kingdom; and a rent would be paid to all those who possessed the most productive machinery.

" The labour of nature is paid not because she does much, but because she does little. In proportion as she becomes niggardly in her gifts, she exacts a greater price for her work. Where she is munificently beneficent she always works gratis." *Principles*, p. 63.

Mr. Ricardo seems to have forgotten that the quality which enables land to afford rent, namely, the power of producing the subsistence of more persons than are required for its cultivation, is an advantage without which rent could not have existed. As the population of any given district becomes more dense, the surplus produce of its soil, or, in other words, the amount of its produce which remains after provision has been made for the subsistence of those by whom it is cultivated, has a constant tendency to increase; either because the increase of agricultural skill and capital increases its positive fertility, or because a diminution of its relative fertility, a diminution of its produce relatively to the numbers of its cultivators, forces the poorer classes to be satisfied with a less amount of raw produce; or from both these causes combined. Of these two causes of rent, one is a benefit, the other an evil. That we have in this Country perhaps a million of acres capable of producing, with average labour, forty bushels of corn an acre, is a benefit; that we have not more than a million such acres is an evil. That the average amount of what an agricultural labourer produces much exceeds what is absolutely necessary for the subsistence of an agricultural family is a benefit. That the extent of our fertile land, and the amount of our capital, in proportion to our population, are not sufficient to enable him to consume, directly or indirectly, for his own advantage and that of his family, *all* that he produces, is an evil. To produce rent, both the benefit and the evil must coexist. The one occasions rent to be demanded; but it is the other which enables it to be paid.

Mr. Ricardo's attention seems to have been confined to the evil. But rent might be enormously increased without the increase of that evil, or even though that evil should be diminished. If the proprietor of a single estate could by a wish triple its produce, he would augment, in a much greater ratio, its rent. Would this increase be owing to the parsimony of nature? It may be said that it would be owing to the comparative unproductiveness of the rest of the Country. It must be admitted that, if we could suddenly triple the productive powers of all the land in this Country, the population remaining the same, the whole amount of rent would fall, and the condition of all classes, except of that comparatively small class which subsists on the rent of land, would be much improved. But if our population were also tripled, rents would be prodigiously increased, the situation of the landlords would be improved, and that of no other class deteriorated. In fact, the condition of all other classes would be improved, as the increased division of labour and ease of communication occasioned by a greater density of population would cheapen and improve our manufactures. If the population, instead of being tripled, were only doubled, the situation of the Country would be still better.   The rise in rent, though not equal to what it would have been if the population had been tripled, would still be very great, and both raw produce and manufactures would be more abundant than they were previously. Now this is, in fact, what *has* occured in England during the last hundred and thirty years.   Since the beginning of the 18th Century the population of England has about doubled.   The produce of the land has certainly tripled, probably quadrupled.   Rent has risen in a still greater proportion; but that rise has been accompanied by a rise of wages, estimated in every commodity consumed by the labourers, excepting a few, such as spirituous and fermented liquors, which have been made the subject of special taxation.   With the same labour the labourer can obtain more corn, and perhaps five times as much of the most useful manufactures.   Can it be fairly said that rents have risen because nature has done little? that the price paid for her assistance has been increased because she has become more niggardly in her gifts?   It is true that, if the productiveness of the land, instead of being tripled, had been centupled, rents might not have risen; but it is equally true that they would not have risen, if instead of being tripled, it had remained stationary.   The condition essential to the payment of the labour of nature is not, as Mr. Ricardo states it, that her assistance shall be little, but that it shall not be infinite.

As rent arises from the agency not of man, but of nature, its amount does not depend on the will or the exertions of its recipient. The owner of the land, or of the natural agent, whatever it be, for the use of which persons are willing to pay rent, receives the sum which their mutual competition forces them to give.   As it is all pure gain, he accepts the largest sum that is offered, however trifling its amount. Nor, on the other hand, does the amount of rent depend on the will or the exertions of those who pay it.   Whatever be the value of the services of an appropriated natural agent, that value must be paid by the person who wishes to use them, as both parties to the bargain are aware, that if it is not hired by one applicant it will be by another. The amount, therefore, is subject to no general rule; it has neither a minimum nor a maximum.   It depends on the degree in which nature has endowed certain instruments with peculiar productive powers, and the number of those instruments compared with the number and wealth of the persons able and willing to hire them.   There is, probably, now land near New York selling for £1000 an acre, which a century ago could have been obtained for a dollar.

PROPORTIONATE AMOUNTS OF PROFIT AND WAGES.

Profits and Wages differ in almost all respects from Rent.   They are each subject to a minimum and a maximum.   They are subject to a minimum, because each of them is the result of a sacrifice.   It may be difficult to say what is the minimum with respect to profit, but it is clear that every capitalist, as a motive to abstain from the immediate and unproductive enjoyment of his capital, must require some remuneration exceeding the lowest that is conceivable. The minimum at which wages can be permanently fixed is of course the sum necessary to enable the existing labouring population to subsist. On the other hand, as the rate of wages depends in a great measure on the number of labourers, and the rate of profit on the amount of capital, both high wages and high profits have a tendency to produce their own diminution. High wages, by stimulating an increase of population, and therefore an increase of the number of labourers, and high profits, by occasioning an increase of capital. It will be seen in a future portion of this Treatise that, if the amount of capital employed in the payment of wages increases, the number of labourers remaining the same, profits will fall; and that if the number of labourers increases, the amount of capital and the productiveness of labour remaining the same, wages will fall; and that, if they both increase in equal proportions, both will have a tendency to fall, in consequence of the larger proportion which they will each bear to the power of the natural agents whose services they each require. And although it may not be easy to fix the maximum of either wages or profits, yet it may be laid down generally, that in no Country have profits continued for any considerable period at the average rate of fifty per cent. per annum, or wages at such a rate as to afford the labourer ten times the amount necessary for the subsistence of a family.

Adam Smith has laid down, that "the whole of the advantages and disadvantages of the different employments of labour and capital must, in the same neighbourhood, be either perfectly equal or continually tending to equality. If in the same neighbourhood there was any employment evidently either more or less advantageous than the rest, so many people would crowd into it in the one case, and so many would desert it in the other, that its advantages would soon return to the level of other employments. This at least would be the case in a society where things were left to take their natural course, where there was perfect liberty, and every man was perfectly free both to choose what occupation he thought proper, and to change it as often as he thought proper. Every man's interest would prompt him to seek the advantageous and to shun the disadvantageous employment." *Wealth of Nations*, Book I. Ch. X.

The truth of these remarks of Adam Smith is obvious. It is obvious also that, in the absence of disturbing causes, the desire of obtaining a more advantageous field for the employment of his mental and bodily faculties, which leads a man to move from one part of the same neighbourhood to another, would lead him from village to village and from Country to Country. For commercial purposes, the whole civilized world is one extended neighbourhood; and the same causes which tend to equalize profits in Liverpool and London tend to equalize them in London and Calcutta. But when we look into the details, we are struck by the difference in the remuneration of persons apparently undergoing equal toils, and exercising equal abstinence. We find a general exempt from more than half the hardships of a private, and receiving more than a hundred times his pay. We find barristers making £10,000 or £15,000 a-year, while a copying clerk is paid for labour as assiduous and more irksome by only £100. We find the purchaser of an Exchequer-bill willing to pay a large premium for the privilege of advancing capital at a profit of three per cent. per annum, while a shopkeeper thinks himself ill paid by less than twenty per cent. We find a London banker satisfied with a profit of seven per cent., while his partner in Calcutta requires fifteen.

Circumstances which decide what, at a given time and in a given place, shall be the average rate of Wages, and the average rate of Profit.— These differences are partly real and partly apparent. So far as they are real, they are occasioned partly by the influence of the different instruments of production, or, in other words, the different sources of revenue, on one another; the influence, for instance, of the rate of profits on the amount of wages, and of the amount of wages on the rate of profits; partly by the greater or less severity of the sacrifices which the labourer and the capitalist must make in addition to the undergoing mere toil or abstinence; and partly by the difficulty with which capital and labour are transferred from one employment to another. A difficulty caused partly by physical obstacles and partly by human habits and institutions. The influence of these causes on the average rates of wages and of profits in the same Country, in different employments of labour and capital, we shall consider hereafter; and having assumed for the purposes of the following discussion that a certain average rate of wages and a certain average rate of profit exists, we shall now endeavour to explain the causes by which these average rates are determined, or, in other words, to explain *the circumstances which decide what, at a given time and in a given place, shall be the average rate of wages and the average rate of profit.* We have already stated as one of the principal sources of difficulty in Political Economy the mutual dependence of its different propositions. A dependence which, as it respects the theory of wages and profits, is so great that it is impossible to give a complete view of the causes which affect the one without adverting to all those which affect the other. We shall endeavour to keep them as distinct as we can, and we shall begin by wages, as that subject is capable of being separately considered to the greatest extent.

MEANINGS OF THE WORDS HIGH AND LOW, AS APPLIED TO WAGES.— We have already defined Wages to be the remuneration received by the labourer in recompense for having exerted his faculties of mind and body. They are said to be *high* or *low*, in proportion to the extent of that remuneration.   That extent has been estimated by three different measures; and the words high and low wages have, consequently, been used in three different senses.

First.   Wages have been termed high or low, according to the amount of *money* earned by the labourer within a given period, without any reference to the commodities which that money would purchase; as when we say that wages have *risen* in England since the reign of Henry VII., because the labourer now receives 1s. 6d. or 2s. a-day, and then received only 4½d.

Secondly.   They have been termed high or low, according to the *quantity and quality of the commodities* obtained by the labourer, without any reference to his receipts in money; as when we say that wages have *fallen* in England since the reign of Henry VII., because the labourer then earned two pecks of wheat a-day, and now earns only one.

Thirdly.   They have been termed high or low, according to the share or proportion which the labourer receives of the produce of his own labour, without any reference to the total amount of that produce.

The first nomenclature, that which measures wages simply by their amount in money, is the popular one.   The second, that which considers wages simply with reference to the quantity and quality of the commodities received by the labourer, or, to speak more correctly, purchasable with his money wages, was that generally adopted by Adam Smith.   The third, that which considers wages as high or low, simply with reference to the labourer's share or proportion of what he produces, was introduced by Mr. Ricardo, and has been continued by many of his followers.

This last use of the words high and low wages has always appeared to us one of the most unfortunate of Mr. Ricardo's many innovations in the language of Political Economy.   In the first place, it has a tendency to withdraw our attention, even when we are considering the subject of wages, from the facts which most influence the labourer's condition.   To ascertain whether his wages are high or low, we are desired to inquire, not whether he is ill or well paid,—not whether he is well or ill fed, or clothed, or lodged, or warmed, but simply what proportion of what he produces comes to his share.   During the last four or five years many a hand-weaver has received only 8s. 3d. for producing, by a fortnight's exertion, a web that the capitalist has sold for 8s. 4d.   A coal merchant often pays his men £2 a-week, and charges his employers for their services £2 10s.   But, according to Mr. Ricardo's nomenclature, the wages of the weaver, at 4s. 1½d. a-week, are much higher than those of the coal-heaver at £2, since the weaver receives 99 per cent. of the value of his labour, while the coal-heaver has only 80 per cent.

And, even if the nomenclature in question were free from this objection, even if the point on which it endeavours to fix the attention

were the most important, instead of being the least important, incident
to wages, it still would be inconvenient, from its tendency to render
the writer who employs it both inconsistent and obscure.   It is almost
impossible to affix to terms of familiar use a perfectly new meaning,
and not from time to time to slide into the old one.   When Mr.
Ricardo says that " nothing can affect profits but a rise of wages,"
p. 118; that " whatever raises the wages of labour lowers the profits
of stock," p. 231; that " high wages invariably affect the employers
of labour by depriving them of a portion of their real profits," p.
129; that, " as the wages of labour fall the profits of stock rise,"
p. 499; he means by high wages, not a large *amount*, but a large
proportion.   But when he speaks of the " encouragement which high
wages give to the increase of population," pp. 88—361, he means by
high wages a large *amount*.   And many of his followers and opponents have supposed the words high and low to be used by him as
indicative of quantity, not proportion.   The consequence has been
that, since the publication of his great Work, an opinion has prevailed
that high wages and high profits are incompatible, and that whatever
is taken from the one is added to the other.   The slightest attempt
to try this theory by an actual example will show its absurdity.   The
usual supposition is, that the capitalist, at an average, advances the
wages of his labourers for one year, and receives, after deducting
rent, one-tenth of the value of what they produce.   We are inclined
to think that in England the average rate of profit is rather greater,
and the average period of advance rather less.   After making many
inquiries on these subjects in Manchester, we found the general
opinion to be, that the manufacturing capitalist turns his capital, at
an average, twice in the year, and receives on each operation a profit
of 5 per cent.; and that the shopkeeper, at an average, turns his
capital four times in a year, and receives on each operation a profit of
about 3½ per cent.   On these data the labourer's share would, of course,
be much greater than according to the ordinary estimate.   We will
suppose, however, that estimate to be correct, and that, after rent has
been deducted, the labourer receives, on an average, nine-tenths of
the value of what he produces.   Under these circumstances a rise in
the amount of wages amounting to one-tenth, or from 10s. to 11s.
a-week, if that rise is to be deducted from the capitalist's share, would
utterly destroy all profit whatever.   A rise of one-fifth, or from 10s.
to 12s. a-week, would occasion to the capitalist a loss equal to the
whole amount of his former profit.   A fall in wages of one-tenth
would double profits; a fall of one-fifth would treble them.   Now we
know that general variations in the amount of wages to the amount
of one-tenth or one-fifth, or to a greater extent, are not of unfrequent
occurrence.   Yet who ever heard of their producing such an effect on
profits ?

And yet this doctrine has received the sanction both of theoretic and practical men.   Mr. Francis Place is asked by the Committee on Artisans and Machinery, (First Report, p. 46,[24]) "Do not the masters in consequence of a rise of wages raise their prices?"—"No," he answers; "I believe there is no principle of Political Economy better established than this of wages; increase of wages must come from profits."

Did Mr. Place ever apply this doctrine when his men asked for higher wages on a general mourning?   Even the Committee appear to have taken this view of the question.   The subject is so important, that we will venture to extract the following passage from the Report made in the following Session:—

"Those eminent persons who, during the last fifty years, have reduced the rules that govern the operations of trade and industry to a Science, undertake to show, by arguments and facts, that the effect of low wages is not a low price of the commodity to which they are applied, but the raising of the average rate of profits in the Country in which they exist.   The explanation of this proposition occupies a large portion of the justly celebrated work of the late Mr. Ricardo, on the Principles of Political Economy; and is also ably set forth in the following evidence of Mr. M'Culloch, to which your Committee particularly desire to draw the attention of the House:—

"'Have you turned your attention to the effect of fluctuations in the rate of wages on the price of commodities?'—'I have.'

"'Do you consider that when wages rise the price of commodities will proportionally increase?'—'I do not think that a real rise of wages has any effect whatever, or but a very imperceptible one, on the price of commodities.'

"'Then, supposing wages to be really lower in France than in this Country, do you think that that circumstance would give the French any advantage over us in the foreign market?'—'No, I do not; I do not think it would give them any advantage whatever.   I think it would occasion a different distribution of the produce of industry in France from what would obtain in England, but that would be all.   In France the labourers would get a less proportion of the produce of industry, and the capitalists a larger proportion.'

"'Could not the French manufacturer, if he gets his labour for less than the English manufacturer, afford to sell his goods for less?' 'As the value of goods is made up wholly of labour and profit, the whole and only effect of a French manufacturer getting his labour for less than an English manufacturer is to enable him to make more profit than the English manufacturer can make, but not to lower the price of his goods.   The low rate of wages in France goes to establish a high rate of profits in all branches of industry in France.'

"'What conclusion do you come to in making a comparison

between wages in England and wages in France?'—'I come to this conclusion, that, if it be true that wages are really higher in England than in France, the only effect of that would be to lower the profits of capital in England below their level in France, but that will have no effect whatever on the price of the commodities produced in either Country.'

" 'When you say that wages do not affect prices, what is it that does affect prices?'—'An increase or diminution of the quantity of labour necessary to the production of the commodity.'

" 'Supposing that there was a free export of machinery, so that France could get that machinery, do you think that under those circumstances we should retain those advantages which we possess at the present moment?'—'Yes, we should; for the export of the machinery would not lower our wages, or increase the wages in France, so that we should preserve that advantage to the full extent that we have it at this moment.'

" 'Will you explain to the Committee why you are of opinion that the French manufacturer would not undersell the English, seeing that his profits are larger than the English manufacturer?'—'Because if he were to offer to undersell the English, he can only do it by consenting to accept a less rate of profit on his capital than the other French capitalists are making on theirs, and I cannot suppose a man of common sense would act upon such a principle.'

" 'Are the Committee to understand, that although a French manufacturer pays half the wages to his men in France which our manufacturers do in England, yet that his wages being on a par, or a level, in general, with the other wages in France, will render his profits on a par with them, and consequently he would not undersell the English merchant by lowering his profits below the average rate of profits in France?'—'Precisely so. I believe, in point of fact, there is no such difference; but he could not undersell the English manufacturer unless he took lower profits than all other producers in France were making. I might illustrate this by what takes place every day in England, where you never find the proprietor of rich land, in order to get rid of his produce, offering it in Mark Lane at a lower rate than that which is got by a farmer or proprietor of the very worst land in the Kingdom.'

" 'Would it not produce a larger sale if the French manufacturer were to sell at a less price?'—'Supposing that to be so, the greater the sale the greater would be the loss of profit.' " [25]

We have extracted this passage as indicating the views of the Committee, not those of Mr. M'Culloch. Mr. M'Culloch, as will appear on turning to his evidence, meant by wages *really high* and *really low*, not a larger or a smaller amount, but a larger or a smaller

[25] Report from Select Committee on Export of Tools and Machinery. Session of 1825, pp. 13, 14.

proportion.   But the Commitee appear to have understood him to mean a larger or a smaller amount.

Mr. Bradbury had previously stated the common day wages in France to be about half the wages paid in England.

He was asked, " In what way do you consider that lower wages in France give the French manufacturers an advantage over English manufacturers?"—" I conceive that if they pay 3*d*. a pound for spinning to the operative spinner, and we pay 6*d*., that would give them an advantage of 3*d*. a pound in the cost."

" You mean to say that the French would be able to sell the article they make, in consequence of paying lower wages, cheaper than the English could sell it ? " — " They could afford it 3*d*. a pound cheaper."

" You mean to say that, according to the rate of wages paid, the price of the article for which they are paid is high or low?"—" It may be afforded higher or lower, I should imagine, as the cost be more or less."

" Therefore the whole reason and ground on which you think that low wages give them an advantage is, that low wages contribute to enable them to sell the article cheaper than if they paid higher wages?"—" Yes, labour constituting a material feature in the cost."

" You conceive that increased cost would be a loss to the party, if the price was not increased in proportion?"—" I should imagine so."

" *Might not the profits of the proprietor be lessened ? "—" They might be lessened, which is in effect a loss."*

" *Might not that enable him to bear the loss which the difference of wages produces ? "* [26]—" *If he chose to make that sacrifice."*

" Might not the profits be lessened until there were no profits at all ?" [27]—" Very easily, I should think."—(Fifth Report of the Select Committee on Artisans and Machinery, pp. 547, 549, 550.)

It was with reference to this evidence that Mr. M'Culloch was examined.   His examination commences thus:—

" Have you read the evidence which has been given before this Committee?"—" I have read portions of it only."

" Have you read the evidence given by Mr. Bradbury?"—" A part of it."

" That part in which he conceives that foreigners have an advantage

[26] In other words, " Might not the loss enable him to bear the loss ?"

[27] This question appears to have come from a different interrogator. In justice to the clear and intelligent evidence of Mr. Bradbury, we should observe that he was far from falling into the common error, that a generally high rate of wages can be unfavourable to a Country. He set out by supposing that, with the assistance of English machinery and English superintendents, the labour of the French spinners might be as productive as that of the English spinners. Under such circumstances, if their wages could remain at one-half of English wages, he believed that the French manufacturer could undersell the English manufacturer. Of the accuracy of this opinion under the possible, though highly improbable hypothesis in question, we entertain no doubt, though, from the tenour of the questions, it appears not to have met with the approbation of the Committee.

over the English manufacturers in consequence of wages being lower in France?"—"Yes, I have read that."

And then follows the question:—

"Have you turned your attention to the effect of fluctuations in the rate of wages on the price of commodities?"

Now if the Committee understood Mr. M'Culloch to mean, by high or low wages, not a great or small amount, but a great or small proportion, his evidence and that of Mr. Bradbury had nothing in common.

The whole of the confusion has been occasioned by the verbal ambiguity which we have pointed out, and would not have arisen if Mr. Ricardo had used any other adjectives than *high* and *low* to express a larger or smaller proportion.

The two other meanings of the words high and low wages, that which refers to the money, and that which refers to the commodities, received by the labourer, are both equally convenient, if we consider the rate of wages *at the same time and place;* for then they both mean the same thing. At the same time and place the labourer who receives the highest wages necessarily obtains the most commodities. But when we refer to different places, or different times, the words high or low wages direct the attention to very different subjects, as we understand them to mean more or less in money, or more or less in commodities. The differences which have taken place in the amount of money wages at different times inform us of scarcely any thing but the abundance or scarcity of the precious metals at those times: facts which are seldom of much importance. The differences in the amount of money wages in different places at the same time are of much more importance, since they indicate the different values of the labour of different Countries in the general market of the world. But even these differences afford no premises from which the positive condition of the labouring classes, in any Country, can be inferred, and but imperfect grounds for estimating their relative condition. The only data which enable us to ascertain the actual situation of the labourers at any given time and place, or their comparative situation at different times and places, are the quantity and quality of the commodities which form their wages, if paid in kind, or are purchasable with their wages, if paid in money. And as the actual or comparative situation of the labourer is the principal object of the following inquiry, we shall use the word wages to express, not the money, but the commodities, which the labourer receives; and we shall consider wages to rise as the quantity or quality of those commodities is increased or improved, and to fall as that quantity or quality is diminished or deteriorated.

It is obvious, too, that the labourer's situation does not depend on the amount which he receives at any one time, but on his average receipts during a given period—during a week, a month, or a year; and that the longer the period taken, the more accurate will be the estimate. Weekly wages have, of course, more tendency to equality than daily ones, and annual than monthly; and, if we could ascertain the amount earned by a man during five, or ten, or twenty years, we should know his situation better than if we confined our attention to a single year.   There is, however, so much difficulty in ascertaining the amount of wages during very long periods, that a single year will probably be the best that we can take. It comprehends what, in most climates, are very different—summer and winter wages; it comprehends also the period during which the most important vegetable productions come to maturity in temperate climates, and on that account has generally been adopted by Political Economists as the average period for which capital is supposed to be advanced.

We should observe that we include, as part of the wages of the married labourer, those of his wife and unemancipated children. To omit them would lead to inaccurate estimates of the comparative situation of the labourers in different Countries, or in different occupations.   In those employments which are carried on under shelter, and with the assistance of that machinery which affords power, and requires human aid only for its direction, the industry of a woman, or a child, approaches in efficiency that of a full-grown man.   A girl of fourteen can manage a power-loom nearly as well as her father; but where strength, or exposure to the seasons, is required, little can be done by the wife, or the girls, or even by the boys, until they approach the age at which they usually quit their father's house.   The earnings of the wife and children of many a Manchester weaver or spinner exceed, or equal, those of himself.   Those of the wife and children of an agricultural labourer, or of a carpenter, or a coalheaver, are generally unimportant—while the husbands, in each case, receives 15s. a-week, the weekly income of the one family may be 40s., and that of the other only 17s. or 18s.

It must be admitted, however, that the workman does not retain the whole of this apparent pecuniary advantage.   The wife is taken from her household labours, and a part of the increased wages is employed in purchasing what might, otherwise, be produced at home.   The evils to the children are still greater.   The infants suffer from the want of maternal attention, and those who are older from fatigue and confinement, from the want of childish relaxation and amusement, and, what is far more important, from the deficiency of religious, moral, and intellectual education.   The establishment of infant and Sunday schools, and laws regulating the number of hours during which children may labour, are palliatives of these evils, but they must exist, to a certain degree, whenever the labour of the wife and children is the subject of sale; and though not, all of them, perhaps, strictly within the province of Political Economy, must never be omitted in any estimate of the causes affecting the welfare of the labouring classes.

Difference between the Amount of Wages and the Price of Labour.— The last preliminary point to which we have to call the reader's attention is, the difference between the *Amount of Wages* and the *Price of Labour*, or, in other words, between the earnings of a labourer during a given time, and the price paid for the performance of a given quantity of work.

If men were the only labourers, and if every man worked equally hard, and for the same number of hours, during the year, these two expressions would be synonymous. If each man, for instance, worked three hundred days during each year, and ten hours during each day, one three-thousandth part of each man's yearly wages would be the price of an hour's labour. But neither of these propositions is true. The yearly wages of a family often include, as we have seen, the results of the labour of the wife and children. And few things are less uniform than the number of working days during the year, or of working hours during the day, or the degree of exertion undergone during those hours.

The established annual holidays in Protestant countries are between fifty and sixty. In many Catholic Countries they exceed one hundred. Among the Hindoos they are said to occupy nearly half the year. But these holidays are confined to a certain portion of the population; the labour of a sailor, or a soldier, or a menial servant, admits of scarcely any distinction of days.

Again, in Northern and Southern latitudes, the hours of out-door labour are limited by the duration of light; and in all climates by the weather. When the labourer works under shelter, the daily hours of labour may be uniform throughout the year. And, independently of natural causes, the daily hours of labour vary in different Countries, and in different employments in the same Country. The daily hours of labour are, perhaps, longer in France than in England, and certainly are longer in England than in Hindostan. In Manchester the manufacturer generally works twelve hours a-day; in Birmingham, ten: a London shopman is seldom employed more than eight or nine.

There is still more discrepancy between the exertions made by different labourers in a given period. They are often, indeed, unsusceptible of comparison. There is no common measure of the toils undergone by a miner and a tailor, or of those of a shopman and an iron-founder. And labour which is the same in kind may vary indefinitely both in intensity and in productiveness. Many of the witnesses examined by the Committee on Artisans and Machinery (Session of 1824,) were English manufacturers, who had worked in France. They agree as to the comparative indolence and inefficiency of the French labourer, even during his hours of employment. One of the witnesses, Adam Young, had been two years in one of the best manufactories in Alsace. He is asked, "Did you find the spinners there as industrious as the spinners in England?" and replies, "No; a spinner in England will do twice as much as a Frenchman.   They get up at four in the morning, and work till ten at night; but our spinners will do as much in six hours as they will in ten.''

" Had you any Frenchmen employed under you?"—" Yes; eight at two francs a day.''

" What had you a day?"—"Twelve francs.''

"Supposing you had had eight English carders under you, how much more work could you have done?"—" With one Englishman I could have done more than I did with those eight Frenchmen.   It cannot be called work they do: it is only looking at it, and wishing it done.''

" Do the French make their yarn at a greater expense."—" Yes; though they have their hands for much less wages than in England.'' —Pp. 580, 582.

The following evidence of Edwin Rose, given on the Factory Inquiry of 1833, relates to a rather later period, and is valuable from the extensive experience of the witness.

" Are wages lower in France, as far as you have seen, than in England?"—" If I have a shop of men in England for any thing, then I have to see how much I have to pay them for the work they turn out of any kind; but if I have the same shop in France, then I must have twice the number of hands to do the same amount of work. It is true I pay them less apiece there; but I have seen that you must have twice as large a building to contain the hands, twice as many clerks and book-keepers, and overlookers to look after them, and twice as many tools to do the same quantity of work as is done here in England; and the master there must have twice as much interest of money on all this; and their minds seem to me to get more bewildered with stress of work there than here.   It seems to me that you have double the number of people there to do the same amount of work, whatever it be; but their wages are lower in money.''

" But do you consider their wages higher in reality?"—" I really do; they are better paid in proportion to the work they turn out than what the English are.''

" What do you think of French workmen, as workmen?"—" I don't think they have that perseverance that English have.   I often have noticed them trying a thing, and then, if it don't answer at first, they seem terrified, and shrug up their shoulders, and throw it aside; but an English workman keeps trying and trying, and won't give up near so soon as the Frenchman.   A house-joiner or carpenter's wages are from thirty-five to forty sous a day.   His work compared with English work is very rough, and but little of it in comparison.   A stonemason's wages are from three francs to four francs.   They are inferior to our masons in laying foundations.   Then, as to time of work, I think two English masons in the same time do more work on an average than three of theirs.''

"In short, do you know any single species of labour that stands a master cheaper in France than in England, quality and quantity of work being considered?"—"I don't know any, unless it be tailors and shoemakers' wages; and I am not sure about them.   Clothes are dearer in France than in England; but shoes are cheaper, the duty being off leather."—*First Report of the Factory Commission*, D. i. p. 121.

Even in the same Country, and in the same employments, similar inequalities are constantly observed.   Every one is aware that much more exertion is undergone by the labourer by task-work than by the day-labourer; by the independent day-labourer than by the pauper; and even by the pauper than by the convict.

It is obvious that the rate of wages is less likely to be uniform than the price of labour, as the amount of wages will be affected, in the first place, by any variations in the price, and in the second place, by any variations in the amount, of the labour exerted.

In England, the average annual wages of labour are three times as high as they are in Ireland; but as the labourer in Ireland is said not to do more than one-third of what is done by the labourer in England, the price of labour may, in both Countries, be about equal. In England, the labourer by task-work earns much more than the day-labourer; but, as it is certainly as profitable to employ him, the price of his labour cannot be higher.   It may be supposed, indeed, that the price of labour is every where, and at all times, the same; and, if there were no disturbing causes,—if all persons knew perfectly well their own interest, and strictly followed it, and there were no difficulties in moving capital and labour from place to place, and from employment to employment,—the price of labour, at the same time, would be every where the same.   But these difficulties occasion the price of labour to vary materially, even at the same time and place; and variations both in the amount of wages and in the price of labour, at different times and in different places, are occasioned not only by these causes, but by others which will be considered in a subsequent part of this Treatise.

These variations affect very differently the labourer and his employer.   The employer is interested in keeping down the price of labour; but while that price remains the same, while at a given expense he gets a given amount of work done, his situation remains unaltered   If a farmer can get a field trenched for £12, it is indifferent to him whether he pays the whole of that sum to three capital workmen, or to four ordinary ones.   The three would receive higher wages than the four, but, as they would do proportionably more work, their labour would come just as cheap.   If the three could be hired at £3 10s apiece, while the four required £3 apiece, though the wages of the three would be higher, the price of the work done by them would be lower.

It is true that the causes which raise the amount of the labourer's wages often raise the rate of the capitalist's profits. If, by increased industry, one man performs the work of two, both the amount of wages and the rate of profits will generally be raised. But the rate of profit will be raised, not by the rise of wages, but in consequence of the additional supply of labour having diminished its price, or having diminished the period for which it had previously been necessary to 'advance that price, or having rendered, as in the instances mentiond by Edwin Rose, the labour previously employed more productive.

The labourer, on the other hand, is principally interested in the amount of wages. The amount of his wages being fixed, it is certainly his interest that the price of his labour should be high, for on that depends the degree of exertion imposed on him. But, if the amount of his wages be low, he must be comparatively poor—if that amount be high he must be comparatively rich—whatever be his remuneration for each specific act of exertion. In the one case he will have leisure and want; in the other toil and abundance. We are far from thinking that the evils of severe and incessant labour, or the benefits of a certain degree of leisure, ought to be left out in any estimate of happiness. But, as we observed in the beginning of this Treatise, it is not with happiness, but with wealth, that we are concerned as Political Economists; we profess to state facts for the information and instruction of the student, not to lay down rules to guide the conduct of the legislator. In explaining the general laws according to which wealth is produced and distributed, we do not assume that all the means by which it can be augmented ought to be encouraged, or even to be permitted. We do not assume even that wealth is a benefit. In fact, however, wealth and happiness are very seldom opposed. Nature, when she imposed on man the necessity of labour, tempered his repugnance to it by making long-continued inactivity painful, and by strongly associating with exertion the idea of its reward. The poor and half-employed Irish labourer, or the still poorer and less industrious savage, is as inferior in happiness as he is in income to the hard-worked English artisan. The Englishman's industry may sometimes be excessive; his desire to better his condition may sometimes drive him on toils productive of disease ill recompensed by the increase of his wages; but that such is not generally the case may be proved by comparing the present duration of life in England with its former duration, or with its duration in other Countries. It is generally admitted that, during the last fifty years, a marked increase has taken place in the industry of our population, and that they are now the hardest-working labourers in the world. But during the whole of that period the average duration of their lives has been constantly increasing, and appears still to increase; and, notwithstanding the apparent unhealthiness of many of their occupations, notwithstanding the atmosphere of smoke and steam, and, what appears to be still more injurious, of dust, in which many of them labour for sixty-nine hours a week, they enjoy, as a community, longer life than the lightly-toiled inhabitants of the most favoured soils and climates.

The average annual mortality in England and Wales is computed by Mr. Rickman at one in forty-nine. In the extensive inquiry instituted by the Poor-Law Commissioners in 1834 into the state of the labouring classes in America and the Continent of Europe, the only Countries in which the mortality appeared to be so small as in England, were Norway, in which it appeared to be one in fifty-four, and the Basses Pyrenees, in which it appeared to be one in fifty. In all the other Countries which gave returns it exceeded the English proportion sometimes by doubling it, and in the majority of instances by more than one-fourth.[28]

Having marked the distinction which really exists between the price of labour and the amount of wages, we shall for the future consider every labouring family as consisting of the same number of persons, and exerting the same degree of industry. On that supposition, the distinction between the price of labour and the amount of wages will be at an end; or rather, the only distinction will be, that the former expression designates the remuneration for each specific exertion; the latter, the aggregate of all those separate remunerations, as summed up at the end of each year. And the question to be answered will be, what are the causes which decide what in any given Country, and at any given period, shall be the quantity and quality of the commodities obtained by a labouring family during a year.

PROXIMATE CAUSE DECIDING THE RATE OF WAGES.

The proximate cause appears to be clear. The quantity and quality of the commodities obtained by each labouring family during a year must depend on the quantity and quality of the commodities directly or indirectly appropriated during the year to the use of the labouring population, compared with the number of labouring families, (including under that term all those who depend on their own labour for subsistence ;) or, to speak more concisely, *on the Extent of the Fund for the maintenance of Labourers, compared with the Number of Labourers to be maintained.*

Discussion of Seven Opinions inconsistent with this Proposition.— This proposition is so nearly self-evident, that if Political Economy were a new Science we should assume it without further remark. But we must warn our readers that this proposition is inconsistent with opinions which are entitled to consideration, some from the number, and others from the authority, of those who maintain them.

[28] Senior, *Preface to Foreign Communications*, p. 238.

First. It is inconsistent with *the doctrine, that the Rate of Wages depends solely on the proportion which the number of Labourers bears to the amount of Capital in a Country.* The word capital has been used in so many senses that it is difficult to state this doctrine precisely ; but we know of no definition of that term which will not include many things that are not used by the labouring classes ; and, if our proposition be correct, no increase or diminution of *these* things can *directly* affect wages. If half the plate glass in the Country were to be destroyed to-morrow the capital of the Country would be diminished ; but the only sufferers would be those who possess or wish to possess plate glass ; among whom the labouring classes are not included. But if half the existing stock of coarse tobacco were destroyed, the immediate consequence would be a fall of wages ; not as estimated in money, but as estimated in the commodities consumed by the labourer. Though receiving the same money wages, the labourer would have less tobacco, or, if he chose to continue undiminished his consumption of tobacco, then less of other things, than he had before. So if a foreign merchant were to come to settle in this Country, and bring with him a cargo of raw and manufactured silk, lace, and diamonds, that cargo would increase the capital of the Country ; silk, lace, and diamonds would become more abundant, and the enjoyments of those who use them would be increased : the enjoyments of the labourers, supposing them not to be consumers of silk, lace, or diamonds, would not be directly increased : indirectly and consequentially, they might be increased. The silk might be re-exported in a manufactured state, and commodities for the use of labourers imported in return ; and then, and not till then, wages would rise ; but that rise would be occasioned, not by the first addition to the capital of the Country, which was made in the form of silk, but by the substituted addition made in the form of commodities used by the labourer.

Secondly. It is inconsistent with *the doctrine, that Wages depend on the proportion borne by the number of Labourers to the whole revenue of the society of which they are members.* In the example last suggested, of the introduction of a new supply of lace or diamonds, the *revenues* of those who use lace or diamonds would be increased ; but as wages are not spent on those articles, *they* would remain unaltered. It is possible, indeed, to state cases in which the revenue of a large portion of a community might be increased, and yet the wages of the labourers might fall without an increase of their numbers. We will suppose the principal trade of Ireland to be the raising of produce for the English market ; and that for every two hundred acres ten families were employed in raising, on half the land, their own subsistence, and on the remainder corn and other exportable crops requiring equal labour. Under such circumstances, if a demand should arise in the English market for cattle, butchers'-meat, and wool, instead of corn, it would be the interest of the Irish landlords and farmers to convert their estates from arable into pasture. Instead of ten families for every two hundred acres, two might be sufficient: one to raise the subsistence of the two, and the other to tend the cattle and sheep. The revenue of the landlords and the farmers would be increased : and, if they employed the whole of that increase in the purchase of Irish labour, all parties would be benefited. But if they devoted the greater part of it to the purchase of English manufactures, the services of a large portion of the Irish labourers would cease to be required ; a large portion of the land formerly employed in producing commodities for their use would be devoted to the production of commodities for the use of England ; and the fund for the maintenance of Irish labour would fall, notwithstanding the increase of the revenue of the landlords and farmers.

Absenteeism.—Thirdly. It is inconsistent with *the prevalent opinion that the non-residence of landlords, funded proprietors, mortgagees, and other unproductive consumers, can be detrimental to the labouring inhabitants of a Country which does not export raw produce.*

In a Country *which exports raw produce,* wages *may* be lowered by such non-residence. If an Irish landlord resides on his estate, he requires the services of certain persons, who must also be resident there, to minister to his daily wants. He must have servants, gardeners, and perhaps gamekeepers. If he build a house, he must employ resident masons and carpenters ; part of his furniture he may import, but the greater part of it must be made in his neighbourhood ; a portion of his land, or, what comes to the same thing, a portion of his rent, must be employed in producing food, clothing, and shelter for all these persons, and for those who produce that food, clothing, and shelter. If he were to remove to England, all these wants would be supplied by Englishmen. The land and capital which was formerly employed in providing the maintenance of Irish labourers would be employed in producing corn and cattle to be exported to England to provide the subsistence of English labourers. The whole quantity of commodities appropriated to the use of Irish labourers would be diminished, and that appropriated to the use of English labourers increased, and wages would, consequently, rise in England, and fall in Ireland.

It is true that these effects would not be co-extensive with the landlord's income. While, in Ireland, he must have consumed many foreign commodities, he must have purchased tea, wine, and sugar, and other things which the climate and the manufactures of Ireland do not afford, and he must have paid for them by sending corn and cattle to England. It is true, also, that while in Ireland he probably employed a portion of his land and of his rents for other purposes, from which the labouring population received no benefit, as a deer park, or a pleasure garden, or in the maintenance of horses or hounds. On his removal, that portion of his land which was a park would be employed, partly in producing exportable commodities, and partly in producing subsistence for its cultivators; and that portion which fed horses for his use might be employed in feeding horses for exportation. The first of these alterations would do good; the second could do no harm. Nor must we forget that, through the cheapness of conveyance between England and Ireland, a portion, or perhaps all, of those whom he employed in Ireland might follow him to England, and, in that case, wages in neither Country would be affected. The fund for the maintenance of labourers in Ireland, and the number of labourers to be maintained, would both be equally diminished, and the fund for the maintenance of labourers in England, and the number of labourers to be maintained, would both be equally increased.

But after making all these deductions, and they are very great, from the supposed effect of the absenteeism of the Irish proprietors on the labouring classes in Ireland, we cannot agree with Mr. M'Culloch that it is immaterial. We cannot but join in the general opinion that their return, though it would not affect the prosperity of the British Empire, considered as a whole, would be immediately beneficial to Ireland, though perhaps too much importance is attached to it.

In Mr. M'Culloch's celebrated examination before the Committee on the state of Ireland, (4th Report, 814, Sess. 1825,) he was asked, "Supposing the largest export of Ireland were in live cattle, and that a considerable portion of rent had been remitted in that manner, does not such a mode of producing the means of paying rent contribute less to the improvement of the poor than any extensive employment of them in labour would produce?—He replies, "Unless the means of paying rent are changed when the landlord goes home, his residence can have no effect whatever."

"Would not," he is asked, "the population of the country be benefited by the expenditure among them of a certain portion of the rent which (if he had been absent) has (would have) been remitted (to England)?" "No," he replies, "I do not see how it could be benefited in the least. If you have a certain value laid out against Irish commodities in the one case, you will have a certain value laid out against them in the other. The cattle are either exported to England, or they stay at home. If they are exported, the landlord will obtain an equivalent for them in English commodities; if they are not, he will obtain an equivalent for them in Irish commodities; so that in both cases the landlord lives on the cattle, or on the value of the cattle: and whether he lives in Ireland or in England, there is obviously just the very same amount of commodities for the people of Ireland to subsist upon."

This reasoning assumes that the landlord, while resident in Ireland, himself personally devours all the cattle produced on his estates; for on no other supposition can there be the very same amount of commodities for the people of Ireland to subsist upon, whether their cattle are retained in Ireland or exported.

But when a Country does *not* export raw produce, the consequences of absenteeism are very different. Those who derive their incomes from such a Country cannot possibly spend them abroad until they have previously spent them at home.

When a Leicestershire landlord is resident on his estate, he employs a certain portion of his land, or, what is the same, of his rent, in maintaining the persons who provide for him those commodities and services, which must be produced on the spot where they are consumed. If he should remove to London, he would want the services of Londoners, and the produce of land and capital which previously maintained labourers resident in Leicester would be sent away to maintain labourers resident in London. The labourers would probably follow, and wages in Leicestershire and London would *then* be unaltered; but until they did so, wages would rise in the one district and fall in the other. At the same time, as the rise and fall would compensate one another, as the fund for the maintenance of labour, and the number of labourers to be maintained, would each remain the same, the same amount of wages would be distributed among the same number of persons, though not precisely in the same proportion as before.

If he were now to remove to Paris, a new distribution must take place. As the price of raw produce is lower in France than in England, and the difference in habits and language between the two Countries prevents the transfer of labourers from the one to the other, neither the labourers nor the produce of his estates could follow him. He must employ French labourers, and he must convert his share of the produce of his estate, or, what is the same thing, his rent, into some exportable form in order to receive it abroad. It may be supposed that he would receive his rent in money. Even if he were to do so, the English labourers would not be injured, for as they do not eat or drink money, provided the same amount of commodities remained for their use, they would be unaffected by the export of money. But it is impossible that he could receive his rent in money unless he chose to suffer a gratuitous loss. The rate of exchange between London and Paris is generally rather in favour of London, and scarcely ever so deviates from par between any two Countries, as to cover the expense of transferring the precious metals from the one to the other, excepting between the Countries which do, and those which do not, possess mines. The remittances from England to France must be sent, therefore, in the form of manufactures, either directly to France, or to some Country with which France has commercial relations. And how would these manufactures be obtained? Of course in exchange for the landlord's rent. His share of the produce of his estates would now go to Birmingham or Sheffield, or Manchester or London, to maintain the labourers employed in producing manufactures, to be sent and sold abroad for his profit. An English absentee employs his income precisely as if he were to remain at home and consume nothing but hardware and cottons. Instead of the services of gardeners and servants, upholsterers and tailors, he purchases those of spinners, and weavers, and cutlers. In either case his income is employed in maintaining labourers, though the class of labourers is different; and in either case, the whole fund for the maintenance of labourers, and the number of labourers to be maintained, remaining unaltered, the wages of labour cannot be affected.

But, in fact, that fund would be rather increased in quantity and rather improved in quality. It would be increased, because land previously employed as a park, or in feeding dogs and horses, or hares and pheasants, would now be employed in producing food or clothing for men. It would be improved, because the increased production of manufactured commodities would occasion an increased division of labour, the use of more and better machinery, and the other improvements which we have ascertained to be its necessary accompaniments.

One disadvantage, and one only, it appears to us would be the result. The absentee in a great measure escapes domestic taxation. We say *in a great measure*, because he still remains liable, if a proprietor of houses or of land, to those taxes which fall upon rent: he pays too, a part of the taxes on the materials of manufactures; and if it were our policy to tax income or exported commodities, he might be forced to pay to the public revenue even more than his former proportion. But, under our present system, which throws the bulk of taxation on commodities produced for internal consumption, he receives the greater part of his revenue without deduction, and, instead of contributing to the support of the British Government, contributes to support that of France or Italy. This inconvenience, perhaps, about balances the advantages which we have just mentioned, and leaves a community which exports only manufactures neither impoverished nor enriched by the residence abroad of its unproductive members.

We ought, perhaps, on this occasion again to remind our readers that it is to wealth and poverty that our attention, when writing on Political Economy, is confined. The *moral* effects of absenteeism must never be neglected by a writer who inquires into the causes which promote the *happiness* of nations, but are without the province of a Political Economist. Nor do we regret that they are so, for they form a subject on which it is far more difficult to obtain satisfactory results. In one respect, indeed, the moral question is the more simple, as it is not complicated by the consideration whether raw produce or manufactures are exported, or whether the non-resident landlord is abroad, or in some town within his own Country. If his presence is to be morally beneficial, it must be his presence on his own estate. To the inhabitants of that estate the place to which he absents himself is indifferent. Adam Smith believed his residence to

be morally injurious. " The residence of a Court," he observes,
(Book ii. Ch. iii.) " in general makes the inferior sort of people
dissolute and poor. The inhabitants of a large village, after having
made considerable progress in manufactures, have become idle in
consequence of a great Lord having taken up his residence in their
neighbourhood." And Mr. M'Culloch, whose fidelity and intelligence
as an observer may be relied on, states, as the result of his own
experience, that in Scotland the estates of absentees are almost
always the best managed. Much, of course, depends on individual
character ; but we are inclined to believe that, in general, the presence
of men of large fortune is morally detrimental, and that of men of
moderate fortune morally beneficial, to their immediate neighbourhood.
The habits of expense and indulgence which, in different gradations,
prevail among all the members of a great establishment, are mischievous as examples, and perhaps still more so as sources of repining
and discontent. The drawing-room and stable do harm to the neighbouring gentry, and the housekeeper's room and servants' hall to
their inferiors. But families of moderate income, including under
that term incomes between £500 and £2000 a year, appear to be
placed in the station most favourable to the acquisition of moral and
intellectual excellence, and to its diffusion among their associates and
dependents. We have no doubt that a well-regulated gentleman's
family, removing the prejudices, soothing the quarrels, directing and
stimulating the exertions, and awarding praise or blame to the conduct
of the villagers round them, is among the most efficient means by
which the character of a neighbourhood can be improved. It is the
happiness of this Country that almost every parish has a resident
fitted by fortune and education for these services ; and bound, not
merely by feelings of propriety, but as a matter of express and professional duty, to their performance. The dispersion throughout the
Country of so many thousand clerical families, each acting in its own
district as a small centre of civilization, is an advantage to which,
perhaps, we have been too long accustomed to be able to appreciate
its extent.

Still, however, we think that even the moral effects of absenteeism
have been exaggerated. Those who declaim against the twelve
thousand English families supposed to be resident abroad, seem to
forget that not one-half, probably not one-quarter, of them, if they
were to return, would dwell any where but in towns, where their
influence would be wasted, or probably not even exerted. What does
it signify to the Northumbrian or Devonshire peasant whether his
landlord lives in London, or Cheltenham, or Rome ? And even of
those who would reside in the country, how many would exercise that
influence beneficially? How many would be fox-hunters or game-
preservers, or surround themselves with dependents whose example
would more than compensate for the virtues of their masters ?

Nothing can be more rash than to predict that *good* would be the result of causes which are quite as capable of producing evil.

The economical effects have been still more generally misunderstood; and we have often been tempted to wonder that doctrines so clear as those which we have just been submitting to our readers should be admitted with reluctance even by those who feel the proofs to be unanswerable, and should be rejected at once by others, as involving a paradox too monstrous to be worth examination.

Much of this, probably, arises from a confusion of the economical with the moral part of the question. Many writers and readers of Political Economy forget that the clearest proof that absenteeism diminishes the virtue or the happiness of the remaining members of a community is no answer to arguments which aim only at proving that it does not diminish their wealth.

Another and perhaps the chief source of error is the circumstance that, when the landlord is present, the gain is concentrated, and the loss diffused, when he is absent the gain is diffused, and the loss concentrated. When he quits his estate, we can put our finger on the village tradesman and labourer who lose his custom and employment. We cannot trace the increase of custom and employment that is consequently scattered among millions of manufacturers. When he returns, we see that the expenditure of £2000 or £3000 a year in a small circle gives wealth and spirit to its inhabitants. We do dot see, however clearly we may infer it, that so much the less is expended in Manchester, Birmingham, or Leeds. The inhabitants of his village attribute their gain and their loss to its causes; and their complaints and acknowledgments are loud in proportion to the degree in which they feel their interests to be affected. No single manufacturer is conscious that the average annual export of more than forty millions sterling has been increased or diminished to the amount of £2000 or £3000. And even if aware of that increase or diminution, he would not attribute it to the residence in Yorkshire or Paris of a given individual, of whose existence he probably is not aware. When to obvious and palpable effects nothing is to be opposed but inferences deduced by a long, though perfectly demonstrative, reasoning process, no one can doubt which will prevail, both with the uneducated, and the educated, vulgar.

Many persons, also, are perplexed by the consideration, that all the commodities which are exported as remittances of the absentee's income are exports for which no return is obtained; that they are as much lost to this Country as if they were a tribute paid to a foreign State, or even as if they were thrown periodically into the sea. This is unquestionably true; but it must be recollected, that whatever is unproductively consumed is, by the very terms of the proposition, destroyed, without producing any return. The only difference between the two cases is, that the resident landlord performs that destruction here; the absentee performs it abroad. In either case, he first purchases the services of those who produce the things which he, for his benefit, not for theirs, is to consume. If he stays here, he pays a man to brush a coat, or clean a pair of boots, or arrange a table; all which in an hour after are in their former condition. When abroad, he pays an equal sum for the production of needles, or calicoes, which are sent abroad, and equally consumed without further benefit to those who produced them. They are, in fact, sold for money to be employed in paying the wages of those foreign servants who now brush the shoes and draw the corks, which, if the landlord had not been an absentee, would have been brushed and drawn in England. The income of unproductive consumers, however paid, is a tribute; and whether they enjoy it here or elsewhere, is their own concern. We know that a man cannot eat his cake and have it; and it is equally true that he cannot sell a cake to another and keep it for himself.

Again, some acute reasoners appear to us to have been led into error on this subject, by perceiving that the income of an absentee is generally remitted to him by means of a trade in which the returns are comparatively slow,[29] and that the expenditure of his income is profitable to those among whom he resides.[30] Now assuming that these circumstances occasion a loss to any body, it is clear that the loss falls solely on the absentee. His rents are, in the first instance, expended as quickly as they are received in the purchase of manufactured commodities, to be exported for his benefit as a means of remittance. They are expended, therefore, in the support of the trade of the English manufacturer, a trade giving quick returns, high wages, and, if we may judge from the additional capital which it is attracting every day, high profits. The absentee, in thus spending his income, gives to England all that an unproductive consumer *can* give, the wages and the profits arising from the expenditure in England of his income as fast as he receives it. Neither the gain nor the loss attending on the remittance or on the subsequent expenditure of its amount are any concern of ours. They effect only the absentee. If he selects ill the place of his residence, he may have to lose by remittances at long dates, or at an unfavourable exchange, or have to pay dearly for bad commodities or unskilful services. If he selects it well, he may be a gainer by the intermediate operations to which his income has been subjected, and receive a larger revenue than he would have obtained at home, or may spend that revenue more agreeably. But with all this England has nothing to do.

The last cause to which we attribute the slow progress of correct

[29] Professor Longfield, *Lectures on Commerce and Absenteeism*, p. 6.

[30] Carey *on Wages*, p. 46. A Work which we regret not to have received until part of this Treatise had been stereotyped, and the remainder was in print.

opinions on this subject is their distastefulness to the most influential members of the community. Nothing can be more flattering to landlords, annuitants, mortgagees, and fundholders, than to be told that their residence is of vital importance to the Country. Nothing can be more humiliating than to be assured that it is utterly immaterial to the rest of the community whether they live in Brighton, or London, or Paris. Those who are aware how much our judgment, even in matters .of Science, is influenced by our wishes, will not be surprised at the prejudices against a doctrine which forbids the bulk of the educated class to believe that they are benefactors to their Country by the mere act of residing within its shores.

We may appear, perhaps, to have dwelt too much on a single subject; but no prevalent error can be effectually exposed until its prevalence has been accounted for. And these are errors which are to be heard in every society, and often from those whose general views in Political Economy are correct. They may be called harmless errors, but no error is, in fact, harmless; and when there is so much in our habits that really requires alteration, we may lose sight of the real and the remediable causes of evil, while our attention is misdirected to absenteeism.

Machinery.—Fourthly. Our proposition that the Rate of Wages depends on the extent of the fund for the maintenance of labourers, compared with the number of labourers to be maintained, is inconsistent with the *doctrine that the general rate of wages can except in two cases, be diminished by the introduction of Machinery.*

The two cases in which the introduction of Machinery can produce such an effect are, first, when labour is employed in the *construction* of machinery, which labour would otherwise have been employed in the production of commodities for the use of labourers; and, secondly, when the machine itself consumes commodities which would otherwise have been consumed by labourers, and *that* to a greater extent than it produces them.

The first case is put by Mr. Ricardo, in his chapter on machinery; but in so detailed a form, that, instead of quoting it, we will extract its substance, with a slight variation of the terms. He supposes a capitalist to carry on the business of a manufacturer of commodities for the use of labourers; or, to use a more concise expression, the business of a manufacturer of wages. He supposes him to have been in the habit of commencing every year with a capital consisting of wages for a certain number of labourers, which we call twenty-six, and of employing that capital in hiring twenty men, to reproduce, during the year, wages for the whole twenty-six, and six to produce commodities for himself. He now supposes him to employ ten of his men during a year in producing, not wages, but a machine, which, with the aid of seven men to keep it in repair and work it, will produce every year wages for thirteen men; that is, wages for six men besides the seven that work it. At the end of the year the capitalist's situation would be unaltered: he would have wages for thirteen men, the produce of the labour of his other ten men during the year; and his machine, also the produce of the labour of ten men during the year, and therefore of equal value. And his situation would *continue* unaltered. Every year his machine would produce wages for thirteen men, of whom seven must be employed in repairing and working it, and six might, as before, be employed for the benefit of the capitalist. But we have seen that, *during the year in which the machine was constructed*, only ten men were employed in producing wages instead of twenty, and, consequently, that wages were produced for only thirteen men instead of for twenty-six. At the end of that year, therefore, the fund for the maintenance of labour was diminished, and wages must, consequently, have fallen. It is of great importance to recollect, that the only reason for this fall was the diminution of the annual production. The twenty men produced wages for twenty-six men, the machine produces wages for only thirteen. The vulgar error on this subject supposes the evil to arise, not from its true cause, the expense of constructing the machine, but from the productive powers of that machine. So far is this from being true, that those productive powers are the specific benefit which is to be set against the evil of its expensiveness. If, instead of wages for thirteen men, the machine could produce wages for thirty, its use, as soon as it came into operation, would have increased instead of diminishing the fund for the maintenance of labour. The same effect would have been produced, if the machine could have been obtained without expense; or if the capitalist, instead of building it out of his capital, had built it out of his profits; if, instead of withdrawing ten men for a year from the production of wages, he had employed in its construction, during two years, five of the men whom he is supposed to have employed in producing commodities for his own use. In either case, the additional produce obtained from the machine would have been an additional fund for the maintenance of labour; and wages must, according to our elementary proposition, have risen.

We have thought it necessary to state this possible evil as a part of the theory of machinery, but we are far from attaching any practical importance to it. We do not believe that there exists upon record a single instance in which the whole annual produce has been diminished by the use of *inanimate* machinery. Partly in consequence of the expense of constructing the greater part of machinery being defrayed out of profits or rent, and partly in consequence of the great proportion which the productive powers of machinery bear to the expense of its construction, its use is uniformly accompanied by an enormous *increase* of production. The annual consumption of cotton wool in this Country, before the introduction of the spinning-jenny, did not exceed twelve hundred thousand pounds; it now amounts to two hundred and forty millions. The number of copies of books extant at any one period before the invention of the printing-press was probably smaller than that which is now produced in a single day. Mr. Ricardo's proposition, therefore, (*Princ.* 474,) that the use of machinery *frequently* diminishes the quantity of the gross produce of a Country, is erroneous, so far as it depends on the case which he has supposed, and of which we have stated the substance.

The other exception, that where the machine itself consumes commodities which would otherwise have been consumed by labourers, and that to a greater extent than it produces them, applies only to the case of horses and working-cattle, which may be termed animated machines. We will suppose a farmer to employ on his farm twenty men, who produce annually their own subsistence, and that of six other men producing commodities for the use of their master. If five horses, consuming we will say, as much as eight men, could do the work of ten men, it would be worth the farmer's while to substitute them for eight of his men, as he would be able to increase the number of persons who work for his own benefit from six to eight. But after deducting the subsistence of the horses, the fund for the maintenance of labourers would be reduced from wages for twenty-six men to wages for eighteen. We cannot refuse to admit that such cases may exist, or to deplore the misery that must accompany them. They are, in fact, now occurring in Ireland, and are occasioning much of the distress of that Country. They seem, indeed, to be the natural accompaniments of a certain period in the progress of national improvement. In the early stages of society, the rank and even the safety of the landed proprietor is principally determined by the number of his dependents. The best mode of increasing that number is to allow the land, which he does not occupy as his own demesne, to be subdivided into small tenements, each cultivated by one family, and just sufficient for their support. Such tenants can of course pay little rent, but they are enabled by their abundant leisure, and forced by their absolute dependence, to swell the retinue, and aid the political influence, of their landlord in peace, and to follow his banner in public and private war. Cameron of Lochiel, whose rental did not exceed £500 a year, carried with him into the rebellion of 1745 eight hundred men raised from his own tenantry. But in the progress of civilization, as wealth becomes the principal means of distinction and influence, landowners prefer rent to dependents. To obtain rent, that process of cultivation must be employed which will give, not absolutely the greatest amount of produce, but the greatest after deducting the expenses. For this purpose a tract of five hundred acres, from which fifty families produced their own subsistence, and produced scarcely any thing more, may be converted into one farm, and with the labour of ten families, and as many horses, may produce the subsistence of only thirty families. Fortunately, however, the period at which these alterations take place is generally one of great social improvement; so that, after a short interval, the increased diligence and skill with which labour is applied occasion an increase of the produce, after deducting the new expenditure. The fund for the maintenance of labourers now becomes increased from two different sources—partly from the increased efficiency of human labour when aided by that of horses and cattle, and partly from the results of a part of the human labour set free by the substitution of brutes. The ultimate consequences of such a change are always beneficial; the change itself must, in general, be accompanied by distress.

But with the exception of these two cases, one of which produces only temporary effects, and the other, though apparently possible, seems never actually to occur, it appears clear that the use of machinery must either raise the general rate of wages, or leave it unaltered.

When machinery is applied to the production of commodities which are *not* intended, directly or indirectly, for the use of labourers, it occasions no alteration in the general rate of wages; we say the *general* rate of wages, because it may diminish the rate of wages in some employments,—a diminution always compensated by a corresponding increase in some others. A small screw was shown to us at Birmingham which, in the manufacture of corkscrews, performed the work of fifty-nine men; with its assistance one man could cut a spiral groove in as many corkscrew shanks as sixty men could have cut in the same time with the tools previously in use. As the use of corkscrews is limited, it is not probable that the demand for them has sufficiently increased to enable the whole number of labourers previously employed in their manufacture to remain so employed after such an increase in their productive power. Some of the corkscrew-makers, therefore, must have been thrown out of work, and the rate of wages in that trade probably fell. But as the whole fund for the maintenance of labourers, and the whole number of labourers to be maintained, remained unaltered, that fall must have been balanced by a rise somewhere else—a rise which we may trace to its proximate cause, by recollecting that the fall in the price of corkscrews must have left every purchaser of a corkscrew a fund for the purchase of labour, rather larger than he would have possessed if he had paid the former price.

If, however, machinery be applied to the production of any commodity used by the labouring population, the general rate of wages will *rise*. That it cannot fall is clear, on the grounds which we have just stated. If the improvement be great, and the commodity not subject to a corresponding increase of demand, some of the labourers formerly employed in its production will be thrown out of employment, and wages, in that trade, will fall—a fall which, as the whole fund for the maintenance of labour is not diminished, must be met by a corresponding rise in some other trade. But the fund *will be increased* by the additional quantity produced of the commodity to which the improvement has been applied: estimated in that commodity, therefore, the general rate of wages, or, in other words, the quantity of commodities obtained by the labouring population, will be increased by the introduction of machinery; estimated in all others, it will be stationary.

The example taken from the manufacture of corkscrews is as unfavourable to the effects of machinery as can be proposed; for the use of the commodity is supposed to be unable to keep up with the increased power of production, and the whole number of labourers employed on it is, consequently, diminished. This, however, is a very rare occurrence. The usual effect of an increase in the facility of producing a commodity is so to increase its consumption as to occasion the employment of more, not less, labour than before.

We have already called the reader's attention to the effects of machinery in the manufacture of cotton and in printing. Each of these trades probably employs ten times as many labourers as it would have employed if spinning-jennies and types had not been invented. Under such circumstances, (and they are the usual ones,) the benefits of machinery are not alloyed by even partial inconvenience.

Those who are little affected by inferences from general propositions may be influenced by a witness who states the results of his own observations. We will support our argument, therefore, by the following extract from Mr. Cowell's valuable preface to the Tables of Wages constructed by him in the performance of his duties as a Commissioner on the Factory Inquiry:—

" As long as the cotton-working continues to extend, the apprehensions entertained by the operatives of a fall in wages, either for adults or children, consequent upon improvements in machinery, are groundless. Their assertion is, (and it was repeated to me innumerable times,) that they have to turn out more work now for less wages than formerly. The *Manchester and Salford Advertiser*, which is the journal of the operatives, scarcely publishes a number which does not ring the changes on this assertion; and in that for the 11th of January, 1834, it asserts, ' that a spinner now turns out double the work for a tenth less wages than in 1804.'

" The matter stands thus: in 1804 a spinner was paid 8s. 6d. for every pound of yarn of the fineness of two hundred hanks to the pound, spinning on a mule of the average productive power of that time. What that productive power was I do not know. But in 1829 he was paid at the rate of 4s. 1d. for spinning the same quality on a mule of the productive power of three hundred and twelve; in 1831, and at present, at the rate of 2s. 5d. and 2s. 8½d. for spinning the same quality on a mule of the productive power of six hundred and forty-eight. These quotations are from the Manchester prices.

" Thus, in 1829, the spinner turned off three hundred and twelve pounds of yarn in the same time that he now takes to turn off six hundred and forty eight. He was paid at the rate of 4s. 1d. per pound in 1829, he is now paid at the rate of 2s. 5d. But three hundred and twelve pounds at 4s. 1d. amount to one thousand two hundred and seventy-four shillings, and six hundred and forty-eight pounds at 2s. 5d. to one thousand five hundred and sixty-six shillings. He receives, therefore, two hundred and ninety-two shillings more than he did in 1829 for equal times of work. It is perfectly true that he does 'more work for less wages than in 1829;' but this is nothing to the purpose, when the proposition to be proved is, that 'wages are lower than formerly.' I mean to say, that a spinner earns a shilling, or a pound, or a hundred pounds, in less time at present than he would have consumed in earning a shilling, or a pound, or a hundred pounds, ten years ago, and with the same or less labour; that this enhancement of his earnings has been owing to improvements in machinery; that the progress of improvements will progressively advance his earnings still higher, and at the same time enable a greater number of individuals to profit by the enhanced rate than actually profits by the actual rate ; (provided that nothing occurs to prevent the cotton business from developing itself for the next thirty years as it has done for the last;) and that any improvement in the machinery in any one of the numerous departments of cotton-working will operate to enhance the rate of wages in all other branches, as well as in that department in which it takes place,) by increasing the actual previous demand for labour in those other branches. I assert that every improvement of cotton machinery, in any department of cotton-working, has hitherto had the effect of enabling ' an operative' (speaking in general of every one, in every department whatever) to earn a greater net amount of money, in any given time, than he would have done if the improvements had never taken place.

"The misconceptions as to the real effect of machinery on the wages of labour which the operatives entertain are the causes of turn-outs and strikes; they produce rankling discontent towards their masters, and I regret that I have not had the opportunity of giving them a fuller exposure.

"I certainly consider it of great consequence that the operatives themselves should be satisfied that improvements in machinery tend to raise the amount of money that they gain individually and generally, for the same number of hours' work. Those who dispute the fact must, I think, admit that I have established it in the cases which I have selected, as far as *spinners* are concerned; and as they must likewise admit that the improvement specified creates a fresh and additional demand for young hands, they must also admit that the wages of young hands are augmented in consequence. They must equally admit, that as the price of the article will be lowered in the market from the effects of the improvement, more of it will be consumed; and hence that, in all the correlate processes connected with spinning of cotton, more hands will be required, and consequently that wages throughout the whole range of cotton-working will be better than they were before. If these considerations should induce operatives to hesitate before they combine and turn out against new machinery, before they again cabal for shortening the hours of work, in order to counteract the (fancied) injurious effect upon wages of improvements in machinery, and should lead them to neglect the advice of those who urge them ' to strike for eight hours' work and twelve hours' earnings,' (and this is the advice they have lately received,) my purpose will be answered.

" The generality of the operatives in cotton-working are well-meaning, respectable, shrewd, and sensible; and I believe that if the real effect of machinery in augmenting the actual rate of their earnings, and in enabling a greater number of persons to benefit by the augmented rate, could be fairly set before them and rendered familiar to their minds, it would have a most beneficial effect upon their actions as members of society."—*Factory Inquiry Commission*, 2d Report, D. I. 119. n. m.

Fifthly. Closely connected with this mistake, and occasioned by the same habit of attending only to what is temporary and partial, and neglecting what is permanent and general; of dwelling on the evil that is concentrated, and being insensible to the benefit that is diffused, is the common error of supposing *that the general rate of wages can be reduced by the importation of foreign commodities.* In fact, the opening of a new market is precisely analogous to the introduction of a new machine, except that it is a machine which it costs nothing to construct or to keep up. If the foreign commodity be not consumed by the labouring population, its introduction leaves the general rate of wages unaffected; if it be used by them, their wages are raised as estimated in that commodity. If the laws which favour the wines of the Cape to the exclusion of those of France were repealed, more labourers would be employed in producing commodities for the French market, and fewer for that of the Cape. Wages might temporarily fall in the one trade, and rise in the other. The clear benefit would be derived by the drinkers of wine, who, at the same expense, would obtain more or better wine. So if what are called the protecting duties on French silks were removed, fewer labourers would be employed in the direct production of silk, and more in its indirect production, by the production of the cottons or hardware with which it would be purchased. The wearers of silk would be the only class ultimately benefited; and as the labouring population neither wear silk nor drink wine, the general rate of wages would, in both cases, remain unaltered. But if the laws which prohibit our obtaining on the most advantageous terms sugar and corn, were altered, that portion of the fund for the maintenance of labour, which consists of corn and sugar, would be increased. And the general rate of wages, as estimated in two of the most important articles of food, would be raised.

Sixthly. The views which we have been endeavouring to explain are inconsistent with the common opinion, *that the unproductive consumption of landlords and capitalists is beneficial to the labouring classes, because it furnishes them with employment.* " Tillage," says Paley, (and this is another form of the same fallacy,) " is preferable to pasturage, not only because the provision which it yields goes much further in the sustentation of life, but because it affords *employment* to a more numerous peasantry." The production of more subsistence is certainly an advantage, but what is the advantage of its requiring more labour? If this be an advantage the fertility of land is an evil. If the thing required be *employment*, we should abandon ploughs and even spades. To scratch up a rood with the fingers would give more employment than to dig an acre. Those who maintain that unproductive consumption does good by affording employment, must forget that it is not employment, but food, clothing, shelter, and fuel, in short, the materials of subsistence and comfort, that the labouring classes require. The word " employment " is merely a concise form of designating toil, trouble, exposure, and fatigue. It is indeed sometimes elliptically used as implying the subsistence which is purchased by enduring it. A poor man complains that he wants *work*. He might work to his heart's content, and with no man's leave, if he chose to carry stones from the bottom to the top of a hill. But what he wants is work as a means of obtaining payment. He would be happy to get the payment without the work. Toil, exposure, and fatigue, *per se*, are evils, and the less of them that is required for obtaining a given amount of subsistence and comfort, or, in other words, the greater the facility of obtaining that given amount, the better, *cæteris paribus*, will be the condition of the labouring classes; indeed, of all classes in the community. What occasions the prosperity of a colony? Not the dearness of subsistence, but its cheapness; not the difficulty of obtaining food, clothing, shelter, and fuel, but the facility. Now how can unproductive consumption increase this facility? How can the fund from which all are to be maintained be augmented by the destruction of a portion of it? If the higher orders were to return to the customs of a century ago, and cover their coats with gold lace, they might enjoy their own finery; but how would that benefit their inferiors? The theory which we are considering replies that they would be benefited by being *employed* in making the lace. It is true that a coat, instead of costing £5, would cost £55. But what becomes *now* of the extra £50? for it cannot be said that, because it is not spent on a laced coat, it does not exist. If a landlord with £10,000 a-year spends it unproductively, he pays it away to those who furnish the embellishments of his house and grounds, and supply his stable, his equipage, and his clothes. Suppose him now to abandon all unproductive expenditure, to confine himself to bare necessaries, and to earn them by his own labour, the first consequence would be, that those among whom he previously spent his £10,000 a-year would lose him as an employer; and beyond this the theory in question sees nothing. But what would he. do with the £10,000 which he would still annually receive? No one supposes that he would lock it up in a box, or bury it in his garden. Whether productively or unproductively, it still must be spent. If spent by himself, as by the supposition it would be spent productively, it must increase, and every year still further increase, the whole fund applicable to the use of the rest of the community. If not spent by himself, it must be lent, as is done by a miser of the present day, to some other person, and by that person it must be spent productively or unproductively. He might, perhaps, buy with it property in the English funds; but what becomes of it in the hands of the person who sells to him that funded property? He might buy with it French rentes; but in what form would the price of those rentes go to Paris? —In the form, as we have seen, of manufactured commodities. *Quâcunque viâ datâ*, every man must spend his income; and the less he spends on himself, the more remains for the rest of the world.

Preference of Services to Commodities.—The seventh and last theory inconsistent with our own views, to which we shall call the reader's attention, is that proposed by Mr. Ricardo in the following passage:—

" The labouring class have no small interest in the manner in which the net income of the Country is expended, although it should, in all cases, be expended for the gratification and enjoyment of those who are fairly entitled to it.

" If a landlord, or a capitalist, expends his revenue in the manner of an ancient Baron, in the support of a great number of retainers or menial servants, he will give employment to much more labour than if he expended it on fine clothes or costly furniture.

" In both cases the net revenue would be the same, and so would be the gross revenue, but the former would be realized in different commodities. If my revenue were £10,000, the same quantity nearly of productive labour would be employed, whether I realized it in fine clothes and costly furniture, &c. &c., or in a quantity of food and clothing of the same value. If, however, I realized my revenue in the first set of commodities, no more labour would be *consequently* employed: I should enjoy my furniture and my clothes, and there would be an end of them; but if I realized my revenue in food and clothing, and my desire was to employ menial servants, all those whom I could so employ with my revenue of £10,000, or with the food and clothing which it would purchase, would be to be added to the former demand for labourers, and this addition would take place only because I chose this mode of expending my revenue.   As the labourers, then, are interested in the demand for labour, they must naturally desire that as much as possible should be diverted from expenditure on luxuries, to be expended in the support of menial servants.

" In the same manner a Country engaged in war, and which is under the necessity of maintaining large fleets and armies, employs a great many more men than will be employed when the war terminates, and the annual expenses which it brings with it cease.

" If I were not called upon for a tax of £500 during the war, which is expended on men in the situations of soldiers and sailors, I might probably spend that portion of my income on furniture, clothes, books, &c. &c., and whether it was expended in the one way or the other, there would be the same quantity of labour employed in production; for the food and clothing of the soldier and sailor would require the same amount of industry to produce them as the more luxurious commodities: but, in the case of war, there would be the additional demand for men as soldiers and sailors; and, consequently, a war which is supported out of the revenue, and not from the capital of a Country, is favourable to an increase of population.

" At the termination of the war, when part of my revenue reverts to me, and is employed as before in the purchase of wine, furniture, or other luxuries, the population which it before supported, and which the war called into existence, will become redundant, and by its effect on the rest of the population, and its competition with it for employment, will sink the value of wages, and very materially deteriorate the condition of the labouring classes." [31]

Mr. Ricardo's theory is, that it is more beneficial to the labouring classes to be employed in the production of services than in the production of commodities; that it is better for them to be employed in standing behind chairs than in making chairs; as soldiers or sailors than as manufacturers.   Now, as it is clear that the whole quantity of commodities provided for the use of labourers is not increased by the conversion of an artisan into a footman or a soldier, either Mr. Ricardo must be wrong, or our elementary proposition is false.

Mr. Ricardo seems to have been led to his conclusions by observing that the wages of servants, sailors, and soldiers, are principally paid in kind—those of artisans in money.   He correctly states, that if a man with £10,000 a-year spends his income in the purchase of commodities for his own use, he retains, after having made those purchases, no further fund for the maintenance of labour; but that if he spends it in the purchase of commodities to be employed in main-

---

[31] *Principles, &c.*, p. 475.

taining menial servants, he has, in those purchased commodities, a new fund with which he can maintain a certain number of menial servants. It appeared to him, therefore, that the landlord would, in the latter case, be able to spend his income twice over; to subsist twice as many persons as before. It did not occur to him that the landlord, by purchasing himself the subsistence of his servants, merely does for them what they would be able to do better for themselves; that, instead of spending his own income twice over, he merely takes on himself the business of spending theirs for them. He did not perceive that all that the landlord spends in purchasing the subsistence and clothing of his servants, is so much deducted from what he would otherwise have to pay to them in money, to be by them employed in the purchase of subsistence and clothing; and that if he were to give to his servants the value of their whole subsistence in money, the whole body of labourers would be just as well maintained as in the supposed case of his purchasing their subsistence, and then giving it to them in exchange for their services. No one would maintain that, if it were the general practice, in this Country, as it is in India, to give to servants board wages, the demand for labour would be lessened; or that if it were the practice, as it is in semi-barbarous Countries, to maintain servants to produce within their masters' walls the commodities which we are accustomed to purchase from shops, such as the fine clothes and furniture to which Mr. Ricardo alludes, the demand for labour would be increased. Still less could it be maintained, that if those servants, instead of producing commodities, were employed in following their master's person, or mounting guard before his door, such a change would create an additional demand for men, and be favourable to an increase of population.

So far are we from concurring in Mr. Ricardo's opinion, that it is the interest of the labourers that revenue should be spent rather on services than on commodities, that we believe their interest to be precisely opposite. In the first place, the labourer can generally manage better his own income than it can be managed for him by his master. If a domestic servant could earn as wages the whole sum which he costs his master, even if he were to spend it as he received it, he would probably spend it with more enjoyment. Secondly, the income spent on services is generally spent in the purchase of what perishes at the instant of its creation; that spent on commodities often leaves results which, when their first purchaser has done with them, are serviceable to others. In this Country the poor are, to a great extent, clothed with garments originally provided for their superiors. In all the better class of cottages may be found articles of furniture which never could have been made for their present possessors. A large portion of the commodities which now contribute to the comfort of the labouring classes would never have existed if it had been the fashion in this Country, during the last fifty years, to prefer retinue and attendance to durable commodities. And, thirdly, the income employed on commodities is favourable to the creation of both material and immaterial capital; that employed on services is not. The duties of a servant are so easily learned, that he can scarcely be termed a skilled labourer; his accumulations are small in amount, and seldom turned to much advantage. The artisan learns a trade, in which every year adds to his skill, and is taught mechanical and chemical processes, often susceptible of indefinite improvement, and in which a single invention may raise the author to wealth, and diffuse prosperity over a whole district, or even a whole nation. An industrious artisan can often save a large portion of his income, and invest it with great and immediate profit. He purchases with his savings a small stock of tools and materials, and, by the vigilance and activity which can be applied only to a small capital, renders every portion of it efficient. The ancestors, and not the remote ancestors, of some of our richest and our proudest families, the authors of some of our most valuable discoveries, were common mechanics. What menial servant has in this Country, and in modern times, been a public benefactor, or even raised himself to affluence? Both history and observation show that those Countries in which expenditure is chiefly employed in the purchase of services are poor, and those in which it is chiefly employed on commodities are rich.

Mr. Ricardo's theory as to the effects of war is still more strikingly erroneous. It is, in the first place, open to all the objections which we have already opposed to his views respecting menial servants. The revenue which is employed in maintaining soldiers and sailors would, even if unproductively consumed, maintain at least an equal number of servants and artisans; and that portion of it which would have been employed in the maintenance of artisans would (as we have seen) have been far more beneficially employed. The demand for soldiers and sailors is not, as he terms it, an additional, it is merely a substituted, demand. But a great part of that revenue would have been productively consumed. Instead of employing some labourers in converting suburbs into fortifications, and forests into navies, to perish by dry rot in harbour, or by exposure at sea, and others in walking the deck and parading on the rampart, it would have employed them in adding more and more every year to the fund from which their subsistence is derived. War is mischievous to every class in the community; but to none is it such a curse as to the labourers.

CAUSES ON WHICH THE EXTENT OF THE FUND FOR THE MAINTENANCE OF LABOUR DEPENDS.

We have now explained the principal errors which are inconsistent with our elementary proposition, namely, that *the quantity and quality*

*of the commodities obtained by each labouring family during the year
must depend on the quantity and quality of the commodities directly or
indirectly appropriated during the year to the use of the labouring
population, compared with the number of labouring families, or, to
speak more concisely, on the extent of the fund for the maintenance of
labourers, compared with the number of labourers to be maintained.*

On what, then, does the extent of that fund depend? In the first
place, on the productiveness of labour in the direct or indirect production of the commodities used by the labourer; and, in the second place,
on the number of persons directly or indirectly employed in the production of things for the use of labourers, compared with the whole
number of labouring families. If we wished to ascertain the comparative wages of the labouring population in two parishes, containing
each, we will say, twenty-four labouring families, these are the only
two points to which we need direct our inquiries. If we found that
in the one parish eighteen families, and in the other only twelve, were
employed in producing commodities for the whole twenty-four, we
should infer that, supposing the labour of each to be equally productive,
wages must be higher by one-fourth in the first than in the second.
But if we found that in the second parish labour was more productive
by one-half than in the first, we should infer an equality of wages in
the two.

Causes which affect Productiveness of labour.—We will begin by
considering the causes which affect the productiveness of labour in the
direct or indirect production of the commodities used by the labourer.
We add the word *indirect*, not with reference to the whole fund which
supplies the maintenance of all the labourers throughout the world,
but with reference to the fund which supplies the wants of the labourers
in a particular Country. If we consider the whole world as forming
one community, it is obvious that the fund for the subsistence of the
labouring portion of that community cannot be increased by the
increased production of those commodities which they do not use; by
the increased production, for instance, of lace or statues.

But the fund for the maintenance of the labourers in any given
Country may be, and often is, materially dependent on the facility
with which they can produce commodities useless to themselves except
as the instruments of exchange. The tea, the tobacco, and the sugar
used by our labouring population are principally obtained in return
for exported commodities unfitted for our climate and our habits. But
the superior facility with which we produce those exported commodities
enables, or, if legislative interference did not prevent it, would enable,
our labouring population to obtain tea, sugar, and tobacco with less
labour than they cost in the Countries of which they are the natural
growth. It is unimportant to the labourer whether his corn is the

produce of the soil of England or of Poland ; whether it is obtained directly by means of the plough, or indirectly by means of the loom.

On what then does the first of these two causes, namely, the productiveness of labour, depend?

First. It depends partly *on the corporeal, intellectual, and moral qualities of the labourer ;* on his diligence, his skill, and his strength of body and mind.   And these depend on causes, many of which are imperfectly understood, and others are too complicated to admit of concise explanation, or to be fully considered without entering into investigations connected indeed with Political Economy, but not within its peculiar province.   Much may depend on race and on climate; much more depends on religion, education, and government.   One cause only we shall slightly dwell on, because it is simple, and has not been sufficiently considered by any writers except M. Quetelet,[32] and Sir F. D'Ivernois,[33] and that is, the mean age of the labouring population.   This depends partly on the average duration of life in a Country, and partly on the rate at which its population is increasing. In England, the average duration of life is supposed to amount to about forty-four years.   In many Countries it does not reach thirty-five ; in some it does not attain twenty-five.   Again, in some Countries the population doubles every twenty-five years.   At the present rate of increase in England it would double in about fifty.   The average period of its doubling throughout Europe is supposed to be about a century.

Now it is obvious that, the number of persons and the rate of increase in any two Countries being given, that Country would have the greater number of adults in which the average duration of life was the longer ; and, the longevity being given, that Country would have the greater proportion of adults in which the rate of increase was the slower. Longevity, and a population stationary or slowly increasing, are therefore favourable to the productiveness of labour.

Secondly.   The corporeal, intellectual, and moral qualities of the labourer being given, the *productiveness of labour* in any Country will partly depend *on the natural agents by which it is assisted,* or, in other words, on the climate, soil, situation, and extent in proportion to its population, of that Country.

To some Countries nature has refused the means of supporting human life ; to others she has refused the means of wealth.   No exertions would enable a community to exist long on Melville Island, or in the Deserts of Africa, or to exist comfortably in Greenland or Nova Zembla.   But, though she can deny riches, she cannot give them. The finest districts in the world are among the poorest.   With all the brute and inanimate sources of affluence profusely scattered before them, the inhabitants of the greater part of Africa, America, and

---

[32] *Sur l'Homme,* Tome I. p. 324.
[33] *Sur la Mortalité Proportionelle, &c.*

Asia want the moral and intellectual qualities by which the raw materials of wealth are to be worked up.   Even the Icelanders seem to be richer than the Guachos.   But, although local advantages are far from being the most efficient causes of the productiveness of labour, their influence must not be disregarded.   They have enabled the colonies of highly civilized nations to advance to opulence with a rapidity of which we have no other example.

Thirdly.   The productiveness of labour partly depends *on the degree in which it is assisted by abstinence*, or, to use a more familiar expression, *by the use of capital.*

We have already explained the advantages afforded by capital, and traced them to the use of implements and the division of labour, and need only remind our readers that, of all means by which labour can be rendered productive, the use of capital is far the most efficient. Without tools, and without the division of employments, man would be an animal less capable of obtaining enjoyment, or even subsistence, than the brutes of the field.

Fourthly.   The last of the causes which influence the productiveness of labour is *the existence or the absence of government interference.*

The essential business of government is to afford defence; to protect the community against foreign and domestic violence and fraud.   Unfortunately, however, governments have generally supposed it to be their duty, not merely to give *security* but *wealth*; not merely to enable their subjects to produce and enjoy in safety, but to teach them *what* to produce and *how* to enjoy; to give them instruction how to manage their own concerns, and to force them to obey that instruction.

Unfortunately, too, the ignorance and folly with which they have attempted to execute this office have been equal to the ignorance and folly which led them to undertake it.   Partly under the influence of what has been called the Mercantile Theory, the theory which teaches that wealth consists of gold and silver, and may be indefinitely increased by exporting commodities, and receiving only money in return; and partly misled by the circumstance, that when an individual, or a class, obtains a monopoly against the public, the loss, however great, becomes imperceptible from its diffusion, and the gain, however trifling, is obvious, because it is concentrated, it has long been the ruling principle of commercial statesmen to favour direct at the expense of indirect production; to refuse participation in the benefits bestowed by nature on foreign Countries, though at the expense of surrendering a portion of what she has conferred on their own; and to force the industry of their subjects from those channels in which they have peculiar advantages, into those for which their climate, their habits, and their soil are inappropriate.

It is under the influence of these causes that the civilized world has lately exhibited the strange spectacle of general peace accompanied by general distress. During the War, the greater part of Southern Europe had coalesced into one vast Empire; a single Sovereign ruled from Hamburgh to Rome; and hundreds of lines of custom-houses and revenue-officers, that had previously interposed against commerce barriers more impassable than seas or mountains, were swept away. Napoleon was deeply steeped in the mercantile theory, and his conduct shows how completely his views were founded on unreflecting prejudice. In obedience to that theory, he believed free trade between independent States to be like gambling between individuals, and therefore mischievous to the one or to the other: mischievous in fact to the one which, in the ultimate settling of accounts, had to pay a balance in money. While France and Italy were under different rulers, he therefore must have believed that the inhabitants of one of the two Countries would be injured by being allowed to purchase the commodities of the other. But the framers of the mercantile theory, blind as they were, had never ventured to object to the freest intercourse between the inhabitants of contiguous districts in the same Empire. When he had forced under his yoke Belgium and France, he allowed them therefore a freedom of intercourse which he still prohibited between France and Austria; totally forgetting that the benefit of an exchange does not depend on the accident, whether the parties to it are, or are not, fellow-subjects. His theories were servile copies of errors unhappily too prevalent, and faded away before his strong common sense on the slightest variation of appearances, though the facts on which the question turns were unaltered.

On the termination of the War, Napoleon's Empire was broken up into independent Kingdoms, and each State set to work to reimpose on itself the fetters which his powerful hand had broken. Douaniers and preventive-service men were found instruments as efficient in wasting the resources of their own Country, and in arresting the improvement of their neighbours, as armies and fleets. The produce of France became contraband in Belgium and Italy, and the produce of Belgium and Italy in France. America solemnized the Peace by a tariff, and England by a corn law. To prohibit whatever is wanted became again the rule in commercial policy. Russia is an agricultural Country: she therefore forbad the import of foreign manufactures. England is abundantly supplied with manufactures: she therefore prohibited corn.

We are inclined to think that the conduct of Russia was practically more mischievous than that of England. She has adhered to the anti-commercial system with far more pertinacity than we have; indeed, every change which she has made has been to add to duties, and to extend prohibitions. But the objections in principle against the exclusion of raw produce seem to us still more forcible than those against the exclusion of manufactures. In the first place, the consumption of the labourer consists principally of raw produce, or slightly worked commodities. No restrictions on the importation of the finer manufactures can affect him. But laws against the importation of raw produce are specifically directed against the labouring population. Their professed object is to diminish, in fact, the principal fund for the maintenance of labour. And, secondly, when an agricultural Country prohibits foreign manufactures, the labourer is, to a certain extent, indemnified by a consequent fall in the price of raw produce. On the other hand, when a manufacturing Country prohibits the importation of raw produce, the price of all commodities, excepting labour, has a tendency to increase, and the labourer finds it more difficult to obtain *every* article of his consumption.

This may require some explanation. We have already shown, that every additional quantity of raw produce is, generally speaking, obtained at a greater proportional expense. To prohibit the importation of manufactures is, of course, to prohibit the exportation of the raw produce, which otherwise would have been employed in purchasing them. As a smaller quantity of raw produce is wanted, a smaller quantity is produced, and that quantity is produced at a less proportionate expense; labour, though less productive in clothes and furniture, becomes more productive in raw produce; the price of raw produce, therefore, falls, and the labourer, in having less to pay for food, obtains some compensation for having more to pay for other commodities. The greater part of the evil falls on the proprietors of the land. On the contrary, every additional quantity of manufactured produce is obtained, so far as the manufacturing of it is concerned, at a less proportionate expense. Every increase of the supply is accompanied by the introduction of more and better machinery, and by a further division of labour. As in the former case, restrictions on the importation of raw produce are, in fact, restrictions on the exportation of manufactures. Fewer manufactured commodities being wanted, and consequently fewer produced, what are produced are produced at the expense of proportionately more labour than would otherwise be necessary. More raw produce must be raised at home, and that also must be raised at a greater proportionate expense of labour. The price of the one kind of commodities rises, because it has become necessary to produce more, and that of the other, because it has become necessary to produce less. The productiveness of labour is diminished each way, and the only person uninjured is the landlord.

To a certain extent, however, the misdirection of industry by government interference is a necessary evil. The duties of government cannot be performed without a public revenue; nor can a considerable public revenue be raised without taxation; and the struggle to escape taxation always tends to divert industry from its natural channels. The tax which is least open to this objection, a tax on rent, must tend to prevent the application of capital to land; a tax on profits to occasion the exportation of capital; a tax on income derived from property to prevent accumulation; a tax on wages to occasion their payment rather in kind than in money, and to prevent the labourer from acquiring durable and visible property in the hope of pleading his poverty as an excuse. Taxes on specific articles are evaded by the substitution of some less burdened or cheaper commodity. The beer and malt duties are avoided by the substitution of spirits. The duties on tea and coffee by the use of roasted corn. Now, every tax, so far as it is evaded, is simply mischievous. A window blocked up to avoid window tax may diminish the light and air enjoyed by a whole family, but adds nothing to the public revenue. A distinct and a still greater injury arises from taxation imposed on the instruments and processes of industry. The salt tax, while it existed, prevented in a great measure the use of salt in agriculture. The duty on advertisements prevents vendors and purchasers from knowing each other's wants and supplies. The duties on leather, on spirits, and on glass, have not only prevented England from attaining, in the manufacture of those commodities, her usual superiority, but have kept her positively behind the improved part of Europe. To prevent fraud on the Excise, the manufacturer is subject to innumerable regulations and prohibitions incompatible with a proper economy of materials and division of labour, and which bend very reluctantly to improvements. To improve is necessarily to alter, and any alteration in the process prescribed by law may entangle the manufacturer within the meshes of a regulating Act of Parliament.

It is commonly supposed that men are sufficiently ready to grumble at taxation; but the fact that they are very imperfectly aware of the degree and kind of evil indirectly inflicted might be proved from many instances. To select only one. Most persons are aware of the far higher price borne by good malting barley above the ordinary barley used only for feeding stock; nor can any one doubt that the price of beer is materially enhanced by this circumstance. But, probably, not one consumer in ten thousand has any idea that this is connected with taxation. Yet, in fact, a large proportion of the barley set aside as unfit for malting would make, as far as nature is concerned, very good malt, but requires a process somewhat different from that which the Excise regulations prescribe, and is consequently rendered by law useless for that purpose. It may easily be conceived that, if the times and modes of ploughing, harrowing, and sowing, were prescribed by law, a large portion of land now productive would lie waste.

A Country which has been forced by the folly or the rapacity of its own government, or by the folly or rapacity of other States, to raise a large public revenue, suffers in general far more from the indirect than from the direct effects of taxation; suffers more by being prevented from producing, than by being obliged to pay.

The causes which determine the productiveness of labour in the direct or indirect production of the commodities used by the labourer appear, therefore, to be four. First, the personal character of the labourer, his corporeal, intellectual, and moral qualities; secondly, the degree in which he is assisted by natural agents; thirdly, the degree in which he is assisted by capital; fourthly, the degree of freedom with which he is allowed to direct his industry.

II. Causes which Divert Labour from the Production of Commodities for the use of Labouring Families.

I. Rent.   II. Taxation.   III. Profit.

If all labourers were employed in the production, direct or indirect, of commodities for their own use, the rate of wages would depend solely on the productiveness of labour. But it is obvious that this could never be the case, unless the labourers themselves were the owners of all the capital and all the natural agents of the country; a state of existence so utterly barbarous as to be without distinction of ranks or division of labour; a state in which a few scattered savage families have sometimes been found, but which exhibits none of the phenomena which it is the business of Political Economy to trace to their causes. A great portion of the labour employed in a civilized community is employed in the production of things in the use of which the labourer is not to participate. In a civilized community, therefore, the extent of the fund for the maintenance of labour depends not only on the productiveness of labour, but also on the number of persons employed in the production of things for the use of labourers, compared with the whole number of labouring families.

It appears to us that there are three purposes to which labour, which might otherwise be employed in supplying the fund for the use of labourers, may be diverted; namely, the production of things, first, to be used by the proprietors of natural agents; secondly, to be used by the government; and thirdly, to be used by capitalists; or, to speak more concisely, though less correctly, Labour, instead of being employed in the production of Wages, may be employed in the production of Rent, Taxation, or Profit.

First, with respect to Rent.

We have already seen that Rent depends in part on the productiveness of the natural agent for the assistance of which it is paid. Now any increase in the productive powers of that agent has a tendency to increase Rent, and can have none to diminish Wages.

The improvements in agricultural skill which have taken place during the last one hundred years have greatly increased the productiveness of the Lowlands of Scotland, and greatly increased the amount of rent; but that increase has been accompanied by an increase, though not in an equal ratio, of the amount of wages. Adam Smith states, that at the time when he wrote, (the period of the American War,) the usual price of common labour there was 8d. a-day, or 4s. a-week. It is now more than 8s. a-week; a sum capable of purchasing one-third more of raw produce, and three or four times as much of manufactured produce, as the former wages. Though the rental of the Lowlands has more than tripled, though a much larger portion of what the labourer produces is produced for the benefit of the landlord, yet the positive increase of the whole produce more than compensates this apparent inconvenience. Instead of producing, we will say, twenty bushels, of which the landlord received ten, the capitalist two, and the labourer eight, he produces perhaps thirty-five, of which the landlord receives twenty, the capitalist three, and the labourer twelve.

It appears, therefore, that the whole fund for the maintenance of labour is not necessarily diminished in consequence of a considerable portion of the labourers in a Country being employed in producing commodities for the use of the proprietors of the natural agents in that Country. Such labourers may, in fact, be considered as existing only in consequence of the existence of natural agents of extraordinary productiveness. They draw their subsistence not from the common fund, such as it otherwise would be, but from the addition made to that fund by that extraordinary productiveness.

Of course, when we speak of the amount of rent as unimportant to the labourer, we must be understood to mean only that rent which arises from the peculiar or increased productiveness of the natural agent in question, not of that which arises merely from an increase of population. We have already stated that, in the absence of disturbing causes, subsistence may be expected to increase in a greater ratio than population. But, as we then remarked, it certainly is possible, and perhaps, under the influence of superstition and misgovernment, it is probable, that the number of inhabitants in a Country might increase without a commensurate increase of the means, direct or indirect, of obtaining raw produce. Under such circumstances, rents would rise, and labour, which, if the population had remained stationary, would have been employed in the production of commodities for the use of labourers, would now be employed in producing commodities for the use of landlords. A rise of rent so occasioned would of course be detrimental to the mass of the community. It must be recollected, also, that the government of every Country has in some measure the power of deciding in what proportions the different classes of its subjects shall contribute to the public burdens. Some governments have attempted to exempt, as far as they could, the labourers from these burdens, and to throw them as far as they could upon the landlords. Others again have charged, or have allowed individuals to charge, the revenue arising from land with an expenditure for purposes in which the landlords were not solely or principally interested; such as the establishment and maintenance of roads and bridges, the supply of religious, moral, and intellectual instruction, the

affording gratuitous medical relief to the sick, and even support to the
able-bodied poor or their families.   Others, on the other hand, have
endeavoured to favour the landlords by imposing public expenditure
on the more defenceless portion of the community, the labourers; and
many have adopted each of these different lines of conduct on different
occasions, or with respect to different portions of their expenditure.
The tendency of every such institution must be to augment or diminish
the proportion of the labourers employed for the benefit of landlords,
compared with that of those who are employed for the benefit of
labourers.

Another cause disturbing these proportions is the attempt by a
government to create rent, if it can be called rent, by forcibly limiting
the bounty of nature.   It is possible that, if we had continued to
prohibit the corn of Ireland, the incomes of English landlords might
have been increased.   So, if no coal were allowed to be burned except
the produce of a single colliery, the possessor of that colliery would
enjoy a princely revenue.   But the gain from such a monopoly is not
strictly rent; it is oppression and robbery.

2. **Taxation:—Direction of Labour to supply the Consumption of
Government.**—The second purpose to which labour may be diverted
from the supply of commodities for the use of labourers is the supply
of the consumption of government.   It is clear that all the labour
that is employed in the support of *unnecessary* establishments, and all
the surplus labour which is employed in supporting on an unnecessary
scale of expense those establishments which are strictly wanted, is so
much taken from the revenue of the whole people.   Still more injurious
is the employment of labour for the purposes not merely useless, but
positively mischievous; in the support of pagodas or bonzes, to keep
up or disseminate a demoralizing superstition; in the support of armies
and navies to plunder the commerce and ravage the territories of
States, which nature enabled to confer mutual benefits, but the folly
or wickedness of their rulers force to inflict mutual evil; or in the
support of barriers and blockades to maintain the commercial war in
which nations are accustomed to spend the breathing time of actual
hostility.   Unnecessary taxation, even when innocently applied, is
fraud or robbery.   It is difficult to find a designation for that which
is applied to ends still more mischievous than the means; for that
which makes plunder and extortion the instruments of still further
injury.

It appears at first sight that only this mischievous or useless expenditure ought to be considered as a deduction from wages, since the
labour which is employed in effecting the legitimate purposes of
government is as much employed for the benefit of the labouring
classes as that which is employed in the direct production of commodities for their use.   The great object of government is to afford

security, and security is of all blessings the most important, and the one least capable of being obtained by uncombined exertions. Those writers who have maintained that whatever is raised by taxation is deducted from the revenue of the Country, seem to have been led to this conclusion, by observing that the object of government is to occasion not positive but negative effects, not to produce good, but to prevent evil. And they have thought it right to deduct what is so spent from the net revenue of the people. But it must be recollected that the mere prevention of evil is one of the principal objects even of individual expenditure. We do not build houses because it is pleasant to breathe the confined atmosphere of a room, but because roofs and walls are the only means by which the inclemency of the seasons can be avoided. We do not buy drugs for our pleasure, but to avert or remove disease. Yet no one ever thought what he spends on medicines and on house rent a deduction from his income. When the members of a Friendly Society raise among themselves a fund for their relief in sickness, they do not consider their contributions a deduction from their wages, but a mode of expenditure. And it may be asked, in what respect does each man's contribution towards the means by which the community is to be protected against internal and external violence and fraud differ from his contribution to a Friendly Society, excepting that those evils are more severe and more constantly imminent than sickness, and less capable of being warded off by individual efforts? It is true that, if the protection could be less expensively obtained, the fund for the maintenance of labour would be increased. But this is merely an exemplification of what we have already stated, that the extent of the fund for the maintenance of labour depends mainly on the productiveness of labour. If fewer fleets, and armies, and magistrates, could preserve the peace, that is, if labour were more productive in affording security, the labouring classes would, *cæteris paribus*, be better off, just as they would be better off if fewer husbandmen or artisans could produce, directly or indirectly, the same quantity of corn ; that is, if labour were more productive in supplying food.

But admitting all this to be true, it is also true, as we have already remarked, that the labourer is interested not only in the amount and application of the public revenue, and in the degree in which its payment affects the productiveness of labour, but also in the manner in which the burthen of supplying it is distributed. If the duty on wine were abolished, and an equal revenue raised by substituting an additional duty on coarse tobacco, the labourers, who are the only consumers of coarse tobacco, would purchase, with the same proportion of their wages, less tobacco than before, and the landlords and capitalists, who are the only consumers of wine, would purchase, with the same proportions of their rent and profits, more wine. The productiveness of our labour and the export of our manufactures would be undiminished ;

even the nature of our exports need not be altered; the only change would be in the returns. More wine and less tobacco would be imported. More labourers, therefore, than before, would be employed in obtaining wine for landlords and capitalists, and fewer in obtaining tobacco for labourers.

Nor must it be forgotten that a part of the taxes received by the government of one Country is often paid by the inhabitants of another. We now purchase annually in China about thirty millions of pounds of tea, at about 1s. a pound. On the tea so purchased we impose in different ways taxes to the amount of about two hundred per cent. Were we to repeal that taxation, and the price in China were to remain unaltered, our consumption would probably quadruple; but it is highly improbable that we could purchase one hundred and twenty millions of pounds of tea at 1s. a pound. The price in China might possibly double; it probably would rise one-half. That rise would have a tendency to raise the rent of land and the wages of labour in the tea-growing districts of China. It must be admitted, therefore, that they are both kept down by the existence of the tax; and that a portion of our duty on tea is, in fact, paid by the inhabitants of the tea-growing districts of China. The same reasoning proves that a part of the English duty on claret is paid by France, and that a part of the duties imposed by foreign nations on some of the commodities which we export, is paid by England. As a portion of the taxes raised by every State is, in fact, paid by the inhabitants of those Countries with which it has commercial relations, and as war and misgovernment are the great causes of taxation, an additional proof is afforded of the degree in which each Country is interested in the freedom and tranquillity of its neighbours.

We have lastly to consider the influence of profits on wages; or, in other words, the extent to which wages may be affected by the employment of labour to produce, instead of wages, things for the use of capitalists. In civilized and well-governed communities, this is the principal purpose to which labour, that otherwise might be employed for the benefit of the labourers, is diverted. The labourers who are employed for the benefit of the owners of natural agents may, as we have seen, be in general considered as a separate class, not withdrawn from the general body, but added to it by the existence of those natural agents. Those who are necessarily employed in effecting the legitimate purposes of government are, in fact, employed for the benefit of the labouring population, and the taxation which supplies their maintenance is not necessarily a deduction from wages, but a mode of expenditure. That few governments have confined themselves to their legitimate office, or employed in effecting that office only the necessary amount of labour, is a melancholy truth; and it is true that the fund for the maintenance of labour may be, and in most Countries has been, and is, more diminished in its amount, and more retarded in its increase, by misgovernment than by all other causes put together. But both misgovernment and that interference of the ruling power between the different classes of its subjects which we have already described as affecting the proportions of rent, profit, and wages to one another, are rather disturbing causes than necessary elements in the calculations of Political Economy; and with these allusions to their influence we shall dismiss them.

3. **Influence of Profit on Wages.**—Rent, then, being considered as something extrinsic, and Taxation a mode of expenditure, the only remaining deduction from Wages is Profit. And the productiveness of labour being given, the extent of the fund for the maintenance of labour will depend on the proportion which the number of labourers employed in producing things for the use of capitalists bears to that of those employed in producing things for the use of labourers; or, to use a more common expression, on the proportions in which the produce of labour is shared between the capitalist and the labourer.

In a previous portion of this Treatise we defined the word "abstinence" to mean the conduct of him who abstains from the unproductive consumption of any commodity, or who employs labour to produce distant results. In fact, the act of deferring enjoyment. And we explained that labour cannot be efficient unless assisted by, what is the result of abstinence, capital; nor abstinence in itself efficient unless assisted by labour; that each is disagreeable, and must therefore be called into exertion by the prospect of its specific remuneration; abstinence by the hope of profit, and labour by the hope of wages: and we stated, that although in fact the same individual often undergoes both abstinence and labour, yet that we thought it more convenient to consider the capitalist and the labourer as different persons. In the absence of rent, and of unnecessary or unequally distributed taxation, it is between these two classes that all that is produced is divided; and the question now to be considered is, what decides the proportion of the shares?

The facts which decide in what proportions the capitalist and labourer share the common fund appear to be two: *first, the general rate of profit in the Country on the advance of capital for a given period;* and, *secondly, the period which in each particular case has elapsed between the advance of the capital and the receipt of the profit.*

General Rate of Profit.—First, as to the General Rate of Profit. We have seen that Profit is the remuneration of abstinence, and that abstinence is the deferring of enjoyment. The commodity which owes its existence or its preservation to abstinence is Capital. Its owner is termed a Capitalist, and he is said to *advance* the means by which it is created or preserved. These means are partly materials and implements, (including, under the last term, not merely the ordinary tools of manual labour, but machinery, ships, and even roads, wharfs, and canals,) and partly labour. The materials and implements are supplied by the capitalist directly, the labour is supplied by him indirectly, by advancing the wages of the labourers. The labourers, aided by their implements, convert the materials into a new and vendible commodity, which is termed the *return* of the capitalist. And the capitalist's profit depends on the difference between the value of the advance and the value of the return. In producing the return, the wages and materials are necessarily consumed; they are parted with by the capitalist, and therefore termed circulating capital. The implements are not necessarily consumed; so far as they are unconsumed they remain the property of the capitalist, and are therefore termed fixed capital. The value of that portion of them which remains unconsumed must be added to that of the other returns before the profit can be estimated. The capital of a builder is almost entirely circulating. It consists principally of the bricks, lime, timber, stone, and slate which are the materials with which the house is to be constructed, and of the money necessary to pay the wages of the workmen. His fixed capital (exclusively of his knowledge) consists merely of scaffolding and ladders. All these he advances, and the result, after a certain interval, is a house, together with the former ladders and scaffolding somewhat the worse for wear. The cotton-spinner's advances consist of raw cotton and wages, which are his circulating capital, and buildings and machinery, which are his fixed capital. His returns are a certain quantity of manufactured cotton, and the old buildings and machinery. So a ship-owner's advances consist of his ship, which is his fixed capital, and of its stores, and the wages of his sailors, which are his circulating capital; his returns are his freight, or, in other words, the hire which he receives for the use of his ship, the ship itself, such as it may be, after the voyage, and the stores, if any of them remain unconsumed. The profit in every case consists, as we have already stated, of the difference between the value of the advances and the value of the returns.

How Profit is to be Estimated.—But in what is this value to be estimated? Of course in something as unsusceptible as possible of variations in its general value. If the value of the advances and returns of the capitalist were estimated in corn or in hops, an abundant season might so reduce the value of either as to make him appear a gainer when in fact a loser. His returns might be worth twenty per cent. more of corn or hops than his advances, and yet be inferior in general value. The commodity least susceptible of variation in its general value, during short periods, is money; and partly from this circumstance, and partly from its general use as a measure of value, it is the medium in which calculations of profit are usually expressed. But, if considerable periods are to be taken, even money is subject to great variations, and any sudden change in the facility of obtaining it, arising from an increased fertility of the mines, or an increased productiveness of labour, or an abuse of banking or paper currency, or from similar causes operating in an opposite direction, may materially raise or depress the general value of money in any one Country, even during short periods.

The best Standard of Value for philosophical purposes appears to be the command of labour. In the first place, labour, next to money, is the principal subject of exchange. And, in the second place, labour, as the principal instrument of production, as the only instrument that can be employed at will in the creation of whatever is most wanted, varies less in its general value than any other article of exchange. Money, and the necessaries of life which approach nearest to it, derive in part their steadiness of value from their constant power of commanding labour, a power belonging to no other commodity. Estimated indeed in one class of objects, and it is the class most coveted by man, we mean power and pre-eminence, the value of the command of labour is almost invariable. Two persons who, at different times or in different places, can each command the labour of one thousand average labourers, may indeed enjoy in very different degrees the comforts and conveniences of life; but in power and pre-eminence in their respective Countries they must be nearly on a par. Each must be one man in a thousand. Each must be a thousand times richer than the mass of his Countrymen. If two shillings in Hindostan will command as many labourers as twenty in England, a Hindoo with £3000 a-year is, generally speaking, as great a man in Hindostan as an Englishman with £30,000 a-year in England.

Philosophically, therefore, we think that the value of the capitalist's advances and returns ought to be estimated in their command of labour; popularly, their value is estimated in money; and, as the reciprocal values of money and labour seldom vary much between the times of those advances and returns, the popular mode of estimation is seldom incorrect; and we shall therefore use both indifferently.

The great difficulty of the subject arises from the circumstance, that the rate of profit is not the subject of contract, but of experiment, and cannot be ascertained even by an individual, except as to his *past* operations. While a transaction is going on, the capitalist may hope that the value of the returns will exceed the value of the advances; he may hope that the excess will be considerable; but he cannot be certain that there will be any excess at all; that there will not be a positive loss. He may say what his profit *has* been, but not what it *is*. Frequently, indeed, he cannot say what it *has* been. A whole series of mercantile or manufacturing transactions may be so linked together that, after having been apparently profitable for years, they may terminate in ruin.

If, however, we could ascertain the value of the returns in all the transactions in this Country which were concluded in the year ending yesterday; and also could ascertain what was the value of the advances, and the average time for which those advances were made before the returns were received, we should know what was the average rate of profit in this Country during the last year. Suppose this point ascertained, and the result to be, that the average rate of profit on an advance of capital for a year was in this Country during the last year ten per cent., the question recurs, what were the causes which determined it to be ten per cent. rather than five per cent. or twenty per cent. ?

It appears to us that it must have depended principally on the previous conduct of the capitalists and of the labourers of this Country; on the value of the capital which at some previous period was appropriated by the capitalists to produce commodities for the use of labourers, or, to use a more concise expression, to produce wages; and the number of labourers whom the previous conduct of the labouring population had caused to exist.

Causes regulating the Rate of Profit.—It will be admitted that, in the absence of disturbing causes, the rate of profit in all employments of capital is equal. If we can ascertain, therefore, what are the causes which regulate the rate of profit in any one of the main employments of capital, we may infer that, in the absence of peculiar disturbance, either the same causes, or, causes of equal force, occasion it to be the same in all others. We will inquire, therefore, into the causes which regulate the rate of profit in one of the main employments of capital,—the advance of wages to the labourers who are themselves employed in producing wages, *using the word wages to signify commodities for the use of the labouring population.*

To simplify the question, we will suppose a small colony settled in a district where there is abundance of fertile land, and protected by situation and character from external and internal violence, so that neither rent nor taxation need be supposed to exist: we will suppose it to be inhabited by ten capitalists and one thousand two hundred labouring families; *that the use of money is unknown;* that all the buildings, the clothes, the furniture, and the food, in fact, the whole consumption of the people, is consumed in one year and reproduced in the next; that each family receives its wages for the year on the first day of the year, and completes its production on the last day, so that all the advances are made on the first day of the year, and all the returns received on the last day; and that, at the time when the situation of the colony was first noticed, each capitalist had in his possession wages for one hundred and twenty families during a year, the produce of the labour of one hundred families during the previous year, (being his capital, and which, to reduce it to one denomination, we will call one thousand quarters of corn;) and commodities for his own use, which we will call twenty casks of wine, the produce of the labour of twenty families during the previous year; (being the stock reserved for his own consumption.)

Under such circumstances, if each capitalist should employ his capital in setting one hundred families to work to reproduce wages, and twenty more to reproduce commodities for his own use, and the labouring population should neither increase nor diminish, the rate of profit would remain stationary at twenty per cent. per annum. The advances every year would be one thousand quarters of corn, being wages produced by the labour of one hundred families, and commanding the labour of one hundred and twenty; the returns would be a stock of wages commanding the labour of one hundred and twenty families during the next year, which would be, in fact, a reproduction of the previous capital of one thousand quarters, and also a stock of commodities for the capitalist's own use, produced by one-sixth of the labour employed in reproducing the capital, and therefore one-sixth of the value of the capital. The value of the returns on an advance of capital for a year would exceed the value of the advances by one-sixth. The rate of profit therefore would, as we said before, remain stationary at twenty per cent. per annum. And five-sixths of the labourers would be employed in producing commodities for their own use, and one-sixth in producing commodities for the use of the capitalists.

We will now consider the effects of any alteration in the proportion of capital to labour. Suppose that emigration or an unhealthy season should diminish by fifty the number of labouring familes: each capitalist would have the same capital; consisting of wages produced by the labour of one hundred families during the year, and which we have called one thousand quarters of corn: but the number of labourers being diminished by one-twenty-fourth, instead of commanding the labour of one hundred and twenty families, they would command the labour of only one hundred and fifteen. The one thousand quarters of corn would be divided among one hundred and fifteen families instead of among one hundred and twenty, and the capitalist would get only fifteen casks of wine during the subsequent year instead of twenty. To take the converse: if immigration or an increase of population should have increased the number of labourers by fifty, each capitalist, instead of one hundred and twenty families, would be able to command the labour of one hundred and twenty-five. The one thousand quarters would be divided among one hundred and twenty-five families, instead of among one hundred and twenty, and the capitalist might employ twenty-five families to produce wine for himself instead of twenty. In the one case, profits rise from twenty to about twenty-five per cent.; in the other, they fall to about fifteen. On the other hand, if we suppose the labouring population to remain stationary at one thousand two hundred families, but the capitalists, instead of employing each one hundred families in the production of wages, and twenty in the production of profits, to employ each one hundred and five in the production of wages, each capitalist would at the end of the year have a capital of one thousand and fifty quarters produced by the labour of one hundred and five families, and commanding the labour of one hundred and twenty; or if they each employed in the production of wages only ninety-five families, and in the production of profits twenty-five, each would have at the end of the year a capital of nine hundred and fifty quarters, produced by the labour of ninety-five families, and commanding the labour of one hundred and twenty. Profits would fall in the first instance from twenty per cent. to less than fifteen; in the second, they would rise to more than twenty-five. If, however, the increase of the number of labourers employed in the production of wages should be accompanied by a proportionate increase in the whole number of labourers; or if, when the number of labourers employed in the production of wages was diminished, the whole number of labourers should be diminished in proportion; or, in other words, if the proportion of capital to labour remained unaltered, the rate of profit would be also unaltered. If each were increased, or each diminished, but in different proportions, profits would rise or fall according to the relative variations in the supply of wages and labour.

It appears, therefore, that, under the most simple state of circumstances, the rate of profits depends, as we said before, on the previous conduct of the capitalists and the labourers in a Country.

In this hypothesis we have supposed all the capitalists to act together. And as every permanent increase of capital while the number of labourers remained the same would, under the supposed circumstances, occasion a proportionate diminution of the rate of profit, it never could be the interest of the capitalists, as a body, to increase their capital, except with a view to increase the number of labourers; or even to keep up their capital, except so far as it should be necessary to keep up the existing number of labourers. It would be their interest, if the population were incapable of increase, to devote to the production of wages labour just sufficient to produce the necessaries of life for that stationary population, if the population were advancing just sufficient to enable it to advance; to treat the labourers, in short, as a farmer treats his horses, or a slave-owner his slaves.

Under such circumstances, supposing the capitalists to be governed solely by their interest, the rate of profit would depend partly on the productiveness of labour, and partly on the period that must elapse between the time of the advances and of the returns. Given the period of advance, it would depend on the productiveness of labour. If a labourer by a year's labour could produce a return which, to reduce it to one denomination, we will call ten quarters of corn, and five quarters were enough for his support, the rate of profit would be one hundred per cent. per annum. By an advance of five quarters the capitalist would obtain a return of ten. If the labourer could produce fifteen, the rate of profit would be two hundred per cent.; by an advance of five the capitalist would obtain fifteen. If the labourer could produce only seven and a-half, profits would be fifty per cent. On the other hand, the productiveness of labour being given, the rate of profit would depend on the period for which the capital must be advanced.   When the labourer receiving five quarters as wages could, by a year's labour, produce ten, a capitalist with a capital consisting of ten quarters could employ two labourers, each of whom would return to him ten quarters every year. But if, instead of returning ten quarters at the end of one year, a labourer returned twenty quarters at the end of two years, a capitalist with a capital of ten quarters would be able to employ only one labourer instead of two; for if he were to employ two his capital would be exhausted before it was reproduced.   Only one-half of the number of labourers could be employed by the same amount of capital, and instead of getting a net revenue of ten quarters every year, the capitalist would get a net revenue of only ten quarters every two years.

Happily, however, the capitalists of a Country do not act as a body. Each pursues his own scheme of aggrandizement, indifferent to its effect on his neighbours, and it is chiefly to their mutual competition that we owe the increase both of capital and of population. To revert to our original hypothesis; suppose one of the capitalists, instead of employing, like each of the others, twenty labourers to produce commodities for his own use and one hundred to produce wages, to employ one hundred and ten labourers in the production of wages. A the end of the year he would have a capital consisting of one thousand one hundred quarters of corn produced by the labour of one hundred and ten families, and commanding, *at the existing rate of wages*, the labour of one hundred and thirty-two families; and the nine others would have each a capital consisting of one thousand quarters, produced by the labour of one hundred families, and commanding, *at the existing rate of wages*, one hundred and twenty families.   The whole capital of the Country, instead of its former amount, namely, ten thousand quarters, being wages for one thousand two hundred families, would amount to ten thousand one hundred quarters, being wages for one thousand two hundred and twelve families. But as there would be only one thousand two hundred families to receive them, profits would fall about one per cent., or from twenty per cent. to a fraction less than nineteen per cent. per annum. This fall of profits would prevent the capitalist to whose conduct it was owing from reaping the full benefit of his accumulation. He would find himself possessed of a capital consisting of one thousand one hundred quarters, being wages produced by the labour of one hundred and ten families, and commanding the labour of one hundred and thirty and a fraction; but every other capitalist would find his capital of one thousand quarters, produced by the labour of one hundred families, commanding the labour of a small fraction less than one hundred and nineteen families. The first, or accumulating capitalist, would find the value of his capital and the amount of his profits increased, though the rate of profits had fallen one per cent.   But all the other capitalists would find both the value of their capital and the amount of their profits diminished.

Now there is nothing to which a capitalist submits so reluctantly as the diminution of the value of his capital.   He is dissatisfied if it even remain stationary.   Capitals are generally formed from small beginnings by acts of accumulation, which become in time habitual. The capitalist soon regards the increase of his capital as the great business of his life; and considers the greater part of his profit more as a means to that end than as a subject of enjoyment.   It is probable, therefore, that the other capitalists in the Country would endeavour to keep the value of their capitals unimpaired, though at the expense of a diminution of the general rate of profit.   One after another would follow the example of the first-mentioned capitalist, and devote to the increase of their respective capitals a portion of the labour previously employed in furnishing commodities for their own use.   In time each capitalist, instead of employing one hundred families in the reproduction of capital, and twenty in supplying his own enjoyments, would employ one hundred and ten in the reproduction of capital, and only ten for his own purposes.   The rate of profit would fall from twenty to ten per cent., and, of the one thousand two hundred labouring families, one thousand one hundred would be employed in producing wages, and only one hundred in producing profits.   The annual produce of the Country, instead of ten thousand quarters of corn and two hundred casks of wine, would consist of ten thousand one hundred quarters of corn and one hundred casks of wine.   Instead of five-sixths of the labourers in the Country being employed in producing commodities for the use of the labourers, and one-sixth for the use of capitalists, eleven-twelfths would be employed for the benefit of the labourers, and only one-twelfth for the benefit of the capitalists.

This fall of profit, however, could take place only on the supposition of the number of labouring families remaining unaltered.   But it is highly improbable that it could remain unincreased.   The increase of wages would enable the labourers to marry earlier, or to raise more numerous families.   If labour should remain equally productive, their numbers might increase until the former proportion of labourers to capital had been restored.   All the results would be beneficial.   The labourers would not be worse off than before the additional accumulation took place, and the capitalists would be better off.   The value of their capitals and the amount of their profits would be increased, and the rate of profit would be again twenty per cent. per annum.

We set out with supposing a Country possessing an abundance of fertile land.   Under such circumstances the productiveness of labour might for a long period continue, or even increase, with every addition to the number of its inhabitants.   But in a densely-peopled Country the powers of labour seldom remain the same during an increase of population.   In manufactures labour becomes proportionably more productive.   In agriculture, unless aided by increased industry or skill, or by permanent improvements of the soil, it becomes proportionably less so.   And, as the labourer consumes chiefly raw or slightly-manufactured produce, the increased facility of obtaining manufactures may not make up for an increased difficulty in obtaining raw produce.   In an old Country, therefore, when the rate of profit has been reduced by an increase of capital, it seldom can be fully restored by a proportionate increase of population, unless either the labourer receives a smaller quantity of raw produce than before, or the necessity of cultivating lands of inferior productiveness is obviated either by permanent improvements, such as draining marshes, or fertilizing bogs, or by additional industry or skill, or by the importation of raw produce.   In such Countries the natural progress seems to be an increase of capital, occasioning a fall of the rate of profit; a check to that fall, occasioned by an increase of the labouring population; a check to that increase, occasioned by an increased difficulty in obtaining raw produce; and a diminution, rarely amounting to a removal, of that difficulty, occasioned by permanent agricultural improvements, increased industry or skill, or foreign importation; leaving, as the general result, a constant tendency towards an increase of capital and population, and towards a fall in the rate of profits.

In our hypothesis we have supposed the whole capital of the Country to be consumed and reproduced every year.   Under such circumstances it has appeared that, the number of labourers remaining the same, no permanent addition could be made to capital without occasioning immediately a proportionate diminution of the rate of profit, since that addition would disappear in a year unless reproduced by a repetition of the sacrifice on the part of the capitalist by whom it was originally created.   But the result would be different if that addition were made in a form requiring no further labour for its reproduction.   Suppose the capitalist, instead of adding five to the hundred families employed in producing wages, were to employ the additional five in the construction of a durable machine enabling one man to do some piece of work that previously required two.   At the end of the first year each capitalist would possess wages for one hundred and twenty families, produced by the labour of one hundred families; commodities for his own use, produced by the labour of fifteen families; and his machine, produced by the labour of five families.   But in every subsequent year he might obtain wages for one hundred and twenty families by employing only ninety-nine families and his machine, and might employ twenty-one families in producing commodities for himself.   Both the rate and the amount of profit would be increased without any diminution of wages.   Such a machine is a new labourer added to the existing number of labourers, but a new labourer whom it costs nothing to maintain.   It adds to the amount of the profit of the capitalist who has constructed it, without either taking from the profits of other capitalists, as must be the case when additional capital is created, which must be kept up and worked by additional labour; or taking from the wages of the other labourers, as must be the case when an additional labourer is added, whose subsistence must be taken from the common fund.   A machine or implement is, in fact, merely a means by which the productiveness of labour is increased.   The millions which have been expended in this country in making roads, bridges, and ports, have had no tendency to reduce either the rate of profit or the amount of wages.   They have, in fact, had a tendency to keep up both, by enabling labour to be more productive, and consequently enabling the circulating capital and the population of the Country to increase in corresponding ratios.

It appears, therefore, that in one of the main employments of capital, namely, the employment of labourers to produce commodities for the use of labourers, or, in other words, to produce wages, the difference between the value of the returns and the value of the advances depends on the amount of labour which at a previous period was devoted to the production of wages, compared with the amount of labour which those wages when produced can command.   And as the rate of profits in every different employment of capital has a tendency to equality, we may infer that all capitals, however employed, yield about the same rate of profit as those which are employed in the production of wages.

AVERAGE PERIOD OF ADVANCE OF CAPITAL.—The first of the two principles which regulate the division of the produce between the capitalist and the labourer, namely, *the rate of profit in the advance of capital for a given time*, having been, in some measure, ascertained, we proceed to inquire into the causes which regulate the second principle, namely, *the average time for which the capital must be advanced*.

It must be recollected, however, that the expression "the capitalist's share," though familiarly used by Economists, is not strictly correct.   When the product is completed, it is the sole property of the capitalist, who has purchased it by paying in advance the labourer's wages.   What is meant, therefore, by " the capitalist's share," is that portion of the product, or of the price for which it sells, which the capitalist can retain and apply for his own purposes, keeping the value of his capital unimpaired.   What is meant by " the labourer's share," is that portion of the produce, or of the price for which it sells, which the capitalist, if he keep his capital unimpaired, cannot employ for his own purposes, but must employ in advancing the price of the labour by which the work of reproduction is to be performed. We have already shown that, the period of advance being given, these proportions are determined by the rate of profit. It is equally clear that, the rate of profit being given, they must be determined by the period of advance. If a capitalist has a return which we will call twelve quarters of corn, and we wish to know how much of it he must retain as capital, and how much he may use as profit, the first inquiry is, For what period must he advance his capital before he can again obtain a similar return? The next inquiry is, What is the current rate of profit? If the answer to the first inquiry be, one year, and to the second, twenty per cent. per annum, it follows that, by constantly employing ten quarters as wages, he will receive two as profit. If the period of advance be only six months, the rate of profit continuing at twenty per cent. per annum, he must employ eleven and a fraction as capital, and will not receive quite one as profit. If the period of advance be two years, the rate of profit continuing at twenty per cent. per annum, rather less than eight quarters will form a sufficient capital, and rather more than four will be profit. With every prolongation of the period of advance, the rate of profit continuing the same, the capitalist's share must increase. With every abridgment of that period it must diminish. And it is equally obvious that, the period of advance being given, the capitalist's share must augment with every increase of the rate of profit, and diminish as that rate decreases.

On what then does the period for which capital is to be advanced depend? To this question no general answer can be given. The period differs according to the accidents of soil and climate; it varies indefinitely in every different business, and even in employments which, in other respects, are perfectly similar.

In Europe the harvest is annual; in Hindostan it recurs every six months. The average period for which agricultural wages are advanced must be at least twice as long in Europe as in Hindostan. A great part of the capital employed in breeding horses must be advanced four or five years; that employed in planting must be advanced forty or fifty. A very small part of the capital of a butcher or a baker is advanced for more than a week. The stock of a fishmonger spoils in a day; that of a Rhenish wine-merchant is improved by being kept a century. As a general rule, the average period is longer or shorter in one Country than in another, in an inverse proportion to the general rate of profit. In the general market of the world, a Country in which the rate of profit is low has over one where it is high an advantage which increases at compound interest, as the period of advance is prolonged. The rate of profit in Russia is supposed to be above twice as high as in England. We will suppose that rate to be five per cent. per annum in England, and ten in Russia. A commodity produced in Russia by an advance of £10 for twenty years would sell for nearly £70. A commodity produced in England by the advance of £20 for the same time would sell for less than £60. The difference in the rate of profit would far outbalance a doubling of the first expenditure. Profits are supposed to be lower in Holland and in England than in any other part of the globe. The English and the Dutch, therefore, have almost a monopoly in those trades in which the returns are distant. Abstinence with them is a cheap instrument of production, and they use it to the utmost. In their commerce with other nations they generally pay in ready money, but give a very long credit. They purchase raw produce, and sell manufactures. In many instances they even advance to the foreign Countries the first expenses of production. The indigo of Bengal, the wines of the Cape, the wool of Australia, and the silver of Mexico, are in a great measure produced by the advance of English capital. The accumulated interest on such advances would be an intolerable addition to the value of the returns if the rate of profit were high. This circumstance occasions a tendency to uniformity in the proportion, in different Countries, in which the produce is shared between the capitalist and the labourer. Where profits are high, the capitalist's share is kept down by the shortness of the period for which his capital is advanced. Where they are low, it is kept up by the prolongation of that period.

The labourer is far more interested in the comparative rate of profit than in the comparative period for which capital is advanced. The productiveness of labour and the period of advance being given, we have seen that the amount of his share of the product depends on the rate of profit. It is his interest, therefore, in the first place, that when capital is employed *in the production of the commodities which he consumes*, all other things remaining the same, the rate of profit should be low. And if it were possible that the rate of profit in other employments could be higher, capital would be diverted from the only production in which the labourer is directly interested—the production of commodities for his own use—and the general fund for the maintenance of labour would be diminished. All other things, therefore, remaining the same, it is the labourer's interest that the rate of profit should be *universally low*. But it must be recollected, first, that the average period for which capital is advanced, especially in the production of the commodities used by labourers, is so short that the capitalist's share is small even when profits are high: if the advance has been for six months, the capitalist's share, at the high rate of twenty per cent. per annum, would be less than one-eleventh : and, secondly, that a high rate of profit is generally found to accompany a great productiveness of labour. And therefore that, in general, the labourer is better paid, or, in other words, receives a larger amount of commodities, when profits are high, that is when he receives a small share, than when profits are low, that is when he receives a large share, of the value of what he produces. The increase of the labourer's share from ten-elevenths to twenty-one-twenty-seconds, which would be the consequence in the case which we have supposed of a fall of profits by one-half, would add very little to the *amount* of his wages.

On the other hand, it is his interest that, when capital is employed in the production of *what he himself consumes*, the period of advance should be short. We will suppose a labourer employed on the least productive soil to produce by a year's labour, employed in hoeing and weeding, an additional produce of twenty-two quarters of corn; the wages of labour to be £20 a-year; the rate of profit to be ten per cent. per annum, and a year to elapse between the advance of the wages and the corn being fit for use; the price of the corn would be £22; the labourer would receive twenty quarters, or, what is the same, £20, with which he could purchase twenty quarters. But if corn were not fit for use until it had been kept for ten years, on the same data, the corn, instead of selling for £22, would sell for above £50; the labourer would receive less than ten quarters instead of twenty, or, what comes to the same, his wages, instead of twenty, would purchase less than ten quarters. To produce the corn would require the same degree of labour as before, but ten times as much abstinence.

Another consequence of the prolongation of the period of advance would be, that with the same amount of capital the capitalist would be able to maintain much fewer labourers than before. If ten quarters were necessary to maintain a labouring family during a year, and they could reproduce eleven in a state fit for consumption at the end of the year, a capital of one hundred quarters would enable a capitalist to keep in constant employ ten labouring families during the first year, and eleven during every subsequent year. But, if the corn were not fit for consumption till the end of ten years, a capitalist starting with a capital of one hundred quarters could not maintain more than a single family, for, if he were to maintain more, the capital would be exhausted before it was reproduced. The prolongation of the period of advance would have precisely the same effect as a diminished productiveness of labour.

But the prolongation of the period of advance of the capital employed in the production of the commodities which the labourer does not consume is utterly indifferent to him. If a labourer by a year's labour can produce twenty-two ounces of lace, his wages being £20 a-year, and advanced for a year, and the rate of profit being ten per cent., he will receive ten-elevenths of the value of the lace, or, in other words, he might purchase with his wages twenty ounces of lace. If the lace required keeping for ten years, his wages would purchase less than ten ounces of the lace in its complete state. But as he never wishes to purchase lace, and as the prolongation of the

period for which capital must be advanced in the production of lace
would not affect either the productiveness of labour, or the rate of
profit, or the period of advance in any other employment, it would
be utterly indifferent to him; it would affect only the consumers of
lace.

We have seen that, although practically high wages and high
profits generally go together, yet, all other things remaining the
same, it is the interest of the labourers that profits should be universally low.   It is equally clear that it is the interest of the capitalists
that they should be universally high.   A fall in the rate of profit in
any one employment has a tendency to force capital into the others.
This diminishes the competition among the first-mentioned capitalists,
but increases it among the others.   The first are relieved, but it is
only by the loss being spread over the whole body.
But a prolongation of the period of advance affects the capitalist
only so far as he uses the specific commodity with respect to which
that prolongation has taken place.   The rate of profit on the advance
of capital for a given period being given, the length of the period
between the bottling of a pipe of port and its being fit for use affects
a wine merchant only so far as he drinks port.   As a consumer, it is
his interest that the period should be short; as a capitalist it is
immaterial to him.

We have now given an outline of the causes which affect the
general rate of wages, the most important and the most difficult of all
the subjects embraced by Political Economy.   It has appeared, first,
that the general rate of wages depends on the amount of the fund for
the maintenance of labourers, compared with the number of labourers
to be maintained.
Secondly, that the amount of that fund depends partly on the productiveness of labour in the production of the commodities used by
the labourer, or, to speak more concisely, in the production of wages,
and partly on the number of labourers employed in the production of
wages compared with the whole number of labourers.
Thirdly, that the productiveness of labour depends on the character
of the labourer, or the assistance which he derives from natural
agents, and from capital, and on his freedom from interference.
Fourthly, that, in the absence of rent and improper or unequally-
distributed taxation, the proportion of the labourers employed in producing wages to the whole number of labourers depends partly on the
rate of profit, and partly on the time for which the capital employed
in the production of wages must be advanced.
Fifthly, that the rate of profit, at any given time, depends on the
previous conduct of capitalists and labourers.
And, sixthly, that the period for which capital must be advanced

is subject to no general rule, but has a tendency to be prolonged when profits are low, and shortened when they are high.

The inquiry into the causes which regulate wages has, in a great measure, ascertained those which affect profits. We have to add only that profits may be considered in three points of view: first, as to their rate; secondly, as to their amount; and, thirdly, as to the amount of desirable objects which a given amount of profit will command. The causes which decide the rate of profit have been already considered. It has been shown that they depend on the proportion which the supply of capital employed in providing wages bears to the supply of labour. The rate being given, the amount of the profit received by any given capitalist must depend, of course, on the amount of his capital. It follows that, when the rate of profit falls in consequence of an increase of capital without a proportionate increase of labourers, the situation of the existing capitalists, as a body, cannot be deteriorated, unless the fall in the rate has been so great as to overbalance the increase of the amount. Two millions, at five per cent., would give as large an amount of profit as one million at ten. At seven and a-half per cent. they would give a much larger. And such is the tendency of an increase of capital to produce, not indeed a corresponding, but still a positive increase of population, that we believe there is no instance on record of the whole amount of profits having diminished with an increase of the whole amount of capital.

Totally distinct from the amount of profit is the amount of desirable objects which a given amount of profit will purchase. A Chinese and an English capitalist, each of whose annual profit will command the labour of ten families for a year, will enjoy in different degrees the comfort and conveniences of life. The Englishman will have more woollen goods and hardware, the Chinese more tea and silk. The difference depends on the different productiveness of labour in China and in England in the production of those commodities which are used by the capitalists in each Country. In the command of labour, and in the rank in society which that command gives, they are on a par. We have seen that, as population advances, labour has a tendency to become less efficient in the production of raw produce, and more productive in manufactures. The same amount of profit, therefore, will enable the capitalist in a thinly-peopled Country to enjoy coarse profusion, or among a dense population moderate refinement. A South American, with an annual income commanding the labour of one hundred families, would live in a log-house on the skirts of a forest, and keep, perhaps, one hundred horses. An Englishman with the same command of labour would live in a well-furnished villa, and keep a chariot and pair. Each would possess sources of enjoyment totally beyond the reach of the other.

VARIATIONS OF THE AMOUNT OF WAGES AND THE RATE OF PROFITS IN DIFFERENT EMPLOYMENTS OF LABOUR AND CAPITAL.

In the previous discussion we have assumed the existence of a certain average rate of Wages and average rate of Profits. We now propose to consider the influence of some specific causes on the amount of wages and the rate of profits in Different Employments of Labour and Capital.

The justly celebrated chapter on this subject in the *Wealth of Nations* begins with the following words:—

"The five following are the principal circumstances which, so far as I have been able to observe, make up for a small pecuniary gain in some employments, and counterbalance a great one in others. 1. The agreeableness or disagreeableness of the employments themselves. 2. The easiness and cheapness, or the difficulty and expense, of learning them. 3. The constancy or inconstancy of employment in them. 4. The small or great trust which must be reposed in those who exercise them. 5. The probability or improbability of success in them." Book I. Ch. X.

As our remarks will be chiefly a commentary on those of Adam Smith, we shall, as far as we can, follow his arrangement. We shall begin, therefore, by the influence of agreeableness or disagreeableness.

1. **Agreeableness.**—The act of labouring implies a sacrifice of ease, and it is chiefly to this sacrifice that our attention is directed when we speak of wages as the remuneration for labour. But, as we have already observed, the indolence which generally indisposes to severe or long-continued bodily exertion is not in all cases the only feeling which the labourer has to conquer. His employment may be dangerous, or physically disagreeable, or degrading. In any one of these cases his wages are the reward not only of the fatigue, but of the hazard, the discomfort, or the discredit which he has encountered. Adam Smith, however, has remarked, that the prospect of hazards from which we can hope to extricate ourselves by courage and address is not disagreeable, and does not raise the wages of labour in any employment. "The dangers and hair-breadth escapes of a life of adventure, instead of disheartening young people, seem frequently to recommend a trade to them. But it is otherwise," he observes, "with those in which courage and address can be of no avail. In trades which are known to be very unwholesome the wages of labour are always remarkably high."[34]

Unwholesomeness, indeed, is generally united to other disagreeable circumstances. Dirt, dust, deleterious atmosphere, exposure to con-

[34] Book I. Ch. X.

tinued heat or cold, or to sudden transitions from the one to the other, which are the principal causes of unhealthiness in any business, are also the principal causes of its being generally disagreeable. When toil, disease, and discomfort, are all to be encountered, the temptation must indeed be high. But this union is not universal. The trade of a house-painter is one of the most agreeable, and one of the most unwholesome, among ordinary occupations. On the other hand, that of a butcher, though brutal and disgusting, is eminently healthy. The wages of each are, we believe, about equal, and considerably exceed the remuneration for the mere labour undergone, which, in fact, is in both cases very trifling. But the fear of popular odium, and, what is always strongest amongst the least educated, the fear of popular ridicule, as they are amongst the most powerful feelings of our nature, are the most effectual means by which the wages of an employment can be increased. To Adam Smith's instance of a public executioner may be added that of a common informer; both of whom are remunerated at a rate quite disproportioned to the quantity of work which they do. They are paid not so much for encountering toil as for being pelted and hissed. The most degrading of all common trades, perhaps, is that of a beggar; but, when pursued as a trade, it is believed to be a very gainful one.

Such appears to be the influence upon wages of danger, discomfort, and disgrace. And it may be supposed that any peculiarly agreeable employment is generally as comparatively underpaid as peculiarly disagreeable ones are overpaid. Adam Smith has accordingly remarked that in a civilized society hunters and fishers, who follow as a trade what other people pursue as a pastime, are generally very poor people. "Fishermen," he observes, "have been poor from the times of Theocritus. The natural taste for these employments makes more people follow them than can live comfortably by them; and the produce of their labour, in proportion to its quantity, comes always too cheap to market to afford any thing but the most scanty subsistence to the labourers." Hunting, however, can scarcely be said to exist as a trade in any well-civilized Country. And we doubt the accuracy of Adam Smith's statement as to fishermen; unless, as perhaps was the case, he intended to confine them to the small number of anglers and poachers on rivers, who do, in fact, follow as a trade what other men enjoy as a pastime. Marine fishery is a business of too much toil and hardship to be very attractive; and if any proof, besides the well-fed persons and ample clothing of the men and their families were required, of its being well paid, it would be found in the fact that the capital employed in it, which is far from inconsiderable, generally belongs to the fishermen themselves.

As a general rule, we fear it must be admitted that the occupations open to those who are not possessed of capital differ only in the degree in which they are disagreeable. The least disagreeable are man's primeval occupations, those of a shepherd and a tiller of the ground. And, accordingly, we believe that in every state of society the lowest wages are those which are paid to agricultural labourers. The current wages of common agricultural labourers may, therefore, in general be considered as representing the value, at the time and place where they are paid, of mere bodily labour. If, at the same time and place, we find the services of any other labourer more highly paid, we may infer either that his employment is subject to some peculiar disadvantage, or that, in fact, rent or profit enter into his remuneration.

Adam Smith states that, in point of agreeableness or disagreeableness, there is little or no difference in the greater part of the different employments of stock, though a great deal in those of labour; and he infers, as we have seen, that average profits are more nearly on a level than average wages. That portion of profit which is simply the remuneration for abstinence is certainly, at the same time and place, nearly on a level; for abstinence, being a negative idea, does not admit of degrees, excepting in the amount of capital from the unproductive use of which the capitalist abstains, and the length of time during which he abstains.

But we cannot admit that the agreeableness or disagreeableness of the greater part of the different employments of capital is about the same. Nor would Adam Smith have stated them to be so unless he had used wages in a wider, and profit in a narrower sense than that which has been adopted in this Treatise. Wages, in the sense in which we have used the word, are paid almost exclusively for undergoing bodily labour or bodily inconvenience, and bodily labour is almost always disagreeable. But the labour of employing capital is principally mental, and mental exertion is often delightful. We frequently hear of men who are devoted to their profession or their business, however generally unattractive. A surgeon once told us that, whatever were his income, his utmost happiness would be to superintend a great military hospital. Half the miseries of mankind have arisen from the delight of statesmen in governing, and of generals in war. Again, the mere labourer receives mere pecuniary wages, or food, shelter, and clothing, of equal value. The capitalist is often paid by power or reputation, and sometimes receives the highest of human rewards, the consciousness that he has been widely and permanently useful. And, on the other hand, there are employments, as for instance the slave-trade, which imply fatigue, hardship, and danger, public execration, and, if a slave trader can be supposed to reflect on the nature of his occupation, self-reproach. It is unnecessary to prove by a formal induction that, when almost all that renders life agreeable, or even endurable, is sacrificed to profit, the profit must be great, or that competition must reduce very low the pecuniary reward or valuable remuneration of occupations which seem to carry with them their own reward.

It may not appear obvious why the extra profit of a disagreeable employment should bear any proportion to the value of the capital employed in it. It must be remembered that, since the number of persons possessed of a given capital becomes rapidly smaller as the amount of the supposed capital is larger, the possessors of any given amount of capital enjoy a sort of monopoly, which becomes stricter and stricter as the given amount is larger; and, secondly, that the larger a man's capital, and consequently his income, the greater must be the temptation necessary to induce him to encounter moral or physical evil in the hope of increasing it. On the other hand, both the trouble and the inferiority of rank that accompany any trade are generally in inverse proportion to the capital employed. Where, indeed, the objection to a trade arises from its moral turpitude, as in the case of the keeper of a gambling-house, or of any place of still more shameful resort, its extent will only increase its infamy. But in the absence of this peculiar objection, the same trade which on a small scale is mean, is respectable in a large way, and almost dignified when carried to its greatest extent. The trouble cannot be so completely got rid of, but, when the capital is large enough to enable the employment of clerks and junior partners of great knowledge and high character, it may often be so far reduced as to occupy a small portion of the principal's daily time. There are at this instant many persons busily engaged, and even distinguished in politics and literature, who are also at the head of great banking, brewing, or mercantile establishments. It is not probable that their occupations in business can employ much of their time.

The result that might be anticipated from these opposing circumstances is, that that part of profit which is the remuneration for the trouble and other sacrifices, independent of abstinence made by the capitalist, though it must positively increase in amount, yet generally bears a smaller proportion to the capital employed as that capital increases in value. And this anticipation is, we think, confirmed by observation. There are, we apprehend, few persons employing in England a capital of £100,000, who would not be satisfied with a profit of less than ten per cent. per annum. A manufacturer of considerable eminence, with a capital of £40,000, complained to us of the smallness of his profits, which he estimated at twelve and a half per cent. About fifteen per cent. we believe to be the average that is expected by men with mercantile capitals between £10,000 and £20,000. Scarcely any wholesale trade can be carried on with a capital of less than £10,000. The capitals of less value, therefore, generally belong to farmers, shopkeepers, and small manufacturers, who, even when their capital amounts to £5000 or £6000, expect twenty per cent., and when it is lower a much larger per centage. We have heard that stall fruit-sellers calculate their gains at 2d. in the shilling, or twenty per cent. per day, or something more than 7000 per cent. per annum. This seems, however, almost too low. The capital employed at any one time seldom exceeds in value 5s., twenty per cent. on which would only be 1s. a-day; a sum which would scarcely pay the wages of the mere labour employed. It is, however, possible that the capital may sometimes be turned more than once in a day; and the capitalists in question, if they can be called so, are generally the old and infirm, whose labour is of little value. The calculation, therefore, may probably be correct, and we have mentioned it as the highest apparent rate of profit that we know.

2. **Facility of learning the Business.**—" Secondly," says Adam Smith, "the wages of labour vary with the easiness and cheapness, or the difficulty and expense, of learning the business.

"When any expensive machine is erected, the extraordinary work to be performed by it before it is worn out, it must be expected, will replace the capital laid out on it with at least the ordinary profits. A man educated at the expense of much labour and time may be compared to one of these expensive machines. The work which he learns to perform, it must be expected, over and above the usual wages of common labour, will replace to him the whole expense of his education with at least the ordinary profits of an equally valuable capital. It must do this in a reasonable time, regard being had to the very uncertain duration of human life, in the same manner as to the more certain duration of the machine. The difference between the wages of skilled labour and those of common labour is founded on this principle." Book I. Ch. X.

We agree with the whole of this admirable passage, except that we think it shows the propriety of rather terming the surplus remuneration of skilled over common labour profit than wages. It is an advantage derived by the skilled labourer in consequence partly of his own previous conduct, and partly of that of his parents or friends ;—of the labour and of the expense which they respectively contributed to his education. It is profit on a capital, though on that sort of capital which cannot be made available without the labour of its possessor.

Adam Smith has remarked that, in the liberal professions, this labour and expense are very inadequately remunerated; and he attributes the slightness of their remuneration first to the desire of the reputation which attends upon superior excellence in any of them; secondly, to the natural confidence which every man has, more or less, not only in his own abilities, but in his own good fortune; and thirdly, as far as literature and the church are concerned, to the number of persons who are educated for those occupations at the public expense.

The two first causes operate very forcibly. The influence of the third he has, we think, exaggerated, or, perhaps, its force may have much diminished since he wrote. In the first place, though our population has nearly doubled in the interval, the number of provisions for affording gratuitously the means of a liberal education has not materially increased. And, secondly, from the change which has taken place in the style of living at the places of education, and in many cases from the nominal value of the provisions having remained unaltered, while money has lost more than half its value, these provisions now afford much less real assistance to the persons who obtain them. Adam Smith seems to have supposed that the greater part of the clergy were educated at the expense of the public, and he expressly states that few were educated altogether at their own. But at present there are scarcely any undergraduates at either of our Universities wholly maintained by a foundation: probably there are not twenty who receive from such a source one-half of their expenditure, and by far the greater number receive no pecuniary assistance except from the relative cheapness of instruction. We say *relative* cheapness, because the sum of money positively paid for instruction is perhaps as great at Oxford and Cambridge as at most other Universities; but the attention bestowed by the teacher on each individual student is considerably greater. In the foreign Universities a lecture is a discourse delivered by the professor; in ours, the College lectures, which are the principal means of instruction, are, in a great degree, examinations undergone by the pupils. There can be no comparison between the labour imposed on the teacher in these two modes of education. But that which is the laborious one necessarily confines each tutor to a small number of pupils. If our foundations did not afford them an income, our tutors must either require a much larger remuneration from each pupil, or adopt the foreign mode of teaching by discourses delivered to large assemblies.

The principal cause which fills the avenues to some of the liberal professions with candidates so numerous as materially to diminish one another's reward is one which Adam Smith has omitted.

The average expense of providing in the cheapest manner for the maintenance of a child until it can maintain itself by ordinary labour may perhaps amount to about £40. This is double the sum for which a parish will indemnify the father of a bastard. The parish, however, speculates on the chances of the child's death. The average expense of giving to a gentleman's son the education which is essential to his holding his father's rank cannot be estimated at less than £2040. But neither the labour which the boy undergoes, nor the expense borne by his father, is incurred principally in order to obtain future profit. The boy works under the stimulus of immediate praise or immediate punishment. It never occurs to the father that it would be cheaper to have his child nursed in the country at 2s. a-week till he is eight years old, and then removed to a farm-yard or a cotton-mill; and that in giving him a more expensive education he is engaging in a speculation which is likely to be unprofitable. To witness a son's daily improvement is, with all well-disposed men, or rather with all men, except a few outcasts, one of the greatest sources of immediate gratification.   The expense incurred for that purpose is as much repaid by immediate enjoyment as that which is incurred to obtain the most transitory pleasures.   It is true that a further object may also be obtained, but the immediate motive is ample.

But the extra expense and labour thus incurred in some cases constitute the whole expense and labour of preparation for a liberal profession, and in all cases constitute the bulk of that expense and labour.   In the church they constitute the whole of the expense, and almost all the labour.   A graduate of Oxford or Cambridge may have a very little more to read before he takes orders, but has absolutely nothing more to pay.   What he obtains, therefore, as a clergyman, after deducting the mere wages of his additional labour, is pure gain. And when we consider how many are the motives for undergoing that labour, besides the merely pecuniary ones, we might be tempted to wonder that the pecuniary rewards should remain so high.   Three circumstances keep them up: two by diminishing the number of candidates, and the third by raising the fund applicable to their use. The two former ones are the indelibility of the clerical character, and the interdiction of clergymen from almost all secular employments, especially from those which offer the most glittering rewards.   Many men would enter the church if they could combine it with other occupations, or if they might quit it at pleasure, who refuse to enter into a path in which it is not permitted to turn back or to diverge. These are probably the principal causes which tend in this Country to keep down the number of clergymen.   The revenue of the existing members is kept up by means of the fund set apart by law for their use, and somewhat equalized by the repeated intervention of the Legislature to raise the remuneration of curates by prohibiting the incumbent from offering, and the curate from accepting, a stipend as low as would have been fixed on mere principles of competition.   The expense of entering the army is probably about equal to that of the church; for though about £600 is to be added for the price of the first commission and for outfit, the difference is about made up by the early age at which the profession can be begun.   The expense of the navy is much less, and either profession may be entered upon without further preparatory study.   The Legislature has fixed the pay and other advantages of the army and navy (moderate as they appear to be) much higher than would have been necessary to keep up the supply of qualified candidates.   The difficulty of obtaining permission to enter either of them is so notorious, that few persons without considerable interest ever think of them.   Yet, notwithstanding the influence of this feeling in diminishing the number of competitors, the Admiralty and the Horse Guards are besieged by candidates for first commissions ten times more numerous than the vacancies.

The same may be said of what are the subjects of almost a distinct profession, public offices. Small as the emoluments are, if they are to be considered as repaying the expenses of education, they are objects of eager competition.

If further proof were wanted that the number of the candidates for the liberal professions is principally kept up by the feeling which forces every parent to endeavour to give to his children at least the education of his own rank rather than by calculation, it may be found in the abundance of governesses. The expense of giving to a girl the education which will fit her to be a governess, though not quite equal to that of educating a boy as a gentleman, is yet very considerable: no part of it is ever supplied by the public; and yet that profession is so overstocked with candidates that the pay scarcely equals that of a servant.

An expense of nearly £1000 beyond the common expense of a regular education may be necessary to start a young man as a physician, and perhaps nearly £1500 as a barrister. The lower branches of the legal and medical professions are about as expensive as the church or the army. But no branch of either law or physic admits of practice till after an apprenticeship of from three to five years, or of success, without three or four years of diligent study. The effect of all these causes has been so much to diminish the number of competitors in the medical and legal professions, that we much doubt whether they are now, as Adam Smith states them to have been in his time, under-recompensed in point of pecuniary gain. We speak more doubtfully as to medicine; but we can say, from the observation of many years, that his statement that, "if you send your son to study the law, it is at least twenty to one if he ever makes such proficiency as will enable him to live by the business," has no resemblance to the existing state of things. We have watched the progress of perhaps a hundred legal students, and, where fair diligence has been employed, success has been the rule, and failure the exception. Many, indeed, have not applied fair diligence; but we have seen much more success among the idle than failure among the laborious. So far from the chances being twenty to one *against* a young lawyer, we should be inclined to rate them at two to one in his favour.

3. **Constancy of Employment.**—A third cause of variableness both in wages and in profits is constancy or inconstancy of employment. The variations which it occasions are, however, rather apparent than real. A London porter, employed for an hour, would think himself ill paid by less than a shilling. A pavior or a hodman, whose labour is much more severe, seldom receives more than 3d. an hour. But the pavior can always find a market for his services. At 3d. an hour, he can at an average earn three shillings a-day, or about £46 a-year. The porter may be sometimes a day without a job. If his employment be less regular by three-fourths than that of the pavior, to make his

annual wages equal, his hourly wages must of course be three times as high. Adam Smith, indeed, thinks that his annual wages ought to be higher than the average, to make him some compensation for those anxious and desponding moments which the thought of so precarious a situation must sometimes occasion. But this evil is compensated, and, in most dispositions, more than compensated, by the diminution of his toil. We believe, after all, that nothing is so much disliked as steady, regular labour; and that the opportunities of idleness afforded by an occupation of irregular employment are so much more than an equivalent for its anxiety as to reduce the annual wages of such occupations to below the common average.

In the employment of capital, however, this compensation does not often exist. The occasional unproductiveness of his capital, generally speaking, affords no relief to the capitalist. It must, therefore, be compensated by a surplus profit, when productive, at least enough to balance its periods of unproductiveness. A house-builder's capital often lies unproductive; there are some places in which the majority of the houses are unoccupied for nine months in the year. The builder's profit during their occupation must be at least four times as great as if they were regularly inhabited. One of the consequences of the effect of irregularity of employment on wages and profits is to occasion many services and commodities to cheapen as the demand for them increases. A man who can count on employment for four hours a-day would be forced by competition to sell his services for nearly half of what he might have asked if he could have reckoned on only two hours. Prices in a watering-place always fall as the season becomes longer.

4. **Trust.**—The fourth cause assigned by Adam Smith for the variation in wages, the small or great Trust which must be reposed in the workman, appears to be in a great measure included in the second of his causes, the expense of education. Occasionally, indeed, we see persons receiving and deserving confidence though brought up under disadvantageous circumstances. The integrity of such persons must arise from a peculiarly happy natural disposition, and its reward may then be considered a species of rent; but, as a general rule, trustworthiness is the result of early moral cultivation, and in that case is as much to be considered a part of a man's immaterial capital as his prudence or his knowledge.

5. **Probability of Success.**—The last of the causes mentioned by Adam Smith, as affecting the remuneration of different employments, is the Probability or Improbability of Success.

Uncertainty of success, in some respects, resembles inconstancy of employment. A few examples will show them to be different. The legal and medical professions are generally thought to be remarkably uncertain, but the employment of a successful physician or barrister is painfully incessant. On the other hand, a man may be morally sure that in a given occupation he will have a day's work forty or fifty times during a year, and that his earnings on those occasions will supply well his annual subsistence. Such an occupation would be certain, notwithstanding its inconstancy.

Uncertainty of success cannot well affect the wages of common labour, since no man, unless he be to a certain extent a capitalist, unless he have a fund for his intermediate support, can devote himself to an employment in which the success is uncertain. But its apparent, and indeed its real effect on *profits*, is very considerable.

Perfect knowledge, of course, excludes the idea of chance; but if all men had sufficient information to enable them to calculate fairly the chances of success, and were subject neither to rashness nor to timidity, it appears clear that even then the average profits of any employment would be raised by uncertainty of success.

When the sums are equal, to lose is obviously a greater evil than to gain is a good. If two men, with each a capital of £2000, toss up for £1000, the gainer augments his fortune by only one-third, and the loser sacrifices one-half. Laplace calculates the disadvantage at twenty-six per cent. At an equal game, he observes, the loss is relatively greater than the gain. Suppose a player with a fortune of 100 francs to risk 50 of them at heads and tails, his fortune, after he has deposited his stake, will be reduced to 87 francs; that is to say, 87 francs unhazarded would procure him as much happiness as 50 unhazarded, with 50 more subjected to the chance of being doubled or lost. Admitting this calculation to be correct, and admitting the existence of the degree of information and prudence which we have supposed, no one possessed of £10,000 would venture £5000 with an even chance of losing it, unless he had an even chance of gaining not merely £10,000, and an adequate profit on his capital of £5000, but could reckon on a further profit of £1300, as the price for undergoing the risk.

It is needless to say that men are far from possessing this degree either of information or of prudence. It is to be observed, however, that there are two sorts of uncertainty. In some cases the hazard is essentially connected with the employment itself, and recurs, in about an equal degree, at every operation. Smuggling, and the manufacture of gunpowder, are instances. Experience and skill may somewhat diminish the risk; but the best smuggler, and the best maker of gunpowder, probably each, suffers an average amount of loss. But there are employments in which success, if once obtained, is permanent. Such is often the case in mining. That mining is generally the road to ruin is notorious in all mining countries; but there are miners who have never suffered a loss. The same may be said of the liberal professions. Granting them to be as uncertain as Adam Smith believed them to be, the evil to which that uncertainty refers is experienced only by those who fail. To those who succeed they afford a revenue eminently safe and regular. Their uncertainty is personal. It arises from the error to which every man is subject when he compares his own qualifications with those of his rivals. If he be found on the actual trial inferior, his failure is irretrievable. In the other alternative his success is as permanent. Where any business is necessarily and permanently hazardous, the fortunes of any one individual engaged in it afford a sample from which we may estimate the fortunes of all. If only one old farmer could give to us all his personal experience, we should probably have a tolerably correct conception of the hazards to which farming is exposed. But, if we were to estimate the chances of legal or medical success from the average of ten or twenty selected instances, we should be likely to be grossly misled. The first sort of uncertainty, therefore, is likely to be estimated with a much greater approach to correctness than the second.

Adam Smith believed both to be under-estimated, and, consequently, that the average profits of all hazardous employments are below the average profits of safe ones. His views are stated with so much force and ingenuity, that we will extract them at considerable length.

" The overweening conceit which the greater part of men have of their own abilities is an ancient evil remarked by the philosophers and moralists of all ages. Their absurd presumption in their own good fortune has been less taken notice of. It is, however, if possible, still more universal. There is no man living who, when in tolerable health and spirits, has not some share of it. The chance of gain is by every man, more or less, overvalued; and the chance of loss is by most men undervalued; and by scarce any man, who is in tolerable health and spirits, valued at more than it is worth.

" That the chance of gain is naturally overvalued we may learn from the universal success of lotteries. The world neither ever saw, nor ever will see, a perfectly fair lottery, or one in which the whole gain compensated the whole loss, because the undertaker could make nothing by it. In the state lotteries the tickets are really not worth the price which is paid by the original subscribers, and yet commonly sell in the market for twenty, thirty, and sometimes forty per cent. advance. The vain hope of gaining some of the great prizes is the sole cause of this demand. The soberest people scarce look upon it as a folly to pay a small sum for the chance of gaining £10,000 or £20,000, though they know that even that small sum is perhaps twenty or thirty per cent. more than the chance is worth. In a lottery in which no prize exceeded £20, though, in other respects, it approached much nearer to a perfectly fair one than the common state lotteries, there would not be the same demand for tickets. In order to have a better chance for some of the great prizes, some people purchase several tickets, and others small shares in a still greater number. There is not, however, a more certain proposition in Mathematics, than that the more tickets you adventure upon, the more likely you are to be a loser. Adventure upon all the tickets in the lottery, and you lose for certain; and the greater the number of your tickets, the nearer you approach to this certainty.

"That the chance of loss is frequently undervalued, and scarce ever valued more than it is worth, we may learn from the very moderate profit of insurers. In order to make insurance either from fire or sea risk a trade at all, the common premium must be sufficient to compensate the common losses, to pay the expenses of management, and to afford such a profit as might have been drawn from an equal capital employed in any common trade. The person who pays no more than this evidently pays no more than the real value of the risk, or the lowest price at which he can reasonably expect to insure it. But, though many people have made a little money by insurance, very few have made a great fortune: and from this consideration alone it seems evident enough that the ordinary balance of profit and loss is not more advantageous in this than in other common trades, by which so many people make fortunes. Moderate, however, as the premium of insurance commonly is, many people despise the risk too much to care to pay it. Taking the whole kingdom at an average, nineteen houses in twenty, or rather perhaps ninety-nine in a hundred, are not insured from fire. Sea risk is more alarming to the greater part of people, and the proportion of ships insured to those not insured is much greater. Many sail, however, at all seasons, and even in time of war, without any insurance. This may sometimes, perhaps, be done without any imprudence. When a great company, or even a great merchant, has twenty or thirty ships at sea, they may, as it were, insure one another. The premium saved upon them all may more than compensate such losses as they are likely to meet with in the common course of chances. The neglect of insurance upon shipping, however, in the same manner as upon houses, is, in most cases, the effect of no such nice calculation, but of mere thoughtless rashness and presumptuous contempt of the risk. The ordinary rate of profit always rises, more or less, with the risk. It does not, however, seem to rise in proportion to it, or so as to compensate it completely. Bankruptcies are most frequent in the most hazardous trades. The most hazardous of all trades, that of a smuggler, though, when the adventure succeeds, it is likewise the most profitable, is the infallible road to bankruptcy. The presumptuous hope of success seems to act here as upon all other occasions, and to entice so many adventurers into those hazardous trades, that their competition reduces their profit below what is sufficient to compensate the risk. To compensate it completely, the common returns ought, over and above the ordinary profits of stock, not only to make up for all occasional losses, but to afford a surplus profit to the adventurers of the same nature with the profits of insurers. But if the common returns were sufficient for all this, bankruptcies would not be more frequent in these than in other trades." Book I. Ch. X.

Whether Adam Smith's conclusions be true or false, they certainly do not follow from his premises. Bankruptcies might be frequent in a trade of extraordinary profit. We will suppose ten merchants each to employ for a year a capital of £10,000 in a remarkably safe trade, and ten others to employ equal capitals for the same period in a hazardous trade; and ten per cent. per annum to be the average rate of profit in undertakings involving similar trouble. The capital of £100,000 engaged in the safe trade would, at the end of the year, be raised to £110,000, but be distributed in the same proportions as before. If the capital engaged in the hazardous trade were also, at the end of the year, to amount to £110,000, it is clear that each trade would have been equally profitable, although a different distribution of the capital might have ruined some, and made the fortunes of others, among the merchants engaged in it. Two might have lost, and two others might have doubled, their whole property. If the capital in the hazardous trade were found, at the end of the year, to have been raised from £100,000 to £120,000, it is clear that the hazardous trade must have been twice as profitable as the safe one, though the whole of the advantage might have fallen to two or three or even to one of the supposed ten merchants, leaving all the others to bankruptcy.

Insurance was a still more unfortunate source of argument; for all the premises that it affords lead to a conclusion directly opposed to Adam Smith's. Insurance is one of the safest of employments. If its profits be remarkably moderate, their moderation can be accounted for only by the extra competition which its safety invites. It affords, therefore, at least one example in favour of the superior profits of hazardous employments. Nor can it be said that the majority of persons despise the risk too much to secure themselves against it by paying a moderate premium. So much do they fear the risk that they are willing to guard against it by paying a most immoderate premium. The sum received by the insurance office must, as Adam Smith has remarked, exceed the value of the risk by an amount sufficient to pay the expenses of management, and afford ordinary profit. The sum received by the office on common insurances against fire is 1s. 6d. per £100; of which at least 6d. must go to pay expenses and profit, leaving 1s. as the value of the risk. But a duty is also paid to Government by the insured of 3s. per £100; so that the whole expense of insurance is 4s. 6d. per £100, or nearly five times the value of the risk. And, even at this extravagant rate, we believe that of good houses not one in a hundred is uninsured. So little do people despise the risk that, with their eyes open, they purchase a security against it at nearly five times its real value.

We suspect the fact to be that the imagination is unduly affected by the prospect either of enormous gain or of enormous loss; and, consequently, that men are ready to purchase the chance of obtaining a very great advantage, or the certainty of not suffering a very great disadvantage, at a price far beyond the value of either contingency. And this appears to be sufficiently proved by the facts which have been stated respecting insurance and lotteries. The English state lotteries of late times, indeed, afforded much more striking proofs of men's tendency to over-estimate the chances of extravagant gain than those which Adam Smith had seen. The tickets were always worth exactly £10 a-piece—£10 for each ticket forming always a sum equal to the aggregate amount of all the prizes; the average price of a ticket was from £21 to £24 a-piece. Instead of twenty or thirty per cent. the purchasers paid more than one hundred per cent. more than the value of their hope, just as, in the case of insurance, they pay nearly five hundred per cent. more than the value of their fear. The purchasers of tickets seem to have considered the relation between £24 and £20,000, not that between £24 and the one two-thousandth chance of getting £20,000. Just as those who insure their houses compare £2 5s. with £1000 instead of comparing it with the one two-thousandth chance of losing £1000. Adam Smith has well remarked, that if the disproportion between the sum paid and the sum attainable were altered, even though the bargain were rendered more favourable, the competition for it would diminish. No one would buy half the tickets in a lottery, even at £12 a ticket; he would at once see the absurdity of paying £120,000 for an even chance of getting £200,000, though, if a state lottery were now opened, a folly just twice as great in kind would be committed by thousands. So if, instead of one in two thousand, which we believe to be about the present average, one house in ten were annually burned down, and the annual expense of insurance were £22 10s. per cent., insurance would diminish, though the terms would be twice as favourable as they now are.

Those employments which offer the possibility of a great return for a small outlay are of the nature of lotteries; and it may be supposed that they attract competition in proportion not so much to the real value of the contingency as to the excess of the possible return over the certain outlay. If that excess be very great, it may be supposed that the number of competitors in proportion to that of prizes will reduce so low the value of each man's contingency as to render such employments on the whole unprofitable. In this Country the church, the army, and the bar, are such employments. They offer prizes that may satisfy to its utmost almost every human desire; and they require, as we have seen, from those who have already received a gentleman's education, a very moderate further outlay: the church and the army scarcely any; the bar perhaps £1500.   Under these circumstances, if the number of barristers were not kept down by the necessity of years of irksome study, and the emoluments of the church and of the army and navy kept up by the funds appropriated to their respective use, we have no doubt that the competition in these professions would reduce their average profit far below even its present moderate amount. We often hear proposals for equalizing, or rather for diminishing, the inequality in ecclesiastical preferments.   At first sight it appears a waste to pay £20,000 a-year to an Archbishop for doing less than is required from the curate of a populous parish with only £100 a-year. But if our object were to obtain an expensively educated clergy on the cheapest terms, that object would probably be best effected, not by diminishing, but by increasing, the value of the highest prizes. The revenues of all the English Bishoprics put together fall short of £150,000 a-year.   This sum, divided among the ten thousand livings, would raise the value of each by £15.   Can any one believe that such a change would not diminish the worldly attractions of the church? Nothing sells so dearly as what is disposed of by a well-constructed lottery, and if we wish to sell salaries dearly, that is, to obtain as much work and knowledge as possible for as little pay as possible, the best means is to dazzle the imagination with a few splendid prizes, and, by magnificently overpaying one or two, to induce thousands to sell their services at half price.

We have been told that it was once proposed at Rome, as the easiest mode of constructing a vast dome, to raise a mound of earth of the required shape, and build over it.   But the expense of then removing the earth appeared enormous.   On the principle which we have endeavoured to illustrate it was proposed that in raising the mound the earth should be irregularly mixed with coins of gold, silver, and copper, amounting in the aggregate to a sum equal to about half the aggregate amount of the wages which it would have cost to remove it by paid labourers, and then to allow the populace to remove it in barrows, without payment.   It was supposed that a sufficient number of persons would offer their services, though, in fact, working, in the aggregate, at half price.

We have already expressed an opinion that the bar is better paid than the church, and we attribute this to its being less of a lottery. The expenditure, as we have seen, is far greater, and the prizes, on the whole, are smaller.   The learned profession which offers the fewest prizes and requires the largest outlay, that of a schoolmaster, as it ceases to be a lottery, is by far the best paid.   There are probably few capitals which in the aggregate yield so certain and at the same time so large a profit.

In some few cases commercial adventures are of the nature of a lottery. Such were the shares which excited the strange fevers of cupidity and speculation which marked the years of 1720 and 1825. Of the thousands who crowded to buy Chili and Peruvian, and Rio la Plata, and Columbian, and Mexican shares, how many can be supposed not to have ascertained, but to have endeavoured to ascertain, or even to have thought of ascertaining, the probability of their Company's success? All they knew was that Real del Monte shares, for which £70 had been given, were selling for £1200: and they bought a few shares in other Companies, because, if the speculation succeeded, they might get one thousand per cent., and if it failed they had only lost one or two hundred pounds.

Generally speaking, however, those commercial adventures which offer a large immediate advantage are more in the nature of ordinary gambling than of a lottery. The possible loss often equals or exceeds, and generally bears a large proportion to, the possible gain. The undue hopes and the undue fears, which we have described as excited by the prospect of enormous gain and enormous loss, may now be supposed to balance one another, and to leave room for the action of Adam Smith's principle, an absurd presumption in our own good fortune. If his theory be correct, if every man in tolerable health and spirits have a tendency to miscalculate the chances in his own favour, it must follow that those speculations, which offer a great gain at the hazard of a great loss, invite so much competition as to be, if not positively unprofitable, at least less advantageous than ordinary employments. And we believe such to be the case. Mining and stock-jobbing are employments of capital which offer splendid success at the hazard of ruinous failure. The former employment is notorious not merely as affording less than average profits, but as affording no aggregate balance of profit at all as productive in the aggregate of loss. Knowledge, diligence, capital, all the materials of success, are applied in Cornwall to one of the richest mineral districts in the world, and yet it is supposed that the aggregate price of the whole of the copper and tin annually raised in Cornwall is not equal to the whole of the expense of raising it. A few capitalists, however, make large fortunes, and their success draws on the rest, generally to loss, often to ruin.

Even if speculation in the funds were attended by no expense, it is mathematically certain that it could in the aggregate afford no profit, as what is gained by one must be lost by another. But it is carried on at a very great expense. Every transfer costs a commission of 2s. 6d. for every £100 stock. A man who annually buys and sells stock to the amount of £800,000, and that is far from a large amount for an habitual speculator, must at an average pay for commission £1000 a-year; and that £1000 exactly represents the amount of his annual loss, supposing him to speculate with average success.

On the whole, however, though we attribute something to men's confidence in their superior good fortune, we attribute much more to their confidence in their superior ability. A confidence which, if universal, would, *on the whole*, produce as much miscalculation as the former, but which is not obviously irrational in *each particular instance*, and on that very account is stronger, and more general.

The third and last class of the employments of capital which are subject to uncertainty comprises those which are just the reverse of a lottery: those in which the gain is in each instance small, but nearly certain; and the loss great, but highly improbable.

If our theory be correct, this remote contingency of great loss must in general be overvalued, and the capitalist who submits to it must, in addition to the profit which would content him if his business were perfectly safe, receive at an average in the first place an extra profit equal to the risk, and in the second place, a further profit to compensate his anxiety, to compensate the excess of evil occasioned by loss over the benefit that attends on gain, and a still further profit to compensate the undue importance which he is likely to attribute to the chances against him.

Now this class comprises almost all those employments of capital which, to distinguish them from those attended by extraordinary risk, are generally termed safe. A merchant or a manufacturer who wishes to be safe must in general give up the hope of obtaining great profit by any single transaction. But no productive employment of capital can be *perfectly* safe. A capitalist may, indeed, *lend* his capital to one who wishes to employ it, on receiving a pledge, and the pledge may so much exceed in value the sum lent as to make the loan secure; but the capital itself, if employed, must be risked. Credit must be given, confidence must be reposed in agents, and when every precaution has been taken, an extraordinary season, an unexpected source of supply, a sudden change in foreign or domestic politics, or a commercial panic, may produce ruin out of the best-arranged operations. No man in business can be perfectly sure that in ten years' time he shall not be a bankrupt. If we are right, this risk of enormous loss, when unbalanced by the hope of enormous gain, must be compensated by an extra profit of something more than its value, just as the chance of enormous gain, when not balanced by the fear of enormous loss, is purchased at more than its value; and as the latter class of employments gives a smaller, so the former must give a greater average return than would be afforded by an employment perfectly safe, if any such there be.

INEQUALITIES IN WAGES AND PROFITS OCCASIONED BY THE DIFFICULTY OF TRANSFERRING CAPITAL AND LABOUR FROM ONE EMPLOYMENT TO ANOTHER.

The inequalities in wages and profits which we have as yet considered arise from causes inherent in the employments themselves which have been the subjects of discussion, and would, generally speaking, exist even if one occupation could at will be exchanged for another. But great inequalities are found which cannot be accounted for by any circumstances leading men to prefer one employment to another, and which therefore continue only in consequence of the difficulties experienced by the labourers and the capitalists in changing their employments.

The difficulty with which labour is transferred from one occupation to another is the principal evil of a high state of civilization. It exists in proportion to the division of labour. In a savage state almost every man is equally fit to exercise, and in fact does exercise, almost every employment. But in the progress of improvement two circumstances combine to render narrower and narrower the field within which a given individual can be profitably employed. In the first place the operations in which he is engaged become fewer and fewer. "In a pin-manufactory," says Adam Smith, "one man draws out the wire, another straightens it, a third cuts it, a fourth points it, a fifth grinds it at the top for receiving the head; to make the head requires two or three distinct operations; to put it on is a peculiar business; to whiten the pins is another; it is even a trade by itself to put them into the paper; and the important business of making a pin is in this manner divided into about eighteen distinct operations." In a large manufactory the man who is engaged in one of these operations has little experience in any of the others.

And, in the second place, the skill which the division of labour gives to each distinct class of artificers generally prevents whatever peculiar dexterity an individual may have from being of any value in a business to which he has not been brought up. A workman whose specific labour has ceased to be in demand finds every other long-established employment filled by persons whose time has been devoted to it from the age at which their organs were still pliable and their attention fresh.

Mr. Ewart, one of the many intelligent witnesses examined by the Commitee on Artisans and Machinery, is asked:—

"Can you state any facts to prove the inefficiency of even the best workmen when they are taken out of the immediate line of their daily business, though in the same trade?"

He replies, "Yes, I can: I should state particularly the case of the clock and watch tool and movement makers in Lancashire; they are considered the best workmen; they use the same sort of tools that the cotton-machine makers use; but they are brought up to no employment but making those clock and watch tools and movements. When those men come to be employed in making cotton machines, we find that they have almost as much to learn as if they had never learnt any working in metal at all. We have found them quite insufficient to do any ordinary filing and turning." [35]

Garnier, in the amusing notes to his translation of Adam Smith, contrasts the comfort of the lower orders in France with the pauperism of England, and ascribes the difference which he discovers to artificial restraints on the circulation of labour in England, and the absence of such restraints in France. " Under a government," he observes, " which does not interfere with the direction of industry, it is impossible that a man in health and strength can be without employment, unless his vices make employment intolerable to him. Let the workman be allowed to choose the market for his labour, and you may be sure that he will find one, and more and more certainly in proportion to the wealth of the Country. The complaint of want of work is the threadbare excuse of the idler who prefers relief to wages. If he were to search for it, he would find it as well as his companions. In France, though our population is one-third more numerous than that of England, and the fund for the support of labour much smaller, the labouring classes are free from want, or even discomfort." [36]

There can be no doubt that we have among our institutions and our habits much that fetters and misdirects the industry of our labourers; and that these causes frequently occasion, and always prolong, the want of employment to which large portions of our labourers are frequently exposed. We believe, too, that from many of these causes France is comparatively free. The monopolies possessed by towns and by incorporated bodies of artificers, with their oppressive bye-laws and duties, were swept away by the Revolution. Much, however, that is productive of evils similar in kind, still remains. Not long ago the number of butchers in Paris was, by an ordonnance of police, restricted to four hundred. The most important of all employments, that of affording education, is a government monopoly; and the commercial code of France is even worse than our own. If, therefore, the labouring classes of France never suffer from want of employment, they do not owe their immunity to a complete, or even a very considerable, freedom from interference. If their employment be actually more constant than that of our labouring classes, we believe that they owe that constancy principally to the inferior extent of their manufactures, and, what is both the cause and the effect of that inferiority, to a much less subdivision of labour.

[35] *Report on Artisans and Machinery*, 1824, p. 251.   [36] Note 25.

Less than one-third of the population of England, and more than two-thirds of the population of France, are employed in the cultivation of the soil.   We are inclined to think that, notwithstanding this dispro-portion, the English labouring classes are better fed than the French. But there is no comparison between their respective enjoyment of clothing and other manufactures.   The greater part of the coarser manufactures are both cheaper and better in England; while the wages in France, both of manufacturing and agricultural labourers, are about half what they are with us.   " A peasant suffering severely from rheumatism," says M. Say, (*Cours Complet*, Tome I. p. 46,) " asked my advice. I recommended to him a flannel waistcoat next the skin. He did not know that there was such a thing as flannel.   I told him then to wear under his shirt a cloth waistcoat turned inside-out. How, he asked, am I to get cloth to wear under my shirt, when I have never been able to afford to wear it above?   And yet he was no worse off than his neighbours."

The French labourer, being employed in more capacities than the Englishman, has more trades to turn to, and for that very reason is less efficient at any one.   The Russian is probably more seldom out of employ than the Frenchman, and the Tartar less frequently than either.   But few principles are more clearly established than that, *cæteris paribus*, the productiveness of labour is in proportion to its subdivision, and that, *cæteris paribus*, in proportion to that subdivision must be the occasional suffering from want of employment.   A savage may be compared to one of his own instruments, to his club, or his adze, clumsy and inefficient, but yet complete in itself.   A civilized artificer is like a single wheel or roller, which, when combined with many thousand others in an elaborate piece of machinery, contributes to effects which seem beyond human force and ingenuity, but, alone, is almost utterly useless.

The difficulty in transferring *material* capital from one employment to another depends principally on the degree in which it has been manufactured, and on the change to be made in the disposition of its parts.   The destination of raw material can, in general, be changed with little inconvenience.   The stones that have been collected for a bridge may easily be employed for a house.   But if they have been formed into a house, or a bridge, the value of the materials would scarcely pay the expense of removing them.   Those costly instru-ments which form the principal part of fixed capital can scarcely ever be applied in their original state to any but their original purposes.   They are employed, therefore, in the same way, long after they have ceased to afford average profit on the expense of their construction, because a still greater loss would be incurred by attempting to use them in a different manner.   It would be a bad speculation to erect a steam-engine at the cost of £20,000, which should return an annual profit of only £100, but it would be a still worse one to sell it as old iron for £500.

There is a considerable resemblance in this respect between mental and inanimate capital. Probity, industry, judgment, elementary knowledge, and the other moral and intellectual habits and acquirements to which we give the general name of a "good education," are a kind of mental raw material, of which the destination can be altered at pleasure. The peculiar knowledge and habits of a given profession are like a steam-engine or a water-mill, of comparatively small value for any but their appropriate purposes. In general, however, mental capital is the more transferable of the two, and becomes more and more so the more exclusively mental it is. The professional knowledge and dexterity of a weaver would be of little use to him in any other employment. A lawyer or a physician, prevented by circumstances from continuing to practise, would find the information and the intellectual habits which he had acquired in his former profession of considerable advantage in any new one. Bodily labour, especially when the labourer is confined to a very few operations, so that a few muscles have too much and the rest too little to do, often weakens, and almost always distorts, the frame. Mr. Shaw, a surgeon of great eminence in the treatment of distortion, told us that, as he walked along the streets, he could in general tell each man's trade by his characteristic deformity. But mental exertion, unless in those rare cases in which it is carried to such an excess as to produce cerebral derangement, never seems to weaken the mind. It may sometimes, perhaps, a little distort it, may sometimes give to one or two faculties an undue preponderance; but even this, to such an extent as to diminish the productiveness of the individual's subsequent exertions, is comparatively rare. And, in general, it will be found, that the more work a man's mind has done, the more he is able to do, and the better he will do it.

DIFFICULTY OF TRANSFERRING LABOUR AND CAPITAL FROM ONE COUNTRY TO ANOTHER.

The obstacles which exist, even within the same neighbourhood and the same Country, to the transfer of labour and capital from one employment to another, are of course aggravated, when not only the occupation but the neighbourhood or the Country is to be changed. Adam Smith states the common price of labour in London and its neighbourhood to have been, when he wrote, 1s. 6d. a-day, and the usual price in the Lowlands of Scotland to have been 8d. " Such a difference of prices," he adds, " which it seems is not always sufficient to transport a man from one parish to another, would necessarily occasion so great a transportation of the most bulky commodities, not only from one parish to another but from one end of the kingdom, almost from one end of the world, to another, as would soon reduce them more nearly to a level. After all that has been said of the levity and inconstancy of human nature, it appears evidently from experience, that a man is, of all sorts of luggage, the most difficult to be transported." Book I. Ch. VI.

When we compare the wages of labour in different Countries, we usually estimate them in money. And we are forced to do this for two reasons: first, because the precious metals are the only important commodities universally distributed throughout the world; and, secondly, because they are the only commodities of which the value is every where the same, or very nearly the same. We should gain little information by comparing the number of pine-apples that can be earned in Java and in England by a week's ordinary labour. And still less by comparing the quantity of pulque earned by a Mexican with the quantity of whisky earned by an Irishman. But money wages, though they measure accurately the value of national labour in the general market of the world, afford a very imperfect test of the degree of comfort and convenience obtained by the labourer in different Countries. Now it is this difference, not the difference in money wages, that leads him to change his residence; and we can ascertain, or rather approximate to ascertaining, these differences only by translating the money wages in different Countries into the commodities used by the labourer. The money wages of labour in North America are about one-third higher than in England; this is in some measure compensated by the higher price of manufactures. But as food, which every where forms the largest portion of the labourer's expenses, is considerably cheaper than with us, the real superiority of the American over the English labourer is greater than is indicated by the difference in their wages. We are told (Crawford's *Embassy*, p. 468) that a day labourer in Bengal can hardly earn £3 a-year. Notwithstanding this low rate of wages, most manufactures are dearer there than in England. Food, of course, is cheaper; for were it at the same price as the cheapest food in England, a family could not exist at about 1s. a-week. And it is obvious that in every Country the average wages of labour must be sufficient to support an average family. In proportion to the quantity of land and labour required, rice is, perhaps, the most abundant food that the earth affords. Rice, therefore, is the food of the Bengallee, and his wages, supposing them to be all laid out in food, would produce him about eight hundred pounds; the same quantity of rice might be purchased *here* for about £10 sterling. Estimated in money, therefore, wages in England, at £30 a-year, are ten times as high as in Bengal; estimated in manufactures, they are more than ten times; estimated in rice, they are about three times as high.

In comparing the rate of profits in two Countries, this difficulty does not exist; both the advances and the returns being always estimated in money, the apparent must be the real difference between the rate of profits in any two Countries.

The great obstacles to the circulation of labour are difference of climate, distance of place, and difference of language. The first is by far the most powerful, and is so great that there is little voluntary emigration of labourers to a very dissimilar climate. Difference of language seems often a greater obstacle than very considerable distance of place. The advance of wages obtained by an English mechanic in France is greater than he can get by going to America; but ten go to America for one who will venture to France. Differences in habits, government, and religion are comparatively weak obstacles, except in those cases where the differences have caused an antipathy, making immigration dangerous. Few Countries differ more in habits and religion than England and Ireland, or in government than Ireland and the United States. Yet we know how great is the emigration from Ireland to both those Countries. In general, however, the physical and moral obstacles to the emigration of single labourers, or even of bodies of labourers, unless supported and directed by a very considerable capital, are such that it seldom takes place unless under peculiar circumstances; such as those of Ireland and England, or Ireland and America, where the temptation is very great, the physical obstacle only a passage of a few weeks in the one case, and a few hours in the other, and the language the same.

But the voluntary migrations of capitalists and labourers united, and the attempts by capitalists to force the involuntary migration of labourers, have been among the principal causes that have advanced and retarded the improvement of mankind. To the first class belong those hostile migrations in which a whole nation, in the hope of obtaining a climate or a soil more favourable to production, has moved in a body to seize the territory of a neighbour. From the invasion of Egypt by the Shepherd Kings to that of Greece by the Turks, these movements have kept the inhabitants of the whole of our hemisphere in a constant fluctuation. Many Countries, and among them our own, have been so covered by successive strata of occupants, that no trace of the first settlers can be discovered; in others, the poor remains of the aborigines are discovered, like the Helots of Laconia, the Fellahs of Egypt, or the Bheels of Hindostan, by their misery and degradation. Europe, in its present state, does not fear these invasions. They could not be attempted by a civilized nation, nor, in the present state of the art of war, could they be successful *against* one. But, until the improvement of military science and the extensive use of machinery in war, gave to wealth and knowledge their present superiority, these attributes seem to have been sources rather of weakness than of strength. The least polished people seem, on the whole, to have had the advantage. Cicero confesses the warlike superiority of the Gauls over the Romans. It was not till after Gaul had become comparatively civilized that her military fame was recalled as a tradition.[37] A few

---

[37] *Gallos in bello floruisse audivimus.*

centuries of peace made the Britons an easy prey to the Saxons, and the Saxons to the Danes. Under such circumstances the permanent improvement of the human race seemed almost hopeless. And if gunpowder had not been brought into use just at the time when those military virtues which belong to semi-barbarism were decaying, it appears probable that another irruption of barbarians might have brought back another middle age, in which Europe might have lost all that she gained between the XIIth and the XVth Centuries.

Resembling in kind these migratory invasions, but very different from them in effect, have been those emigrations on a smaller scale, to which we give the name of COLONIZATION; in which a portion of a comparatively civilized nation have gone out, with their knowledge and wealth, their material, and moral, and intellectual capital, and settled in an unoccupied or thinly peopled district. It is a remarkable and a most unhappy circumstance that, notwithstanding the progress of political knowledge, the true principles of Colonization have been less and less understood, or, if understood, less and less acted on, as civilization has advanced. The earliest Colonies with which we are acquainted, those founded by the Phœnicians and the Greeks, seem to have been founded for the benefit of the Colonists. They were allowed to appoint their own governors, to direct their own industry, and to manage their own concerns; and they relied on themselves for their defence. They were children, but emancipated children; and their progress was in proportion to their independence. The Phœnician Colonies in Africa and Syria, and the Grecian Colonies in Italy, Thrace, Sicily, and Asia, seem quickly to have risen to an equality with, or to have surpassed, their Mother Countries; to have obtained, in fact, all the wealth and power which their extent of territory, and the religion and knowledge of the times, made it possible to acquire. The Roman Colonies scarcely deserve that name. They were generally formed by grants of the lands, the capital, and the persons of conquered Tribes, almost as civilized as their conquerors, to the armies or to the populace of Rome, as a reward for services in foreign or civil war, or for sedition and riot in the forum. It may be a question whether they accelerated or retarded the improvement of the world.

The Colonies of modern Europe have been established partly for the benefit of the Colonists, and partly, as it was supposed, for that of the parent state. The latter has, in general, contributed a part of the expense of outfit, and almost all the expense of protection against foreign aggression. She has also, in general, given to her Colonies a monopoly, or something approaching to a monopoly of her market. On the other hand, she has, in general, required her Colonies to give to her own productions a much stricter monopoly. She has, in general, required her Colonies to receive European productions solely from the Mother Country, and to export only to the Mother Country colonial productions. She has, in general, appointed the principal officers,

and interfered in the internal management of her Colonies. She has
not only prohibited the Colonists from purchasing in any other market
what could be produced in the Mother Country, but has prohibited
them from producing for themselves. She has peopled them with the
refuse of her gaols, and governed them by the refuse of her aristocracy.
The Court of Spain commanded the vineyards of Mexico to be rooted
up ; the English Parliament forbade Jamaica to discontinue the slave-
trade, prohibited the establishment of iron, woollen, and hat manufactures in our North American Colonies, and even now forbids the
West Indians to refine their own sugar. The Mother Country dragged
the Colonists into all her wars, and, from their comparatively defenceless situation, exposed their trade to more loss, and their persons and
property to more danger, than she encountered herself. And when
the rising strength of the Colony rendered these oppressions intolerable,
no Mother Country has yet had the good sense to submit quietly to a
separation, which, even if it could have been avoided, might have been
desirable ; and which, whether expedient or not, was inevitable.
England, France, Portugal, and Spain have all wasted, in the vain
attempt to retain their Colonies, ten times more wealth than was
expended in founding them.

But, mismanaged as Colonies have been, they have, without
doubt, been one of the principal means by which civilization has been
diffused.

The separate attempts by independent capitalists to procure the
voluntary EMIGRATION of labourers have generally been made on a
small scale, and have been unprofitable to the undertakers, in consequence of the difficulty of compelling or inducing the labourers to
perform their engagements, and work diligently at a rate of wages
sufficiently inferior to the current rate of the Colony to repay the
expense and risk of the capitalist. Sir R. Wilmot Horton's plans for
effecting Emigration on an extended scale, and as a national undertaking, have not received the attention which the magnitude of the
probable advantage, and the unwearied diligence and public spirit of its
proposer, deserved. And the scheme for founding in Australia a Colony
in which the first price of all the land shall be employed in transporting
labourers, has not yet been submitted to the test of experience.

The attempts by capitalists to force the involuntary migration of
labourers have been productive of almost unmixed evil. They produced, and have continued, the abominable traffic in which *man* is the
commodity ;—a traffic which, partly by its direct effects, and partly
by the wars and general insecurity which are its necessary accompaniments, retarded more than any other cause the early civilization of
Europe ; has kept, and continues to keep, the greater part of Asia,
and the whole of Africa, in hopeless barbarism ; and has divided the
inhabitants of the most fertile portions of the Continent of America,

and, until lately, those of almost all her islands, into two classes only, the oppressors and the oppressed.

The transfer of *Capital* from one Country to another is subject to less difficulty. When the exchange is at par between any two Countries, Capital can be transmitted in the shape of money without any expense. And as the occasional loss which occurs when the exchange is against the Country to which it is to be exported is compensated by the occasional gain when it is in favour of that Country, it may fairly be said that monied Capital is transferred from Country to Country without expense. The chief obstacle is the unwillingness of Capitalists either to trust their Capital out of their own superintendence, or to encounter a change of government, habits, climate, and language, by accompanying it. Difference of language, however, is felt as a slight objection by educated men. Nor is difference of government of great importance to those who propose only a transitory residence. The difference indeed is often considered an advantage. During the late war, London was filled by foreign Capitalists, whose principal motive was to escape the tyranny of Napoleon. Differences of habits and climate are more material, especially the latter; but even those do not seem to counterbalance a great increase of profit. There is scarcely a port in the civilized world in which a considerable part of the mercantile class does not consist of the natives of Great Britain. The inequality in the rate of profit throughout the civilized world is, therefore, much less than the inequality of wages. And as the general progress of improvement tends more and more to equalize the advantages possessed by different Countries in government and habits, and even in salubrity of climate, the existing inequalities of profits are likely to diminish.

APPENDIX

On certain terms which are peculiarly liable to be used ambiguously in Political Economy

from *Elements of Logic*
by Richard Whately, D.D.

The foundation of Political Economy being a few general propositions deduced from observation or from consciousness, and generally admitted as soon as stated, it might have been expected that there would be as little difference of opinion among Political-Economists as among Mathematicians;—that, being agreed in their premises, they could not differ in their conclusions, but through some error in reasoning, so palpable as to be readily detected.   And if they had possessed a vocabulary of general terms as precisely defined as the mathematical, this would probably have been the case.   But as the terms of this Science are drawn from common discourse, and seldom carefully defined by the writers who employ them, hardly one of them has any settled and invariable meaning, and their ambiguities are perpetually overlooked.   The principal terms are only seven: *viz.* VALUE, WEALTH, LABOUR, CAPITAL, RENT, WAGES, PROFITS.

1. VALUE. As value is the only relation with which Political Economy is conversant, we might expect all Economists to be

agreed as to its meaning.   There is no subject as to which they
are less agreed.

The popular, and far the most convenient, use of the word,
is to signify the capacity of being given and received in exchange. So defined it expresses a relation. The value of any
one thing must consist in the several quantities of all other
things which can be obtained in exchange for it, and never
can remain fixed for an instant. Most writers admit the
propriety of this definition at the outset, but they scarcely
ever adhere to it.

Adam Smith defines Value to mean either the *utility* of a
particular object, or the power of *purchasing other* goods which
the possession of that object conveys. The first he calls "Value
in use," the second " Value in exchange." But he soon afterwards says, that equal quantities of labour at all times and
places are of equal Value to the labourer, whatever may be the
quantity of goods he receives in return for them; and that
labour never varies in its own Value. It is clear that he affixed,
or thought he had affixed, some other meaning to the word;
as the first of these propositions is contradictory, and the
second false, whichever of his two definitions we adopt.

Mr. Ricardo appears to set out by admitting Adam Smith's
definition of Value in exchange. But in the greater part of his
Principles of Political Economy, he uses the word as synonymous
with *Cost*: and by this one ambiguity has rendered his great work
a long enigma.

Mr. Malthus * defines Value to be the power of purchasing.
In the very next page he distinguishes absolute from relative
Value, a distinction contradictory to his definition of the term,
as expressive of a *relation*.

Mr. M'Culloch † distinguishes between real and exchangeable,
or relative Value. And in his nomenclature, the exchangeable,
or relative, Value of a commodity consists in its capacity of

---

* *Measure of Value*, p. 1.
† *Principles of Political Economy*, Part III. sect. I.

purchasing;—its real Value in the quantity of labour required for its production or appropriation.

All these differences appear to arise from a confusion of cause and effect. Having decided that commodities are Valuable in proportion to the labour they have respectively cost, it was natural to call that labour their Value.

2. WEALTH. Lord Lauderdale has defined Wealth to be " all that man desires." Mr. Malthus,* " those *material* objects which are necessary, useful, or agreeable." Adam Smith confines the term to that portion of the results of land and labour which is capable of being accumulated. The French Economists, to the net product of land. Mr. M'Culloch † and M. Storch,‡ to those material products which have exchangeable value; according to Colonel Torrens § it consists of articles which possess utility, and are produced by some portion of voluntary effort. M. Say ‖ divides wealth into natural and social, and applies the latter term to whatever is susceptible of exchange. It will be observed that the principal difference between these definitions consists in the admission or rejection of the qualifications " exchangeable," and " material."¶

It were well if the ambiguities of this word had done no more than puzzle philosophers. One of them gave birth to the mercantile system. In common language, to grow rich is to

* *Principles of Political Economy*, p. 28.

† *Supplement to the Encyclopædia Britannica*, Vol. VI. p. 217.

‡ *Cours d'Economie Politique*, Tome I. p. 91. Paris edit.

§ *Production of Wealth*, p. 1.

‖ *Traité d'Economie Pol.* Liv. II. Chap. ii.

¶ " In many cases, where an exchange really takes place, the fact is liable (till the attention is called to it) to be overlooked, in consequence of our not seeing any actual transfer from hand to hand of a material object. For instance, when the copyright of a book is sold to a bookseller, the article transferred is not the mere paper covered with writing, but the exclusive *privilege* of printing and publishing. It is plain, however, on a moment's thought, that the transaction is as real an exchange, as that which takes place between the bookseller and his customers who buy copies of the work."—*Introd. to Pol. Econ.* Lect. I.

get *money*; to diminish in fortune is to lose *money*: a rich man is said to have a great deal of *money*; a poor man, very little: and the terms Wealth and Money are in short employed as synonymous. In consequence of these popular notions (to use the words of Adam Smith) all the different nations of Europe have studied every means of accumulating gold and silver in their respective countries. This they have attempted by prohibiting the exportation of money, and by giving bounties on the exportation, and imposing restrictions on the importation, of other commodities in the hope of producing what has been called a " favourable balance of trade;" that is, a trade in which, the imports being always of less value than the exports, the difference is paid in money. A conduct as wise as that of a tradesman who should part with his goods only for money; and instead of employing their price in paying his workmen's wages, or replacing his stock, should keep it for ever in his till. The attempt to force such a trade has been as vain, as the trade, if it could have been obtained, would have been mischievous. But the results have been fraud, punishment, and poverty at home, and discord and war without. It has made nations consider the Wealth of their customers a source of loss instead of profit; and an advantageous market a curse instead of a blessing. By inducing them to refuse to profit by the peculiar advantages in climate, soil, or industry, possessed by their neighbours, it has forced them in a great measure to give up their own. It has for centuries done more, and perhaps for centuries to come will do more, to retard the improvement of Europe than all other causes put together.

3. LABOUR.—The word Labour signifies both the *act* of labouring, and the *result* of that act. It is used in the first sense when we talk of the wages of labour; in the second when we talk of accumulated labour. When used to express the act of labouring, it may appear to have a precise sense, but it is still subject to some ambiguity. Say's definition * is " action suivie,

* *Traité*, &c. Tome II. p. 506.

dirigée vers un bût;" Storch's,* " l'action des facultés humaines dirigée vers un bût utile." These definitions include a walk taken for the purposes of health, and even the exertions of an agreeable converser.

The great defect of Adam Smith, and of our own economists in general, is the want of definitions. There is, perhaps, no definition of Labour by any British Economist. If Adam Smith had framed one, he would probably have struck out his celebrated distinction between " productive " and " unproductive " labourers; for it is difficult to conceive any definition of Labour which will admit the epithet " unproductive " to be applied to any of its sub-divisions, excepting that of *misdirected* labour. On the other hand, if Mr. M'Culloch or Mr. Mill had defined Labour they would scarcely have applied that term to the growth of a tree, or the improvement of wine in a cellar.

4. CAPITAL.—This word, as might have been expected, from the complexity of the notions which it implies, has been used in very different senses.

It is, as usual, undefined by Adam Smith. The general meaning which he attached to it will however appear from his enumeration of its species. He divides it † into *Fixed* and *Circulating*: including in the first what the capitalist retains, in the second what he parts with. *Fixed* Capital he subdivides into—1. Machinery; 2. Shops and other buildings used for trade or manufacture; 3. Improvements of land; 4. Knowledge and skill. *Circulating* Capital he subdivides into— 1. Money; 2. Provisions in the hands of the provision-venders; 3. Unfinished materials of manufacture; 4. Finished work in the hands of the merchant or manufacturer; such as furniture in a cabinet-maker's shop, or trinkets in that of a jeweller.

The following is a list of the definitions adopted by some of the most eminent subsequent economists:

Ricardo ‡—" that part of the wealth of a country which is

* *Cours*, &c. Liv. 1. Chap. iv.   † Book II. Chap. i.
‡ *Principles of Political Economy*, p. 89, 3rd edit.

employed in production; consisting of food, clothing, tools, raw materials, machinery, &c., necessary to give effect to labour."

Malthus *—" that portion of the material possessions of a country which is destined to be employed with a view to profit."

Say †—" accumulation de valeurs soustraites à la consomption improductive." Chap. iii. " Machinery, necessaries of the workman, materials."

Storch ‡—" un fonds de richesses destiné à la production matérielle."

M'Culloch §—" that portion of the produce of industry which can be made directly available to support human existence or facilitate production."

Mill ‖—" something produced, for the purpose of being employed as the mean towards a further production."

Torrens ¶—" those things on which labour has been bestowed, and which are destined, not for the immediate supply of our wants, but to aid us in obtaining other articles of utility."

It is obvious that few of these definitions exactly coincide. Adam Smith's (as implied in his use of the term; for he gives no formal definition) excludes the necessaries of the labourer, when in his own possession; all the rest (and perhaps with better reason) admit them. On the other hand, Adam Smith admits (and in that he seems to be right) those things which are incapable of productive consumption, provided they have not yet reached their consumers. All the other definitions, except perhaps that of Mr. Malthus, which is ambiguous, are subject to the inconsistency of affirming that a diamond, and the gold in which it is to be set, are Capital while the jeweller keeps them separate, but cease to be so when he has formed them into a ring; almost all of them, also, pointedly exclude knowledge and skill. The most objectionable, perhaps, is that of Mr. M'Culloch, which,

---

* *Principles*, &c. p. 293. † *Traité*, &c. Tome II, p. 454.
‡ *Cours*, &c. Liv. II. Chap. i. § *Principles*, &c. p. 92.
‖ *Elements*, &c. p. 19, 3rd edit. ¶ *Production of Wealth*, p. 5.

while it excludes all the finished contents of a jeweller's shop, would include a racing stud.

Adam Smith, however, is far from being consistent in his use of the word; thus, in the beginning of his second book he states, that all Capitals are destined for the maintenance of productive labour only. It is difficult to see what labour is maintained by what is to be unproductively consumed.

5. RENT. 6. WAGES. 7. PROFIT.

Adam Smith first divided revenue into Rent, Wages, and Profit; and his division has been generally followed. The following definitions will best show the degree of precision with which these three terms have been employed.

ADAM SMITH.

1. Rent. What is paid for the licence to gather the produce of the land.—Book I. Chap. vi.

2. Wages. The price of labour.—Book I. Chap. v.

3. Profit. The revenue derived from stock by the person who manages or employs it.—Book I. Chap. vi.

SAY. (*Traité d'Economie Politique.*) 4ème Edit.

1. Rent. Le profit résultant du service productif de la terre.—Tome II. p. 169.

2. Wages. Le prix de l'achat d'un service productif industriel.—Tome II. p. 503.

3. Profit. La portion de la valeur produite, retirée par le capitaliste.—Tome I. p. 71, subdivided into intérêt, profit industriel, and profit capital.

STORCH. (*Cours d'Economie Politique.*) Paris, 1823.

1. Rent. Le prix qu'on paye pour l'usage d'un fonds de terre.—Tome I. p. 354.

2. Wages. Le prix du travail.—p. 283.

3. Profit. The returns to capital are considered by Storch, under the heads, rente de capital, and profit de l'entrepreneur. The first he divides into loyer, the hire of fixed capital, and intérêt, that of circulating capital. The second he considers as composed of, 1st, remuneration for the use of capital; 2nd, assurance against risk; 3rd, remuneration for trouble.—Liv. III. Chap. ii. viii. xiii.

SISMONDI. (*Nouveaux Principes, &c.*)

1. Rent. La pars de la récolte annuelle du sol qui revient au propriétaire après qu'il a acquitté les frais qui l'ont fait naître; and he analyzes rent into, 1st, la compensation du travail de la terre; 2d, le prix de monopole; 3d, la mieux valeur que le propriétaire obtient par la comparaison d'une terre de nature supérieure à une terre inférieure; 4th, le révenu des capitaux qu'il a fixés lui-même sur la terre, et ne peut plus en retirer.— Tome I. p. 280.

2. Wages. Le prix du travail.—p. 91.

3. Profit. Le valeur dont l'ouvrage achevé surpasse les avances qui l'ont fait faire. L'avantage qui résulte des travaux passés. Subdivided into intérêt and profit mercantile.—p. 94, 359.

MALTHUS. (*Principles, &c.*)

1. Rent. That portion of the value of the whole produce of land which remains to the owner after payment of all the outgoings of cultivation, including average profits on the capital employed. The excess of price above wages and profits.—p. 134.

2. Wages. The remuneration of the labourer for his personal exertions.—p. 240.

3. Profit. The difference between the value of the advances necessary to produce a commodity, and the value of the commodity when produced.—p. 293.

Mill. (*Elements, &c.*)   3rd Ed.

1. Rent. The difference between the return made to the most productive, and that which is made to the least productive portion of capital employed on the land.—p. 33.

2. Wages. The price of the labourer's share of the commodity produced.—p. 41.

3. Profit. The share of the joint produce of labour and stock which is received by the owner of stock after replacing the capital consumed. The portion of the whole annual produce which remains after deducting rent and wages. Remuneration for hoarded labour.—Chap. 2, 3.

Torrens. (*Corn Trade.*)   3rd Ed.

1. Rent. That part of the produce which is given to the land-proprietor for the use of the soil.—p. 130.

2. Wages. The articles of wealth which the labourer receives in exchange for his labour.—p. 83.

3. Profit. The excess of value which the finished work possesses above the value of the material, implements, and subsistence expended. The surplus remaining after the cost of production has been replaced.—*Production of Wealth*, p. 53.

M'Culloch. (*Principles, &c.*)

1. Rent. That portion of the produce of the earth which is paid by the farmer to the landlord for the use of the natural and inherent powers of the soil.—p. 265.

2. Wages. The compensation paid to labourers in return for their services.—*Essay on Rate of Wages*, p. 1.

3. Profit. The excess of the commodities produced by the expenditure of a given quantity of capital, over that quantity of capital.—*Principles*, p. 366.

RICARDO.   (*Principles, &c.*)   3rd Ed.

1. Rent.   That portion of the produce of the earth which is paid to the landlord for the use of the original and indestructible powers of the soil.—p. 53.

2. Wages.   The labourer's proportion of the produce.— Chap. v.

3. Profit.   The capitalist's proportion of the produce.— Chap. vi.

The first observation to be made on these definitions, is, that the Rent of *land*, which is only a *species* of an extensive genus, is used as a genus, and that its cognate species are either omitted, or included under genera to which they do not properly belong. Wages and Profits are of human creation; they imply a sacrifice of ease or immediate enjoyment, and bear a ratio to that sacrifice which is indicated by the common expressions of " the rate of wages," and the " rate of profits:" a ratio which has a strong tendency to uniformity.   But there is another and a very large source of revenue which is not the creation of man, but of nature; which owes its origin, not to the will of its possessor, but to accident; which implies no sacrifice, has no tendency to uniformity, and to which the term " rate " is seldom applied.   This revenue arises from the exclusive right to some instrument of production, enabling the employment of a given amount of labour or capital to be more than usually productive.   The *principal* of these instruments is land; but all extraordinary powers of body or mind,—all processes in manufacture which are protected by secrecy or by law,—all peculiar advantages from situation or connexion,—in short, every instrument of production which is not universally accessible, affords a revenue distinct in its origin from Wages or Profits, and of which the Rent of land is only a species.   In the classification of revenues, either Rent ought to have been omitted as a genus, and considered only as an anomalous interruption of the general uniformity of wages and profits, or all the accidental sources of revenue ought to have been included in one genus, of which the Rent of land would have formed the principal species.

Another remark is, that almost all these definitions of Profit include the *wages of the labour of the Capitalist.* The continental Economists have in general been aware of this, and have pointed it out in their analyses of the component parts of Profit. The British Economists have seldom entered into this analysis, and the want of it has been a great cause of obscurity.

On the other hand, much of what properly belongs to Profit and Rent is generally included under Wages. Almost all Economists consider the members of the liberal professions under the class of labourers. The whole subsistence of such persons, observes Mr. M'Culloch,* is derived from Wages; and they are as evidently labourers as if they handled the spade or the plough. But it should be considered, that those who are engaged in any occupation requiring more skill than that of a common husbandman, must have expended capital, more or less, on the acquisition of their skill; their education must have cost something in every case, from that of the handicraft-apprentice, to that of the legal or medical student; and a Profit on this outlay is of course looked for, as in other disbursements of capital; and the higher profit, in proportion to the risk; *viz.* the uncertainty of a man's success in his business. Part, therefore, and generally far the greater part, of what has been reckoned the wages of his labour, ought more properly to be reckoned profits on the capital expended in fitting him for that particular kind of labour. And again, all the excess of gains acquired by one possessing extraordinary talents, opportunities, or patronage (since these correspond to the possession of land,—of a patent-right,—or other monopoly,— of a secret, &c.) may be more properly regarded as Rent than as Wages.

Another most fruitful source of ambiguity arises from the use of the word Wages, sometimes as expressing a *quantity,* sometimes as expressing a *proportion.*

* *Principles,* &c. p. 228.

In ordinary language, Wages means the *amount of some commodity*, generally of silver, given to the labourer in return for a given exertion; and they rise or fall, as that amount is increased or diminished.

In the language of Mr. Ricardo, they usually mean the labourer's *proportion of what is produced*, supposing that produce to be divided between him and the Capitalist. In this sense they generally rise as the whole produce is diminished; though, if the word be used in the other sense, they generally fall. If Mr. Ricardo had constantly used the word " Wages," to express a *proportion*, the only inconvenience would have been the necessity of always translating this expression into common language. But he is not consistent. When he says,* that " whatever raises the Wages of labour lowers the Profits of stock," he considers Wages as a *proportion*. When he says,† that " high Wages encourage population;" he considers wages as an *amount*. Even Mr. M'Culloch, who has clearly explained the ambiguity, has not escaped it. He has even suffered it to affect his reasonings. In his valuable essay, *On the Rate of Wages*,‡ he admits that " when Wages are high, the Capitalist has to pay a larger share of the produce of industry to his labourers." An admission utterly inconsistent with his general use of the word, as expressing the *amount* of what the labourer receives, which, as he has himself observed,§ may increase while his *proportion* diminishes.

A few only have been noticed of the ambiguities which attach to the seven terms that have been selected; and these terms have been fixed on, not as the most ambiguous, but as the most important, in the political nomenclature. " Supply and Demand," " Productive and Unproductive," " Overtrading," and very many others, both in political economy, and in other subjects, which are often used without any more explanation, or any more

---

* *Principles*, &c. p. 312.   † Ibid. p. 83.   ‡ P. 161.
§ *Principles of Political Economy*, p. 365.

suspicion of their requiring it, than the words " triangle " or
" twenty," are perhaps even more liable to ambiguities than
those above treated of. But it is sufficient for the purpose of
this Appendix to have noticed, by way of specimens, a few of
the most remarkable terms in several different branches of
knowledge, in order to show both the frequency of an ambiguous
use of language, and the importance of clearing up such
ambiguity.

BIBLIOGRAPHICAL NOTE

The title-page of the present edition is a reduced facsimile of the quarto first edition which appeared as part of the *Encyclopedia Metropolitana*, 1836. A few copies only of the quarto edition were "struck off separately for private distribution." The title of the second and following editions which appeared separately was shortened to *Political Economy*.

The Appendix "On certain terms which are peculiarly liable to be used ambiguously in Political Economy" appeared for the first time in 1826 in the separate, revised edition of Richard Whately's *Elements of Logic* (originally the section on Logic of the *Encyclopedia Metropolitana*, with no appendix) and has been reprinted unchanged in all its subsequent editions. It was introduced by Whately with this note:

"N.B. As the words which follow are all of them connected together in their significations, and as the explanations of their ambiguities have been furnished by the kindness of the Professor of Political Economy, it seemed advisable to place them by themselves, and in the order in which they appeared to him most naturally to arrange themselves."

HEADLINES ADDED TO AND ALTERED IN THE SECOND (AND SUBSEQUENT) EDITIONS

Page 1   Line 2:   "Introduction."

6   1:   "Nature of Wealth" instead of "Wealth."

6   2:   "Wealth defined."

6   17:   "Constituents of Wealth."

6   18:   "I. Utility."

7   11:   "II. Limitation in Supply."

8   24:   "III. Transferableness."

11   9:   "Limitation in Supply the most Important."

14   2:   "Value Defined."

14   40:   "Demand and Supply."

15   24:   "Demand."

16   3:   "Supply."

16   18:   "Intrinsic and Extrinsic Causes of the Value of a Commodity."

20   33:   "Steadiness in Value, on what it depends."

22   31:   "OBJECTIONS TO THE DEFINITION OF WEALTH CONSIDERED" instead of "Objections to Definition of Wealth considered."

27   1:   "DEVELOPMENT OF THE FIRST ELEMENTARY PROPOSITION OF THE SCIENCE, NAMELY, THAT ON . . ."

29   42:   "DEVELOPMENT OF THE SECOND ELEMENTARY PROPOSITION OF THE SCIENCE, NAMELY, THAT ON the Causes which Limit Population" instead of "Population."

50   24:   "DEVELOPMENT OF THE THIRD ELEMENTARY PROPOSITION OF THE SCIENCE, NAMELY, That the powers of Labour, and of the other Instruments which produce Wealth, may be indefinitely increased by using their Products as the means of further Production."

50   34:   "Product."

51   8:   "Products divided into Services and Commodities."

53   3:   "Service and Commodity Discriminated."

53   27:   "Consumption defined."

54   27:   "Productive and Unproductive Consumption."

60   14:   "Different Modes in which Capital may be Employed."

61   30:   "Fixed and Circulating Capital."

Page 66   Line 6:   "CAPITAL MAY AGAIN BE DIVIDED, ACCORDING TO THE PURPOSES TO WHICH IT IS APPLICABLE, INTO REPRODUCTIVE, SIMPLY PRODUCTIVE, AND UNPRODUCTIVE" (appears in capitals in second edition).

67   17:   "STATEMENT OF ADVANTAGES DERIVED FROM THE USE OF CAPITAL."

67   21:   "I. The Use of Implements."

73   10:   "II. Division of Labour."

81   35:   "DEVELOPMENT OF THE FOURTH ELEMENTARY PROPOSITION OF THE SCIENCE, NAMELY, That Agricultural Skill remaining the same, Additional Labour employed on the Land within a given district produces in general a Less Proportionate Return. Additional Labour when employed in Manufactures is MORE, when employed in Agriculture is LESS, efficient in proportion" instead of "Productiveness of Labour in Agriculture and Manufactures. Fourth Elementary Proposition."

87   1:   "DISTRIBUTION OF WEALTH" instead of "Distribution."

88   30:   "SOCIETY DIVIDED INTO THREE CLASSES— LABOURERS, CAPITALISTS AND PROPRIETORS OF NATURAL AGENTS."

89   6:   "Nomenclature applicable to the First Class, the Labourers."

89   17:   "Nomenclature applicable to the Second Class, the Capitalists."

89   32:   "Nomenclature applicable to the Third Class, the Proprietors of Natural Agents."

101   3:   "Cost of Production defined."

111   5:   "Effects of the Cost of Production on Price."

114   38:   "Effects of Monopolies on Price."

118   44:   "Consequences of the Proposition that Additional Labour when employed in Manufactures is MORE, and when employed in Agriculture is LESS, efficient in proportion."

124   12:   "Tithes."

135   33:   "CAUSES ON WHICH THE PROPORTIONATE AMOUNT OF RENT DEPENDS" instead of "Proportionate Amount of Rent."

141   30:   "Circumstances which decide what, at a given time and in a given place, shall be the average rate of Wages and the average rate of Profit."

Page 149 Line 17: "Difference between the Amount of Wages and the Price of Labour."

154 11: "Discussion of Seven Opinions inconsistent with this proposition" instead of "Erroneous Opinions."

162 38: "Machinery" instead of "Machines."

168 38: (Heading "Population" only appears in first edition.)

174 10: "CAUSES ON WHICH THE EXTENT OF THE FUND FOR THE MAINTENANCE OF LABOUR DEPENDS."

174 37: "Causes which affect Productiveness of Labour" instead of "Productiveness of Labour."

180 20: "II. CAUSES WHICH DIVERT LABOUR FROM THE PRODUCTION OF COMMODITIES FOR THE USE OF LABOURING FAMILIES. 1. RENT. 2. TAXATION. 3. PROFIT" instead of "Proportion of Persons employed in the Production of Commodities for the Use of Labourers to the whole Number of Labouring Families."

186 46: "How Profit is to be Estimated" instead of "How to be estimated."

220 28: "DIFFICULTY OF TRANSFERRING LABOUR AND CAPITAL FROM ONE COUNTRY TO ANOTHER."

INDEX

[The Author of the article on POLITICAL ECONOMY is not accountable for the contents of this INDEX.—EDITOR ENCY. MET.]

Absenteeism, 155.
———————, Considered by M'Culloch to be immaterial, 156.
———————, Economical Effects, 160.
———————, Effects of, 156.
———————, Its importance exaggerated. 159.
———————, Moral Effects, 158.
Abstinence, a Principle of the Production of Wealth, 58.
——————— Defined, 58, 89.
——————— from Marriage, 35.
Additional Labour, when employed in Manufactures is *more*, when employed in Agriculture is *less*, efficient in proportion, 81.
Advance of Capital, 194.
Agricultural compared with Manufacturing Industry, 81, 109.
Agricultural Produce, Effects of Increased Demand on the Price of, 119.
Agricultural Produce of Great Britain more than doubled during the last century, 86.
——————————, Effect of Taxation on the Price of, 121.
Agriculture, possible improvements in, 82.
Amount of Wages and Price of Labour differ, 149.
Anarchy worse than Tyranny, 75.
Anti-Commercial System, 177.
Applications of Capital, 66.
Appropriated Natural Agents, 90
Artisans and Machinery, Report of the Committee on, 144.

Bankruptcies in hazardous Trades, 211.
Bill-Broking, business of, 131.
Bishoprics, Policy of preserving, 214.
Books, a commodity very subject to gluts, 28.

Capital and Labour, Difficulty of Transferring them from one Employment to another, 217.
——————————, Difficulty of Transferring them from one Country to another, 220.
———, Average period of Advance of, 194.
———, Defined, 60.
———, Different Modes in which it may be employed, 60.
———, Divisible according to the Purposes to which it is applicable, into Reproductive, Simply Productive, and Unproductive, 66.
———, Fixed and Circulating, 61.
———, ——— Estimated Differently by Political Economists :—
  Adam Smith, 61.
  Malthus, 64.
  Mill, 62.
  Ricardo, 62.
———, one of the Instruments of Production, 59.
———, statement of Advantages derived from the use of, 67.
Capitalists, 88.
Causes of the Productiveness of Labour, 174.
——— regulating the Rate of Profit, 188.
——— which limit Population, 30.
——— which limit Supply, 97.
Chances, Calculation of, 209.
Checks to Population, 31.
Circulating Capital, 61.
Circulation of Labour impeded by difference of climate, distance of place, and difference of language, 222.
Circumstances which decide the average rate of Wages and average rate of Profits, 141.
Colonies, Mismanagement of, 224.

Colonization, 223.
Colony, Progress of a, 106.
Coloured Neckcloth, History of a, 79.
Commercial Speculation, 18.
Commodities, 51, 170.
————————— Discriminated from Services, 53, 170.
Consumption Defined, 53.
By Malthus, 53.
M'Culloch, 54.
Say, 53.
Consumption, Productive and Unproductive, 54.
Corn Law, English, 177.
Cost of Production, 97.
——————, its effects on Price, 111.
Cotton Trade, increase of, 83.

Decencies Defined, 36.
Demand, Defined, 14, 15.
Difference between the Amount of Wages and the Price of Labour, 149.
Different effects of Increased Demand on the Prices of Manufactured and Raw Produce, 119.
Different effects of Taxation on the Prices of Manufactured and Raw Produce, 120.
Distribution of Wealth, 87.
Division of Labour, 73.
——————— Dependent on the Use of Capital, 78.
——————— Government, an example, 75.
Evils to which Government is subject, 75.
——————, Retailers a consequence of the, 77.
——————, Territorial, (Foreign Trade) 76.
——————, The Post Office, an example, 74.
Dunlop, remarks on American Machinery, 72.

Education, Expense of, for the Professions, 206.
Effects of Absenteeism, 156.
——— ——— Foreign Importation, 168.
——— ——— Increased Demand on Price, 119.
——— ——— Machinery on Wages, 162.
——— ——— Monopolies on Price, 114.
——————— the Cost of Production on Price, 111.
——— ——— the Unproductive Consumption of Landlords and Capitalists, 169.

Emigration insufficient to keep down Population, 42.
Emigration of Labourers, 224.
Employments afford different Rates of Wages, according to their Agreeableness, Unhealthiness, &c., 200.
Exchange, 6, 87.
——————, Laws of, 88, 95.
Expenditure, superfluous, use of, 40, 42.

Factory Commission, Report of, 151.
Famine, a check to Population, 32.
Fixed Capital, 61.
Food, Production of, Rate at which it is capable of being increased, 31.
Foreign Trade, 76, 168.
Fund for Maintenance of Labour, 173.

General Desire for Wealth, 27.
General Rate of Profit, 185.
Gold and Silver, why chosen as Money or standard Instruments of Exchange, 97.
Government, its consumption supplied by Labour, 182.
——————, subject to evils, 75, 182.
——————, utility of a, 74, 87.
Glut, Partial, 29.
——, Universal, 28.

High and Low, meaning of the words as applied to Wages, 141.
Holdsworth on Cotton Spinning Machinery, 71.
Holidays, number of, in different Countries, as affecting the Price of Labour, 149.

Implements, use of, 67.
Importation of Foreign Commodities, its effects on Wages, 168.
Inequalities in Wages and Profits occasioned by the Difficulty of Transferring Capital and Labour from One Employment to another, 217.
Infanticide supposed to be favourable to the Increase of Population, 34.
Instruments of Production, 57.
Insurances, 211.
Jenner, Dr., Value of his discovery, 91.

Labour, a primary Instrument of Production, 57, 88.
——————, Causes which divert it from the Production of Commodities for the use of Labouring Families, 180.

Labour, Command of, 187.
——— Defined, 57.
———, Difficulty of Transferring it from one Employment to another, 217.
and from one Country to another, 220.
———, Division of, 73.
———, Effect of additional, in Manufactures and Agriculture compared, 81.
———, Fund for the Maintenance of, Causes on which its extent depends, 173.
———, Productiveness of, 174.
Labourers, 88, 89.
Lace, History of a piece of, in its progress from Tenessee to Bond-Street, 79.
Land, Labour, and Capital—the three Instruments of Production, 59, 88.
———, Monopoly of, 105.
———, the principal Appropriated Natural Agent, 90.
Landlords, 88, 92.
Laplace on Chances, 209.
Life, Average duration of, as affecting Population, 34.
Limitation, causes of, 97.
——— in Supply, one of the constituents of Value, 7.
Limits of the Science of Political Economy, 2.
London, the making of the first Roads to, opposed by neighbouring Landlords, 108.
Lotteries, 210, 213.
Luxuries defined, 36.

Machines, Use of, 67.
Machinery, American, 72.
———, Effects of, on Wages, 162.
———, Holdsworth's, 71.
———, Marsland's, 70
M'Culloch, Definitions by:—
Consumption, 53.
Political Economy, 1.
M'Culloch, his opinions on Population, 43.
Malthus, Definitions by:—
Consumption, 53.
Cost of Production, 98.
Malthus, his Principle of Population, 45.
Manufactured Produce, Price affected by Increased Demand, 119.
———, and by Taxation, 120.

Manufactures compared with Agriculture, 81.
Marriage, Abstinence from, a Check to Population, 31, 35.
Marsland, power of his Machinery at Stockport, 70.
Mercantile Theory, 176.
Mill on the Increase of Population, 44
Mines, 90.
Mining, 209.
Money, Nature of, 96.
Monopolies, Divided into four kinds, 103.
———, Effects on Price, 114.
———, Nature of, 103.
Monopoly of Land, 105.
Mortality in certain Countries, 34.
Moving Powers, Ancient, 70.
———, Modern, 70.

Napoleon's Continental System, 177.
Natural Agents, Appropriated, 90.
———, Defined, 58.
———, Proprietors of, 88.
Nature of Wealth, 6.
Necessaries Defined, 36.
Non-Residence of Landlords, 155.

Opening of a new trade generally followed by Gluts, 29.
Over-production, Doctrine of, 28.

Political Economy, Definitions of:—
De la Riviere's, 1.
M'Culloch's, 1.
Say's, 1.
Sir J. Steuart's, 1.
Sismondi's, 1.
Storch's, 1.
Politics, 76.
Population and Food, human happiness or misery is dependent on their Relative Advance, which is under human control, 49.
Population and Food, relative Increase of, 30.
Malthus's Opinion, 45.
M'Culloch's, 43.
Mill's, 44.
Scrope's, 43.
Population, Causes which limit, 30.
———, Checks to, Divided by Mr. Malthus into the preventive and the positive, 31.
———, Rate of Increase, 30.

Ports, 90.

Post Office, 74.

Power, Instruments which produce. 70.

Preference of Services to Commodities, 170.

—————— Recommended by Ricardo to the Labouring Classes, 171.

His reasoning fallacious, 171.

Price affected by Cost of Production, 111.

——, —————— Increased Demand, 119.

——, —————— Monopolies, 114.

——, —————— Taxation, 120.

—— of a Manufactured Commodity diminished with increased Production, 84.

—— of Labour different from the Amount of Wages, 149.

——, or Value in Money, 96.

Principle of Population, 43.

Produce divided into Wages, Profit and Rent, 88.

Product, 51.

Production, Cost of, 97.

—————————, Defined, 101.

By Malthus, 98.
— Mill, 98.
— Ricardo, 98.
— Torrens, 98.

—————, Instruments of, 57.

—————, or the means by which wealth is produced, 50.

Productive and Unproductive Classes (of men), not an accurate principle of division, 56.

—————— Capital, 66.

—————— Consumption, 54.

Productiveness of Labour, Causes which affect it, 174.

Products divided into Services and Commodities, 51.

Professions, Expense of Education for the, 206.

Professions, Prospect of Remuneration in the, 213.

Profit and Wages, Proportionate amount of, 139.

——, Average Rate of, 141.

——, Causes regulating the Rate of, 188.

——, General Rate of, 185.

——, How to be estimated, 186.

——, Influence of, on Wages, 180, 185.

——, Nature of, 89, 128.

Profit, Rate of, Variations in different employments, 200.

Proportionate amount of Rent, 135.

Promiscuous Intercourse, a Check to Population, 31, 35.

Proportionate Amounts of Profit and Wages, 139.

Proprietors of Natural Agents, 88, 89.

Proximate Cause deciding the Rate of Wages, 153.

————— Opinions inconsistent with the given explanation, 159.

Prudence the Preventive Check on Population, 36.

Relative Proportions of Rent, Profit, and Wages, 128.

Rent, Nature of, 91, 115, 128.

—— Produced by Labour, 180.

——, Proportionate amount of, Causes on which it depends, 135.

Reproductive Capital, 66.

Retailers, Use of, 77.

Ricardo, Definitions by :—
Fixed and Circulating Capital, 63.
Cost of Production, 98.

Ricardo on Rent, 137.

Risks, Calculation of, 209.

Rivers, 90.

Say, Definitions by :—
Consumption, 53.
Political Economy, 1.

Services, 51, 170.

Slavery, 224.

Smith's (Adam) Discrimination of Fixed and Circulating Capital, 62.

Smuggling, 209.

Society divided into three Classes, 88, 128.

Speculations in Commerce, 18.

Standard of Value, 187.

Statement of the Four Elementary Propositions of the Science of Political Economy, 26.

Steadiness in Value, on what it depends, 20.

Supply Defined, 14, 15.

—————, Limitation in, 7.

Tariffs, 177.

Taxation, Supported by Labour, 180, 182.

——————, Unnecessary, is fraudulent, 182.

Tea Trade, 76.

Time of Advance of Capital, 194.

Tithes, 124.

———, probable effect of their abolition, 124.

Tools, use of, 67.

Torrens's (Colonel) definition of Cost of Production, 98.

Trades afford different Rates of Wages, according to their disagreeableness, &c., 200.

Transferableness a quality necessary to give a thing Value, 8.

Transfer of Capital and Labour from one Country to another, difficult, 220.

Transfer of Capital and Labour from one Employment to another, difficult, 217.

The monopolies possessed by English Incorporations often mischievous in this respect, 218.

Unhealthiness of climate or situation, effects on Population, 34.

United States of America, Increase of Population there, 30, 39, 43, 48.

Unproductive Consumption, 54.

————, Effect on Wages, 169.

Unproductive or Distributive Capital, 66.

Use of Capital, 67.

Use of Implements, 67.

Utility, 6.

Value Defined, 13.

——— of a Commodity, Intrinsic and Extrinsic Causes of, 16.

———, Standard of, 187.

———, Steadiness in, 20.

Variations of the Amount of Wages, and the Rate of Profits in different Employments of Capital and Labour, 201.

Wages, Amount of, differs from the Price of Labour, 149.

———, ————, variations in different employments, 200.

———, ————, compared with amount of work done, 150.

———, Average Rate of, 141.

———, Defined, 88, 89, 128.

Wages Different according to the circumstance of the Employment or Business :—

1. Its Agreeableness, 200.
2. Facility of Learning it, 204.
3. Constancy of Employment, 207.
4. Trust, 208.
5. Probability of Success, 208.

———, Inequalities in, occasioned by the difficulty of transferring Labour from one employment to another, 217.

———, Effects of Absenteeism on, 156.

———, Effects of Foreign Importation on, 168.

———, Effects of Machinery on, 162.

———, Effects of Unproductive Consumption on, 169.

———, High and Low, meaning of these terms, 141.

———, ———, Ricardo's opinions, 142.

———, ———, Place's, 144.

———, ———, M'Culloch's, 144.

———, ———, Bradbury's, 146.

———, Rate of, Proximating cause deciding it, 153.

———, Profit, and Rent, Difficulty of Discrimination, 128.

War, a Check to Population, 33.

Watch, Progress of the Manufacture of a, 112.

Wealth, articles of, divided into Necessaries, Decencies, and Luxuries, 36.

Wealth, Constituents of, 6.

———, Definition of, 6.

———, Defined by Malthus, 22.

———, ——— M'Culloch. 23.

———, ——— Torrens, 23.

———, ——— Ricardo, 22.

———, Distribution of, 87.

———, General Desire for, 27.

———, Nature of, 6.

———, Objections to this Definition, 22.

———, Production of, 50.

Whately on the Increase of Population, 47.

Workmen, French compared with English, 150.